Choking Goats

N.C. Bishop

Lightway Illumination, LLC
Omaha, NE

Copyright © 2017 by N.C. Bishop

All rights reserved. No part of this publication may be reproduced, distributed or transmitted in any form or by any means, including photocopying, recording, or other electronic or mechanical methods, without the prior written permission of the publisher, except in the case of brief quotations embodied in critical reviews and certain other noncommercial uses permitted by copyright law. For permission requests, write to the publisher, addressed "Attention: Permissions Coordinator," at the address below.

Lightway Illumination, LLC
13110 Birch Dr. Suite 148-205
Omaha, NE 68164

Book Layout ©2017 BookDesignTemplates.com

Scripture quotations taken from the New American Standard Bible® (NASB), Copyright © 1960, 1962, 1963, 1968, 1971, 1972, 1973,
1975, 1977, 1995 by The Lockman Foundation
Used by permission. www.Lockman.org

Scripture quotations marked (NIV) are taken from the Holy Bible, New International Version®, NIV®. Copyright © 1973, 1978, 1984, 2011 by Biblica, Inc.™ Used by permission of Zondervan. All rights reserved worldwide. www.zondervan.com The "NIV" and "New International Version" are trademarks registered in the United States Patent and Trademark Office by Biblica, Inc.™

Scripture quotations marked (NLT) are taken from the Holy Bible, New Living Translation, copyright ©1996, 2004, 2015 by Tyndale House Foundation. Used by permission of Tyndale House Publishers, Inc., Carol Stream, Illinois 60188. All rights reserved.

Choking Goats/+N.C. Bishop
ISBN 978-0-692-13730-7

Contents

Introduction 3
   Givens 3
   Yeshua and Torah 15
   Twenty Questions 29

Torah, Obedience, and Salvation 59
   The Truth About Torah 61
   Obedience: Requirement or Response? 75
   Life and Death 91

Liberty or Bondage 109
   The Pattern of Paul 111
   Three Torah Tests 123
   A Philosophical Perspective 139

Rest, Feasts, and Food 161
   His Ways His Way 163
   Remembering the Sabbath 171
   Holidays or Holy Days 191
   There's No Such Thing as Junk Food 211

Conclusion 225
Bibliography 230

To my mother, who taught me to believe the Bible but to question everything.

Special thanks to Rachel, Anne, Monica, and John for your encouragement and support, and for taking the time to contribute as editors.

"To be entirely safe from the devil's snares, the child of God must be completely obedient to the word of the Lord. The driver on the highway is safe, not when he reads the signs; but when he obeys them."

—A.W. Tozer

Section I

Introduction

CHAPTER 1

Givens

In mathematics, the word "givens" describes things that are known. Facts that are given to us prior to any attempt to solve a problem. For instance, imagine we're presented with an equation like A + B = C and told to solve for C, given A=1 and B=2. The givens tell us what we need to know to arrive at the correct solution, C = 3.

Everything I've written in the following pages is my attempt to solve a theological problem, and as such, it's helpful to establish some givens. It's my firm belief, having spent so much time sorting these things out, that an enormous amount of confusion has crept into contemporary Christianity for two reasons. First, the givens have been poorly explained or illustrated if they're explained or illustrated at all. Also, words are used without consensus about how those words are defined. As a result, I'd like to take some time in this first chapter simply getting on the same page, as it were; agreeing on the definitions of terms used throughout this book so as to minimize confusion. After all, in the above equation, if I use the terms A and B thinking A is 1 and B is 2 but you think A is 3 and B is 4, we're never going to agree on what C is.

First and foremost, I'd like to make a brief statement about English Bible translations. In an attempt to avoid conflict, suffice to say none of them are perfect. Some of the discussion that follows about my use of certain names and words will illustrate that it's not possible to go from one language to another without losing meaning or clarity leading to ambiguity. Furthermore, I don't believe anyone needs to learn Hebrew or Greek to understand the Bible, however, in the absence of sound teaching, some basic knowledge and a good concordance would be helpful to everyone. On the spectrum of word-for-word translations and thought-for-thought translations, I prefer to stay on the word-for-word side as much as possible. For this reason, unless otherwise noted, all Scripture references in this book will be from the New American Standard Bible (NASB). I'm not endorsing that translation nor am I asserting it's my preference or closest to the original text although I do appreciate many of their conventions. For instance, Old Testament quotes that appear in the New Testament are printed in all caps, which I find makes it much easier to recognize when New Testament authors are making reference to Old Testament passages and underscores just how often the Old Testament is referred to. I also appreciate that the NASB puts disputed verses in square brackets instead of moving those verses to the footnotes, letting the reader decide whether or not they fit with the context of the passage. I appreciate this because by moving disputed verses to the footnotes, it's almost impossible to even notice anything is missing. For example, how many of you who use an NIV or ESV have noticed that in Acts 8 the text skips from verse 36 to 38?

That said, there's great wisdom in consulting several translations in one's studies but for the sake of consistency I wanted to pull Scripture from a single version and to that end I've chosen the NASB. There are certain situations that benefit from quoting a different translation for clarity or to better illustrate a point but wherever this is done the version will be identified. Additionally, it's sometimes helpful to add emphasis to a certain part of quoted text or replace an English word with the original Hebrew or Greek word or meaning. If you see bold text in quoted passages the emphasis is mine and for word replacements the alternate text will be placed between curly brackets {like this}. I want to be clear that when you see these conventions, they are NOT part of the source text. Beyond this, I've placed Scripture quotations in grey boxes when they appear on their own, or in italics when they appear in line with other text, so that they stand out a bit better. Quotes from sources other than Scripture are formatted the same as the rest of the text.

I'd also like to make clear a few of the precepts I use personally when reading and studying Scripture. These are approaches to Bible study that I've gleaned from men wiser than me. For instance, Alistair Begg commonly says, "The main thing is the plain thing and the plain thing is the main thing". What he means by this is the plain language of the Bible generally expresses the plain meaning of a passage with no mental gymnastics or logic leaps required. In other words, while there may be several layers of meaning to a passage, it means what it plainly says. David Platt has said, "The Bible cannot mean what the Bible never meant", by which he means modern viewpoints and contemporary culture cannot be used to apply meaning retroactively when the original author didn't intend that meaning when it was written. While I'll go into this in much more depth in the following chapters, a good example is Romans 14:1-10. Today, many teach that in this passage, Paul is supporting the abolishing of God's instructions regarding what is and isn't food, but it was written to address optional fast days. In other words, Paul's meaning when he penned this passage 2000 years ago has not changed, regardless of what we're told. If Paul's words were not meant to convey a particular idea when he wrote them, they cannot be said to convey that idea today. Lastly, one should let the Bible define the Bible. For instance, we can wax philosophic all day long about what sin is, but the Bible defines it (1 John 3:4) and we should use the Bible's definition in place of whatever clever meaning we've learned to ascribe to words or ideas.

There is a fair amount of confusion about "the Law" as it's referred to by New Testament figures like Paul and Jesus. We need to be very careful about how we parse passages that deal with the Law because there were legitimately two forms of law. Based on one's cultural understanding of ancient Israel, not discerning the difference results in confusion.

On one side stands the written Torah. The set of instructions Yah gifted to His people at Mt Sinai, although there are indications that Torah existed prior to Mt. Sinai in some non-written form. For instance, in Genesis 7:2, when Noah received instruction to gather animals, he was told how many of each clean and unclean animal to collect. Somehow, Noah was aware of the distinction between clean and unclean creatures. Similarly, in Genesis 14:18-20 we learn of Melchizedek, referred to as a *"priest of God Most High"*, who made offerings for and blessed Abraham. This indicates some form of a priesthood as well as the knowledge of how to make offerings. Again, this suggests that Torah existed in some form before it was imparted to the mixed multitude at Mt. Sinai and of course long before it was written on our hearts (Jeremiah 31:33).

On the other side stands the Rabbinic law of the Pharisees and Sadducees. These are rules that were not given by Yah but were put in place by Rabbis and High Priests to form a sort of fence around Torah. These were not instructions given by God, but the priesthood enforced them with equal weight. As I'll show, in every case where Jesus, Paul and others spoke against the law, they are speaking against the additional regulations that had been put in place around Torah itself. Unfortunately, today, no such distinction is made between what was given by God and what was added by man. We're taught passages that speak negatively against the man-made rules are referring to God-given instruction when they are not.

I would also like to explain my use of the names Yah and Yeshua for the persons most Western Christians know as God and Jesus. I've chosen to use these names primarily for the sake of clarity and personal preference but also in an attempt to avoid offending anyone. My use of Yeshua rather than Jesus is simply a reflection of my own personal beliefs. The name Jesus is an English transliteration of a Greek transliteration of a Hebrew name. To put it another way, from language to language translators didn't translate the word so as to retain the meaning, they tried to mimic the sound of the syllables. That's not a problem in and of itself, but there's an inherent difference between the nature of names in modern Western culture and the nature of names in Biblical Hebrew culture. In modern culture, a name is little more than what someone is called but from a Hebrew mindset, names are intimately tied to the meaning of a Hebrew word and that word, meaning included, is applied to a person. It's a fine distinction but it is an important one. For instance, the name Elijah in Hebrew is Eliyahu, a compound word that means Yah is my God. The name John in Hebrew is Yochanan which means Yah is gracious. The English name Elijah doesn't really mean anything in the sense that the name doesn't have a definition per se, it's just a name. The same is true for the name John; there isn't a definition of the word John.

By contrast Eliyahu and Yochanan are compound Hebrew words with distinct and important meanings used as names.

This difference between Western names and Biblical names makes sense if we understand that the very word "name" in Hebrew is the word "shem". Shem means much more than the common usage of the English word name. It connotes reputation or authority. One might say, "don't tarnish my good name". The word shem has the same sense. A "shem", or "name", as it's used in the Bible tells us more than just what sound one uses to address a person, it tells us something about their character, their reputation, perhaps their future or destiny. In the same way, the word Jesus has no intrinsic meaning. As a word, it doesn't have a definition. It's a name used to refer to a specific person but there's no real translation of the name Jesus. The word yeshua though is the Hebrew word for salvation and is loaded with Biblical implication (I've left the word "yeshua" un-capitalized to indicate that this is the word and not the name as I'm using it here – keep in mind though, there is no such concept as capital and lower-case characters in the Hebrew aleph-bet). Consider the account in Matthew 1:

> [18] Now the birth of Jesus Christ was as follows: when His mother Mary had been betrothed to Joseph, before they came together she was found to be with child by the Holy Spirit. [19] And Joseph her husband, being a righteous man and not wanting to disgrace her, planned to send her away secretly. [20] But when he had considered this, behold, an angel of the Lord appeared to him in a dream, saying, "Joseph, son of David, do not be afraid to take Mary as your wife; for the Child who has been conceived in her is of the Holy Spirit. [21] **She will bear a Son; and you shall call His name Jesus, for He will save His people from their sins.**"

In the last verse, the original language says, *"you shall call His name Yeshua"*, or *"you shall call His name Salvation, for He will save His people from their sins."* By using the proper Hebrew name and knowing the meaning of the word, the description of why this should be His name is much clearer. He will save us from our sins, so His name should be Salvation. Interestingly, in the very next verses there's a reference to Old Testament prophecy that does exactly this - it refers to the Hebrew word Immanuel, translates it for us as *"God with us"*, and thus makes clear that this is not just a newborn man, but is literally God with us!

This understanding sheds new light on Old Testament passages as well. In almost every case where you see the English word "salvation" in the Old Testament the original Hebrew word is "yeshua". In Psalm 9 we find the following:

> [11] Sing praises to the Lord, who dwells in Zion;
> Declare among the peoples His deeds.
> [12] For He who requires blood remembers them;
> He does not forget the cry of the afflicted.
> [13] Be gracious to me, O Lord;
> See my affliction from those who hate me,
> You who lift me up from the gates of death,
> [14] That I may tell of all Your praises,
> That in the gates of the daughter of Zion
> I may rejoice in Your **salvation**.

If we leave that last word untranslated, David is literally saying *"I may rejoice in Your yeshua"*. Considering the ideas in verses 12 and 13, I'd suggest it fits quite well that David is, whether knowingly or not, speaking of the coming Messiah by name. There's a similar passage in Isaiah 12:

> [1] Then you will say on that day,
> "I will give thanks to You, O Lord;
> For although You were angry with me,
> Your anger is turned away,
> And You comfort me.
> [2] "Behold, God is my **salvation**,
> I will trust and not be afraid;
> For the Lord God is my strength and song,
> And He has become my **salvation**."
> [3] Therefore you will joyously draw water
> From the springs of **salvation**.
> [4] And in that day you will say,
> "Give thanks to the Lord, call on His name.
> Make known His deeds among the peoples;
> Make them remember that His name is exalted."

In each of the instances above, replace the English word "salvation" with the original Hebrew word "yeshua" and some interesting depth emerges.

Would you agree the last half of verse 2 is explicitly describing that God will become man in the person of Yeshua? Extending this exercise to verse 3 gives us a rendering that says, *"Therefore you will joyously draw water from the springs of yeshua"*. In light of the accounts in John, this is extraordinary. Consider the following statements by Yeshua himself:

> John 4:13-14 - *Jesus answered and said to her, "Everyone who drinks of this water will thirst again; but whoever drinks of the water that I will give him shall never thirst; but the water that I will give him will become in him a well of water springing up to eternal life."*
>
> John 7:37-38 - *Now on the last day, the great day of the feast, Jesus stood and cried out, saying, "If anyone is thirsty, let him come to Me and drink. He who believes in Me, as the Scripture said, 'From his innermost being will flow rivers of living water.'"*

With all of this in mind, I've chosen to use Yeshua rather than Jesus throughout the following chapters to honor the depth of meaning found in the original language that doesn't just name but also describes the coming Messiah.

It's not my intention to be snobbish or create divisiveness about the proper name of the Messiah, nor is it my intention to convince everyone they should use Yeshua instead of Jesus. There's actually quite a bit of debate about how His Hebrew name should be written and pronounced. Further, I do not wish to assert that the Messiah Himself has a preference – perhaps He does, perhaps He doesn't – all of that is outside the scope of this book. For me, knowing and using the name Yeshua has brought new depth to several areas of Scripture and new understanding to both Old and New Testament passages so it's the name I use.

When referring to God the Father, I'll use the name Yah throughout the remainder of this book. Yah is an abbreviation of the sacred name, YHVH (in Hebrew, the letters Yod-Hey-Vav-Hey) using the first two Hebrew characters of that name, Yod and Hey. This abbreviated form of His name is first used in a song of praise sung by Moses and the Israelites in Exodus 15:2:

> *{Yah} is my strength and song, and He has become my salvation;*

Most Christian's have been using this name for their entire Christian lives, perhaps without really knowing it, by using the fairly common expression, Hallelujah. Hallelujah is a Hebrew phrase consisting of two words, "hallelu", roughly meaning praise, and the name Yah, rendered not quite correctly with a "j" instead of a "y" as jah. Literally, it means praise Yah.

As an aside, remember that the word Yeshua means salvation, so here, the song is saying Yah is my strength and song, and He has become my yeshua. What an appropriate verse to sing just after being delivered from the bondage of Egypt, and what a blessing to be able to sing the exact same verse when we are delivered from the bondage of sin because Yah became our Yeshua.

There are several reasons I prefer to use Yah, most notably that it's a name and not a title as the word "God" is. Further, I think the term God/god is, quite frankly, just not that clear a term. It's a title used not to translate but to replace the Hebrew word "elohim" but throughout Scripture the word "elohim" is applied to people and beings other than God the Father. Elohim means "strong leader" and, in most cases, is definitely talking about the deity Jews and Christians believe created all things, but that's not true in all cases. In 1 Samuel 5:7 for example we see the word "elohim" used twice, once in reference to the God of Israel and once for the pagan's god, Dagon.

> *When the men of Ashdod saw that it was so, they said, "The ark of **God** of Israel must not remain with us, for His hand is severe on us and on Dagon our **god**."*

Similarly, in 1 Kings 11:33 we see a goddess and two gods referred to. In all three instances, god is used in place of the original word elohim.

> *...because they have forsaken Me, and have worshiped Ashtoreth the **goddess** of the Sidonians, Chemosh the **god** of Moab, and Milcom the **god** of the sons of Ammon; and they have not walked in My ways, doing what is right in My sight and observing My statutes and My ordinances, as his father David did.*

Of course, we're accustomed to differentiating between the two uses by the capitalization, but this doesn't work in every case. For instance, in Exodus 4:16 and 7:1, Moses is referred to as an elohim, but the English "capital G" God is used, I believe in error.

> Exodus 4:16 - Moreover, he shall speak for you to the people; and he will be as a mouth for you and you will be ~~as~~ **God** to him.
>
> Exodus 7:1 - Then the Lord said to Moses, "See, I make you ~~as~~ **God** to Pharaoh, and your brother Aaron shall be your prophet.

Most English translations add some articles, so it reads "as God" or "like God" but in the original text these articles aren't actually there and, as such, I've struck them out in the quoted passages above to better illustrate the next point. These passages are simply conveying the idea that Moses will be a "strong leader" to Aaron and that Moses has been set as a "strong leader" over Pharaoh, respectively. It isn't supposed to connote, as it seems to in most English translations, that Moses will be anything like, or stand in the place of, God the Father.

Another reason I don't use the title on its own is the popular, but incorrect, Western philosophy that all religions are basically the same or are all describing the same god in different ways. The best illustration of this is ecumenical efforts to foster peace between Christianity and Islam by asserting that they are both talking about the same god. Nothing could be further from the truth. You've likely heard people say that Allah means god and that's true in a sense. It's believed to be an ancient Arabic derivation of the word elohim, but it's really a half truth. As we've seen, elohim in the Bible is applied to the true God as well as false gods (and angels, and people). It's important to know that Allah is the name of the god of Islam as distinct from the God of Abraham, Isaac, and Jacob. If we all just use the title, God/god, especially when speaking, where no distinction can be made between the words "capital G God" and "lowercase g god" we blur the lines between belief systems and open ourselves up to believing all kinds of untrue things. The topics I'll be discussing are important so it's vital to avoid confusion and equally vital to avoid any pretense that I'm trying to trick anyone by playing word games the way the "all religions are the same" crowd tries to do (i.e.

Christians call their deity God. Muslims say Allah means god. They must be the same thing).

For these reasons, I believe it's important to use a name. I suppose I could just keep saying the God of Abraham, Isaac, and Jacob but that would become cumbersome very quickly, which leaves me with two choices: using His proper name or using His abbreviated name. Using the full proper name has its own issues including deep division over how it's to be pronounced and if it should be pronounced and/or written at all, which leads to some using the altered written form "L-rd" or "G-d". Out of respect for the beliefs of my Jewish friends I've chosen not to use this name, so that leaves Yah as the name I'll use from here forward.

With names and their meanings as I'll be using them firmly established, there's one more word that is of critical importance to the following subject matter and that's the word Torah. Most of the following text is a discussion of the place Torah has in the daily lives of believers in Yeshua. This word is most often translated as the English word "law" and, as with the other words I've discussed, the word "law" is just not very accurate or precise; certainly not accurate or precise enough for us to wade through the discussion to come. A quote I came across online captures and summarizes the problem eloquently saying,

> "Almost all English translations of the Bible translate the Hebrew word Torah as law. Modern Western Christians often have, as a result, received a distorted perspective of Torah from uninformed preaching and Sunday school teachings. It is indeed a legal code with strict requirements, and in its most narrow sense, sometimes Torah can mean law, but law can also be a very misleading translation. To understand Torah strictly as law would be like translating the word parent as disciplinarian". (Young, 39)

Throughout the Bible, New and Old Testament, there are references to Yah's laws, statutes, ordinances, and testimonies. Torah comprises all of these things. As the quote above indicates, Torah includes a legal component but isn't limited to that. If one insists on a single word translation a more accurate choice would be instruction. Torah is Yah's instruction, or teaching, about how one should live in the world He has created. The reason I want to be clear on this is because I believe much of the tension between grace and law is the simple result of the word "law" being a poor translation for Torah which results in a catastrophic misunderstanding of what Torah is and what its purpose has been from the beginning. Here's a hint: It was never about salvation. Sadly, hundreds of years of doctrine and dogma have been built on the foundation of this misunderstanding and the results have been tragic to say the least. Much more will be explained regarding this topic as it's central to the case I'm making so I will belabor it no further at this time, but I want the reader to understand that, wherever possible, I'll use the word Torah instead of referring to God's law or "the Law" or any other similar derivation.

Having established a clear foundation, I'm confident that while we may not end up agreeing on every point in the discussion that follows, we can at least be reasonably sure any disagreement won't be the result of simply meaning different things when we use certain terms. With these givens in mind, let us proceed.

CHAPTER 2

Yeshua and Torah

The subject of this book is Torah and its relevance in the lives of Christians today but, at its core, that's not what this book is about. While Torah is a significant part of the Bible, the Bible is not the story of Torah, it's the story of Yah's interaction with and plan of redemption for His people. In short, it's the story of Yeshua. In Isaiah 46, the prophet tells us that Yah *"tells the end from the beginning"*:

> ⁹ *"Remember the former things long past, For I am God, and there is no other; I am God, and there is no one like Me,* ¹⁰ *Declaring the end from the beginning, And from ancient times things which have not been done, Saying, 'My purpose will be established, And I will accomplish all My good pleasure';*

Knowing this it shouldn't be surprising that we find a framework for salvation described in the first chapters of Genesis. In Genesis 3:7-21 we learn that because of man's transgression, man needs to be cleansed, or covered. We learn that, despite our best efforts, the covering we try to make for ourselves (the fig leaves), the cleansing we attempt by our own efforts, is insufficient and we learn that only the covering Yah provides (the animal skins) will be acceptable in His sight. We also learn in this ancient history that the covering requires sacrifice (the animals from which the skins were taken are the first sacrifices recorded in Scripture). True to His word, Yah has told us the end from the beginning, but the story of Yeshua starts much earlier than that.

I'll come back to this point, but I'd first like to establish that if what I've written doesn't relate to Yeshua it's nothing more than anecdotally interesting. Nothing is more important than our personal relationship with Yeshua, and all of Scripture points us squarely to Him, so I'd like to take some time to illustrate the relationship between Yeshua and Torah to drive home the point that what I'm advocating is not obedience for the sake of obedience. I'll discuss at length how obedience was never intended to, nor can it ever, secure salvation. Obedience, properly understood from a Biblical perspective, is always a response to salvation, never a means to salvation. Even as a response to salvation though, following Torah with the wrong motive is as empty as not following Torah at all and the point is relationship. By learning what Torah is and how that instruction bears on our lives, we come to learn about Yeshua, and as our understanding of the way He walked deepens, the deeper our relationship with Him becomes.

Moses says in Exodus 33:13:

> "Now therefore, I pray thee, if I have found grace in thy sight, shew me now thy way, that I may know thee, that I may find grace in thy sight: and consider that this nation is thy people." (KJV)

There are a lot of interesting things to note in that verse. For instance, Moses says, *"if I have found grace, show me thy way"*. This is an early illustration of the idea that grace always comes before instruction (i.e. salvation before obedience), but what's of particular relevance is the reason Moses asks Yah to show him the way. *"That I may know thee"*, he says. Moses, if he has found grace in the sight of Yah, wants to know Yah's ways so he can know the one who provided the way through the one that IS the way. Moses is not seeking a body of rules to follow or a lifestyle to adopt, he's seeking relationship and understands that Yah's instructions provide the path to, or mechanism for, relationship.

Two particular statements made by Yeshua are important to this discussion. These statements are recorded in the gospel of John, chapters 8 and 14:

> John 8 - ¹² Then Jesus again spoke to them, saying, "I am the Light of the world; he who follows Me will not walk in the darkness, but will have the Light of life."
>
> John 14 - ¹ "Do not let your heart be troubled; believe in God, believe also in Me. ² In My Father's house are many dwelling places; if it were not so, I would have told you; for I go to prepare a place for you. ³ If I go and prepare a place for you, I will come again and receive you to Myself, that where I am, there you may be also. ⁴ And you know the way where I am going." ⁵ Thomas said to Him, "Lord, we do not know where You are going, how do we know the way?" ⁶ Jesus said to him, "I am the way, and the truth, and the life; no one comes to the Father but through Me.

I'd like to focus on the statements, *"I am the light..."* and *"I am the way, and the truth, and the life...."* In these two passages, Yeshua describes Himself in four ways: As the light, the way, the truth and the life. If anyone has done a study of how Torah is described in the Old Testament, these words will stand out. Let's look at each one.

Torah is consistently referred to as "the way" in the Old Testament. In Exodus 18, Moses' father-in-law tells Moses:

> ¹⁹ Now listen to me: I will give you counsel, and God be with you. You be the people's representative before God, and you bring the disputes to God, ²⁰ then teach them the statutes and the laws, and make known to them the way in which they are to walk and the work they are to do.

"The way in which they are to walk" is, of course, according to Yah's instruction – Torah. Later, in Deuteronomy 10, Moses says the following:

> ¹² "Now, Israel, what does the Lord your God require from you, but to fear the Lord your God, to walk in all His ways and love Him, and to serve the Lord your God with all your heart and with all your soul, ¹³ and to keep the Lord's commandments and His statutes which I am commanding you today for your good?

Again, we see a reference to walking in *"His ways"*, which includes keeping Yah's commandments and statutes, another reference to the body of instruction we know as Torah.

Joshua reiterates this point in Joshua 22:5:

> [5] Only be very careful to observe the commandment and the law which Moses the servant of the Lord commanded you, to love the Lord your God and walk in all His ways and keep His commandments and hold fast to Him and serve Him with all your heart and with all your soul." [6] So Joshua blessed them and sent them away, and they went to their tents.

The same advice is relayed to Solomon by David as David approaches the end of his life in 1 Kings 2:1-3:

> [3] Keep the charge of the Lord your God, to walk in His ways, to keep His statutes, His commandments, His ordinances, and His testimonies, according to what is written in the Law of Moses, that you may succeed in all that you do and wherever you turn, [4] so that the Lord may carry out His promise which He spoke concerning me, saying, 'If your sons are careful of their way, to walk before Me in truth with all their heart and with all their soul, you shall not lack a man on the throne of Israel.'

Notice that this passage really hammers home that "the way" is a reference to Torah when David relates His ways, statutes, commandments, ordinances, and testimonies as *"what is written in the {Torah} of Moses"*. Also notice that all of this is summarized in verse 4 as *"walking in truth"*.

The first verse of Psalm 119 also makes clear the relationship between "the way" and Torah saying, *"Blessed are the undefiled in the way, who walk in the law of the Lord" (KJV)*. Proverbs 6:23 says, *"For the commandment is a lamp; and the law is light; and reproofs of instruction are the way of life"*, not only referring to Yah's instruction as "the way" of life but also, remembering that the word law is translated from the word Torah, Proverbs 6:23 is literally saying that Torah is light.

In Isaiah 2 we're given a prophecy describing what will happen when Yeshua returns to reign on Earth and the way is again directly related to Torah:

> [2] Now it will come about that in the last days the mountain of the house of the Lord will be established as the chief of the mountains, and will be raised above the hills; and all the nations will stream to it.
> [3] And many peoples will come and say, "Come, let us go up to the mountain of the Lord, to the house of the God of Jacob; that He may teach us concerning His ways and that we may walk in His paths." For the law will go forth from Zion and the word of the Lord from Jerusalem.

And in Malachi 2, the prophet contrasts the good and true instruction of the Levitical priesthood against the priesthood of his day saying:

> "*8 But as for you, you have turned aside from the way; you have caused many to stumble by the instruction; you have corrupted the covenant of Levi," says the Lord of hosts. 9 "So I also have made you despised and abased before all the people, just as you are not keeping My ways but are showing partiality in the instruction."*

All of this helps us take hold of the cultural setting into which Yeshua was born. It was common knowledge that "the way" was a euphemism for living according to Torah and with this in mind we can better understand some of the things we find in the New Testament. For instance, we know Yeshua taught Torah because those who opposed Him declared as much in Mark 12:14 saying:

> *13 Then they sent some of the Pharisees and Herodians to Him in order to trap Him in a statement. 14 They came and said to Him, "Teacher, we know that You are truthful and defer to no one; for You are not partial to any, but teach the way of God in truth. Is it lawful to pay a poll-tax to Caesar, or not?*

Contrary to their false accusations during His trial, they acknowledge here that Yeshua teaches the way of Yah truthfully, a phrase they clearly understood as teaching Torah.

Finally, in Acts, Paul says during his trial,

> "*14 But this I admit to you, that according to the Way which they call a sect I do serve the God of our fathers, believing everything that is in accordance with the Law and that is written in the Prophets...".*

Here again, "the way", is described as everything in accordance with Torah and the Prophets. Some of you may be thinking that Paul is using "the way" to mean something different because he says it's called a sect. Remember, though, that the Judaism of his day included all of the man-made rules and regulations that had been added to Torah, so while Paul does mean Torah when he uses the term "the way", those who believed Yah's instructions stood on their own without any need for the man-made additions would have indeed been a minority and seen as a sect.

As we just saw in 1 Kings 2:1-3, Torah is referred to as the way, but is also said to be walking in truth. Psalm 119:142 further establishes the link between Torah and truth: *"Your righteousness is an everlasting righteousness, and Your law is truth."* What's remarkable here is the same thing that's remarkable about Yeshua's statement in John 14:6. To paraphrase Michael Ramsden, Yeshua didn't say He said true things, although it's true that He did. What's remarkable is that He says He IS truth and we see the same thing here. Not just that Torah is true, which it is, but that Torah is truth itself.

In the passage from Malachi 2 we looked at earlier, we saw the contrast between the priesthood that had strayed from "the way" and the Levitical priesthood. On the other side of that contrast we have the description of the righteousness of Levi:

> [6] *The law of truth was in his mouth, and iniquity was not found in his lips: he walked with me in peace and equity, and did turn many away from iniquity.* [7] *For the priest's lips should keep knowledge, and they should seek the law at his mouth: for he is the messenger of the L*ORD *of hosts.* (KJV)

If we replace "law" with the original word "Torah", the first few words use the description *"the {Torah} of truth"*. Once again, this insight into the cultural understanding of the relationship between Torah and truth, namely that Torah is truth, helps us understand some of the passages we find in the New Testament. For example, in Romans 2:20, Paul describes Torah as *"the embodiment of knowledge and truth"*.

> [17] *But if you bear the name "Jew" and rely upon the Law and boast in God,* [18] *and know His will and approve the things that are essential, being instructed out of the Law,* [19] *and are confident that you yourself are a guide to the blind, a light to those who are in darkness,* [20] *a corrector of the foolish, a teacher of the immature, having in the Law the embodiment of knowledge and of the truth,* [21] *you, therefore, who teach another, do you not teach yourself? You who preach that one shall not steal, do you steal?* [22] *You who say that one should not commit adultery, do you commit adultery? You who abhor idols, do you rob temples?* [23] *You who boast in the Law, through your breaking the Law,*

> do you dishonor God? ²⁴ For "the name of God is blasphemed among the Gentiles because of you," just as it is written.

This provides another example of Torah being described as truth toward the end of verse 20 and light in verse 19, which we'll discuss in a moment.

Having shown Torah referred to as the way and the truth I'll move on to the life. This one is interesting because Torah isn't described as life itself. There are two sides to Torah. Life if one obeys and death if one does not. Another way of saying this might be, following Torah leads to life while choosing to depart from it leads to death, and isn't that the case with Yeshua? It's not the mere fact of Yeshua's existence or His sacrifice on our behalf that leads to life, it's accepting His free gift and following Him that does. After all, as it's been said, even demons believe in Jesus. Following Him is what makes all the difference. The most explicit reference to Torah in this sense comes from Deuteronomy 30:15-18:

> ¹⁵ "See, I have set before you today life and prosperity, and death and adversity; ¹⁶ in that I command you today to love the Lord your God, to walk in His ways and to keep His commandments and His statutes and His judgments, that you may live and multiply, and that the Lord your God may bless you in the land where you are entering to possess it. ¹⁷ But if your heart turns away and you will not obey, but are drawn away and worship other gods and serve them, ¹⁸ I declare to you today that you shall surely perish. You will not prolong your days in the land where you are crossing the Jordan to enter and possess it.

There are a variety of single references describing obedience as leading to life. For example, Proverbs 6:23:

> For the commandment is a lamp; and the law is light; and reproofs of instruction are the way of life.

Possibly the most surprising reference comes from Revelation, specifically verse 14 of chapter 22,

> "Blessed are they that do his commandments, that they may have right to the tree of life, and may enter in through the gates into the city (KJV)".

Although other passages in Revelation pair faith in Christ with obeying the commandments as both being attributes of the saved (Revelation 12:17 and 14:12), it's surprising to find here the distinction of having right to the tree of life doesn't hinge on simply believing in Yeshua as so many teach, but on following the commandments, or, in other words, walking as Yeshua walked.

To be fair, there are basically two translations of Revelation 22:14 with some translations, including the NASB, using the phrase *"they who wash their robes"* instead of *"they that do his commandments"*. It's not my intention to delve into the nuances of this difference but, personally, I believe the KJV rendering, being derived from Erasmus' Greek text, is more trustworthy than the *"wash their robes"* translation. I'll leave it to the reader to look into this and come to his or her own conclusion, but I will say that this passage in Revelation, if the KJV translation is correct, is completely consistent with Yeshua's own words in Matthew 19:

> [16] *And someone came to Him and said, "Teacher, what good thing shall I do that I may obtain eternal life?"* [17] *And He said to him, "Why are you asking Me about what is good? There is only One who is good; but if you wish to enter into life, keep the commandments."*

Back to the original point, in each of these passages the relationship between Torah and life is described in the same way. Life if you walk according to Torah's instruction and death if you go another way. Likewise, in Yeshua, Yah has placed a fulcrum on the landscape of human history and everyone's future is balanced upon it. Follow and you will live and multiply. Refuse, turning to other endeavors or avenues of living, and you will perish. For instance, notice that eternal life is given to those who follow Him in John 10:27-28:

> *"My sheep hear My voice, and I know them, and they follow Me; and I give eternal life to them, and they will never perish; and no one will snatch them out of My hand".*

The passage that ends with the popular verse, Romans 6:23, illustrates the same contrast between life and death:

> [20] *For when you were slaves of sin, you were free in regard to righteousness.* [21] *Therefore what benefit were you then deriving from the things of which you are now ashamed? For the outcome of those things is death.* [22] *But now having been freed from sin and enslaved to God, you derive your benefit, resulting in sanctification, and the outcome, eternal life.* [23] *For the wages of sin is death, but the free gift of God is eternal life in Christ Jesus our Lord.*

Paul says when we were yoked with sin we could not practice righteousness, but now, being yoked with Yeshua, having Torah written on our hearts, we have been freed from our inability to walk in His ways – the way of life. All these references taken together, show Yeshua and Torah described as the life in the same way; that life and death hinge on our choice to follow or not, rounding out the way, truth, and life triad as descriptions of both Yeshua and Torah.

Finally, we have the light. Yeshua is described as the light in several places, for instance John 1:6-9 says of John the Baptist's witness to Yeshua:

> [6] *There came a man sent from God, whose name was John.* [7] *He came as a witness, to testify about the Light, so that all might believe through him.* [8] *He was not the Light, but he came to testify about the Light.* [9] *There was the true Light which, coming into the world, enlightens every man.*

And, of course, there's the statement we looked at toward the beginning of this section in John 8:12:

> *Then Jesus again spoke to them, saying, "I am the Light of the world; he who follows Me will not walk in the darkness, but will have the Light of life."*

Knowing that Yeshua and Torah are described as the way, truth and life, the same result shouldn't be surprising as it relates to Yeshua, Torah, and light. To not walk in darkness is to walk in the light, which is quite interesting considering a passage we looked at a few paragraphs ago during the discussion of Torah's description as "the way". A prophecy in Isaiah 2 that speaks of Yeshua's future reign says in verse 3:

> *"And many peoples will come and say, "Come, let us go up to the mountain of the Lord, to the house of the God of Jacob; that He may teach us concerning His*

ways and that we may walk in His paths." For the law will go forth from Zion and the word of the Lord from Jerusalem."

In verse 5 of the same passage it continues:

"Come, house of Jacob, and let us walk in the light of the Lord".

This directly ties walking in the light to walking according to Torah. Later in Isaiah 8 we find the same relationship expressed in the negative in verse 20:

"To the law and to the testimony: if they speak not according to this word, it is because there is no light in them."

Similarly, Job 24:13 says of non-believers:

"Others have been with those who rebel against the light; they do not want to know its ways nor abide in its paths."

Notice that this verse describes the light as having its own ways and paths. Very similar to the descriptions we've already discussed casting Torah as the way.

In the New Testament, we find all of these concepts woven together in a passage from John that begins with the popular verse 16 from chapter 3:

[16] "For God so loved the world, that He gave His only begotten Son, that whoever believes in Him shall not perish, but have eternal life. [17] For God did not send the Son into the world to judge the world, but that the world might be saved through Him. [18] He who believes in Him is not judged; he who does not believe has been judged already, because he has not believed in the name of the only begotten Son of God. [19] This is the judgment, that the Light has come into the world, and men loved the darkness rather than the Light, for their deeds were evil. [20] For everyone who does evil hates the Light, and does not come to the Light for fear that his deeds will be exposed. [21] But he who practices the truth comes to the Light, so that his deeds may be manifested as having been wrought in God."

While verse 18 talks about the importance of believing, it's interesting that the focus of verses 19-21 is on actions not beliefs. It's about lifestyle and behavior. When verse 21 refers to practicing the truth it should be obvious that one cannot practice Yeshua, but one can practice Torah, which we know, like Yeshua, is described as truth.

Torah is also described as walking in the light in other passages we've seen previously, for instance, Proverbs 6:23 which says:

> "For the commandment is a lamp and the teaching is light; and reproofs for discipline are the way of life."

And Psalm 119:105 which says:

> "Your word is a lamp to my feet, and a light to my path"

The use of the imagery of a lamp is quite compelling as this is the same language used in Revelation 21:23 which says of the new Jerusalem:

> "And the city has no need of the sun or of the moon to shine on it, for the glory of God has illumined it, and its lamp is the Lamb."

Clearly the relationship between Torah, Yeshua and "the light" is as inseparable as Torah, Yeshua, and "the way, the truth, and the life".

The story of salvation from Genesis to Revelation paints a picture of this, dare I say, evolution of instruction. We see a steady progression from an initial unwritten state of Torah to Yeshua. We're not told much about the form it originally took, whether oral or something else but we have examples like Noah knowing the difference between clean and unclean animals, Job offering sacrifices for his children, and Melchizedek being described as a priest of Yah long before Torah was given at Mt. Sinai.

When we get to Mt. Sinai the same Torah that was evidently known by the patriarchs was written down, but the people had corrupt hearts and this corruption made obedience impossible. To remedy this, Torah was made flesh in the person of Yeshua, who demonstrated perfect practice of Yah's instruction for us and implores us to walk in the way He demonstrated. Finally, upon Yeshua's death and resurrection His Spirit was given whereby Torah is written on our hearts which finally frees us to live in liberty through obedience being freed from our flesh to walk in His Spirit. Is there any other way His Spirit would have us walk but according to the Father's instructions?

Taken as a whole, the parallels and language used throughout the Bible to describe Yeshua and Torah make the two inseparable. A case cannot be made that one can live a life walking as He walked without Torah being the reference point for one's lifestyle and behavior. As I said at the beginning of the chapter, nothing is more important than our personal relationship with Yeshua, but to believe that one must discern what the Christian life looks like from clues and reiterations in the New Testament is a lie. There are many believers out there who wonder what Yah's will for their life is, but I believe most people, when pondering that question, have the mechanism and the result reversed. What most people seem to mean is, what does Yah want me to do in my life, or how can I be involved in Yah's movement in this world, and they go after that result, rather than simply leveraging the mechanism Yah has provided. The answer to the question, what is Yah's will for my life is very simple and can be found at the end of Ecclesiastes, chapter 12, verse 13:

> [13] *Let us hear the conclusion of the whole matter: Fear God, and keep his commandments: for this is the whole duty of man.*

When we are in relationship with Yeshua, and that relationship deepens as we learn to walk as He walked we will find ourselves more and more in the center of Yah's will. The entire reason He left us His true instruction is so that those with wisdom to hear, and by hearing obey, would be walking according to His plan. What you end up doing along the way will be what Yah has intended for you as a natural result of your walking His way. The opposite though is also true. If we choose to go our own way or try to find our own path, even if our goal is to serve Yah, we will land squarely outside of what He has planned for us and are, at the very worst, at risk of being among those to whom Yeshua says in Matthew 7:21-23:

> [21] *"Not everyone who says to Me, 'Lord, Lord,' will enter the kingdom of heaven, but he who does the will of My Father who is in heaven will enter.* [22] *Many will say to Me on that day, 'Lord, Lord, did we not prophesy in Your name, and*

> in Your name cast out demons, and in Your name perform many miracles?' ²³ And then I will declare to them, 'I never knew you; depart from Me, you who practice lawlessness.'

Remembering that Yeshua spoke Aramaic, that last phrase would have literally been, *"you who practice {torahlessness}"*. Yeshua is pointing out that it's not enough to do a variety of what might be considered good works in His name if Torah has no place in your life. Yeshua, Yah's Wisdom, the Word and Torah are as inseparable as are the Father, Son and Holy Spirit. You see, if I have an idea, and I speak that idea, then write that idea down, and then practice that idea, can one separate the oral, written and physical demonstration of that idea from the idea itself? Are these four distinct and different things or are they the same thing expressed in four ways?

Of course, it's the latter, and so it is with Yeshua and Torah. Torah is the wisdom of God and that wisdom was expressed as "the Word" which Yah spoke in the beginning. Looking back at the first few verses of Genesis we find the first word of Yah recorded in Scripture from Genesis 1:3:

> Then God said, "Let there be light"; and there was light.

This is another place where the translation is ok but not great. The original Hebrew says something closer to, "and God spoke, 'light', and light was". The account of creation throughout the Bible makes clear that Yah creates through speech, and the true nature of Genesis 1:3 is that Yah spoke light into His creation. What He spoke, became. If we then jump to the first few verses of John, we see the progression I've spoken of described.

> ¹ In the beginning was the Word, and the Word was with God, and the Word was God. ² He was in the beginning with God. ³ All things came into being through Him, and apart from Him nothing came into being that has come into being. ⁴ In Him was life, and the life was the Light of men. ⁵ The Light shines in the darkness, and the darkness did not comprehend it...
>
> ¹⁴ ...And the Word became flesh, and dwelt among us, and we saw His glory, glory as of the only begotten from the Father, full of grace and truth.

Among other things, this passage points out that the Word existed before the creation of the universe. *"In the beginning the word was with God and was God"*, John says, and that word was "light". From the passages we've looked at, this was when Yeshua, having pre-existed, entered creation, but what form did He take? John also said in 1:14 that the Word, or light, became flesh and dwelt among us, indicating that from creation until Yeshua's birth, the Word was in the world in some non-flesh form. Given the descriptions of Torah as the way, truth, life and as light, and the fact that those descriptions are used in reference to Yeshua, combined with these assertions by John that the Word was eventually made flesh, this inseparable relationship between the Word, Light, Torah and Yeshua is undeniable.

Admittedly this is all a bit complex. Anyone who has tried to describe the trinity will understand that no analogy is perfect. We can't describe the Father, Son and Holy Spirit as three parts of a whole because they are all equally Yah. We can't describe a deity that takes any one of three forms, like ice, water, and steam are three forms of water, because all three are equally Yah at all times. I mention this to illustrate that there are things difficult to describe simply because they aren't like anything else in the human experience.

That Torah and Yeshua are different ways of describing the same person is as complex an idea as the Father, Son and Holy Spirit being equally Yah, but the Bible's descriptions of the Torah and Yeshua leave no room to separate the two. You can no more follow Yeshua without following Torah than you can have a relationship with the Father without a relationship with the Son. Please don't misunderstand me here. I believe most Christian's follow most of Torah, whether they would acknowledge it or not. Caring for the poor, treating other's as equals, and refraining from theft, murder, and adultery are all Torah instructions most Christian's follow without batting an eye. What I'm saying is that Torah and Yeshua are inextricably linked and the extent to which a person departs from one is the extent to which one remains distant from the other. My purpose in writing this book, is to encourage everyone reading this to close the gaps that have been created by misunderstanding and misinterpretation so that we all might draw nearer to Yeshua.

CHAPTER 3

Twenty Questions

There's a wonderful scene in Peter Jackson's film adaptation of the Lord of the Rings where a cadre of living trees called Ents attack the castle of Saurumon, a wizard turned evil. During this scene, a dam is broken and a river floods into the valley below sweeping away the army and infrastructure of Saurumon. To weather the deluge, the Ents sink their roots deep into the ground and lean into the rush of water, not swayed or moved by the oncoming torrent.

I always think of this scene in relation to a biblical theme illustrated in Ephesians 4, specifically verse 14:

> [11] *So Christ himself gave the apostles, the prophets, the evangelists, the pastors and teachers,* [12] *to equip his people for works of service, so that the body of Christ may be built up* [13] *until we all reach unity in the faith and in the knowledge of the Son of God and become mature, attaining to the whole measure of the fullness of Christ.*
>
> [14] *Then we will no longer be infants, tossed back and forth by the waves, and blown here and there by every wind of teaching and by the cunning and craftiness of people in their deceitful scheming.* [15] *Instead, speaking the truth in love, we will grow to become in every respect the mature body of him who is the head, that is, Christ.*

In our world, we face an increasing deluge of ideas and philosophies about what the Bible says and means. According to this passage in Ephesians we've been provided with teachers who, presumably, will teach good doctrine. Being grounded in good doctrine we will be equipped to stand firm in the face of a flood of craftiness and scheming. Just as the Ents were able to stand because of their roots, we, too, can stand in the faith by firmly establishing our own roots. As it says in Colossians 2, also referring to false doctrine:

> [6] *Therefore as you have received Christ Jesus the Lord, so walk in Him,* [7] *having been firmly rooted* and now *being built up in Him and established in your faith, just as you were instructed,* and *overflowing with gratitude.*
>
> [8] *See to it that no one takes you captive through philosophy and empty deception, according to the tradition of men, according to the elementary principles of the world, rather than according to Christ.*

It is with this basic principal in mind that I intend to expose a fatal misconception that has permeated almost all of Western Christianity; a misconception that has successfully severed Christianity from its root and left it vulnerable to being "*...tossed back and forth by the waves, and blown here and there by every wind of teaching...*"; a misconception that has left us with some 40,000 Christian denominations across the world! This misconception is itself rooted in the most ancient of deceptions, *"Did God really say...?"* In the garden, the serpent tempted Eve asking her *"Did God really say you mustn't eat of any tree in the Garden?"* Today this question is echoed in mainstream Christianity's approach to Torah. Did God really say I have to obey Him? Did God really say His laws and statutes were forever? Did God really say we should observe His feasts *"throughout our generations"*?

It's not only my goal to expose this false teaching, but to illustrate that it was, from the beginning, designed to create a counterfeit Christianity that is a sort of conglomeration of religious ideas and Hellenistic philosophies that lends itself to change according to a particular culture or time; a Christianity with no power to convict and thus no power to save, but so close to the real thing as to fool the average well-meaning church-goer into a false sense of relationship with the Messiah.

The misconception to which I'm referring takes many forms and is expressed in many ways but, in summary, it is the assertion that Torah has been done away with. If you've been a Christian for even a small amount of time you've probably heard this idea supported with references like "We're not under law but under grace" (a reference to Romans 6:14), or "the Law was nailed to the cross" (a mischaracterization of Colossians 2:14).

In the following chapters, I'll show how these verses, and others, have been taken out of context, and how they're not actually saying what mainstream Christianity teaches they're saying. I'll further illustrate that throughout the New Testament encouragement toward obedience to Torah permeates every author's writing including Paul and, more importantly, the words of Yeshua himself. I'll also highlight the incongruities that emerge between the Old and New Testament as a result of this false doctrine. In fact, these incongruities are unavoidable and irreconcilable if Torah has indeed been done away with. Conversely, I'll show that one should expect consistency throughout Scripture and suspicion should arise when there appear to be contradictions or changes from one part of the Bible to another.

With these lofty goals in mind, I'll start with a series of questions that come from my own walk through these spiritual waters. Problematic passages I kept finding in the Bible that ended up not being problems with the Bible but problems with my own understanding. My hope is by starting here I'll be able to drive past any offense you may be tempted to take in response to what I'm saying and establish that there are questions which deserve answers if we are to believe that Torah has been abolished. I won't answer these questions here. That's what the rest of this book is for, but I do at least want to encourage you to keep reading by demonstrating there are valid questions that deserve the attention and careful consideration of every believer trying to *"follow after Christ"* (1 Peter 2:21).

Because the majority of those who read this are likely "New Testament Christians" I'll limit the scope of my questions to the latter two-thirds of Scripture, Matthew to Revelation.

Question 1: If Torah has been done away with, what is Yeshua saying in Matthew 23?

> *[1] Then Yeshua spoke to the crowds and to His disciples, [2] saying: "The scribes and the Pharisees have seated themselves in the chair of Moses; [3] **therefore all that they tell you, do and observe**, but do not do according to their deeds; for they say things and do not do them.*

The chair of Moses or the seat of Moses, depending on the translation, is a reference to one's authority to teach Torah. Just as Moses received Torah from Yah and taught it to the Israelites at Mt. Sinai, so too were the scribes and Pharisees responsible for teaching Torah to the people in Yeshua's day. This authority for teaching is described as "sitting in the seat of Moses". Knowing that these men were teaching Torah, it seems very strange that Yeshua would tell the people to do and observe all that they instruct if Yeshua's intention was to abolish Torah through His death and resurrection in the very near future.

Questions 2-4: What is meant by Yeshua in John 14?

> [10] *Do you not believe that I am in the Father, and the Father is in Me? The words that I say to you I do not speak on My own initiative, but the Father abiding in Me does His works.* [11] *Believe Me that I am in the Father and the Father is in Me; otherwise believe because of the works themselves.* [12] *Truly, truly, I say to you, he who believes in Me, the works that I do, he will do also; and greater works than these he will do; because I go to the Father.* [13] *Whatever you ask in My name, that will I do, so that the Father may be glorified in the Son.* [14] *If you ask Me anything in My name, I will do it.*
>
> [15] *"If you love Me, you will keep My commandments.*

Question 2: This whole exchange is very confusing if Torah is no longer relevant. Regarding verse 12, it's hopefully well understood that the distinction of Yeshua's life was that of perfect obedience to Torah so what is meant when he says, *"the works that I do, [he who believes] will do also"*?

Question 3: Moving to verse 15, what does Yeshua mean when he says, *"if you love me, you will keep my commandments"*?

Question 4: Most will refer to the beatitudes or the vice/virtue lists in Paul's letters as "Yeshua's commandments" but Yeshua clearly says in verse 10 that what He's saying aren't His words but the words of the Father. Yeshua is doing the Father's work. Where do we find the words of the Father and the work of the Father recorded if not in Torah?

To avoid being accused of taking these words to mean something Yeshua didn't intend, this concept is expressed more directly later in the same chapter:

> ²³ *Yeshua answered and said to him, "If anyone loves Me, he will keep My word; and My Father will love him, and We will come to him and make Our abode with him.* ²⁴ *He who does not love Me does not keep My words; and the word which you hear is not Mine, but the Father's who sent Me.*

That last phrase is interesting. The common understanding is that Yeshua came on the scene with a new message. A message of liberty instead of law, but he's clearly saying here that His words are not His, but the Father's. Again, in John 15:

> ¹⁰ *If you keep My commandments, you will abide in My love; just as I have kept My Father's commandments and abide in His love.*

Taken together, this would seem to pose a big problem for those who say Yeshua brought, in a sense, his own commandments to replace Torah.

Questions 5-7: How shall we explain Yeshua's statements in Matthew 5?

> ¹⁷ *"Do not think that I came to abolish the Law or the Prophets; I did not come to abolish but to fulfill.* ¹⁸ *For truly I say to you, until heaven and earth pass away, not the smallest letter or stroke shall pass from the Law until all is accomplished.* ¹⁹ *Whoever then annuls one of the least of these commandments, and teaches others* to do the same, *shall be called least in the kingdom of heaven; but whoever keeps and teaches* them, *he shall be called great in the kingdom of heaven.*

Question 5: In verse 17, are we to believe that the words "abolish" and "fulfill" have the same practical meaning? Yeshua says he did not come to abolish the law, abolish of course meaning "to do away with". Mainstream Christian teaching says Yeshua did away with the law by fulfilling it. If we paraphrase with this in mind, is Yeshua saying *"I did not come to {do away with the law}, but {to do away with the law}?"* That doesn't just seem odd, it seems nonsensical.

Question 6: Further, in verse 18, Yeshua states clearly that nothing from Torah will pass away until heaven and Earth pass away. Since that hasn't happened, how can Torah have been abolished?

Many will assert that, "until all is accomplished" was satisfied with Yeshua's death on the cross. After all, didn't Yeshua say *"It is finished"*? Unfortunately, you have to separate *"until all is accomplished"* from the phrase *"until heaven and earth pass away"* to make this work, but that means Yeshua references two points in time and we're left to wonder which is the correct one. Will *"...not the smallest letter or stroke...pass from the Law..."* until all is accomplished or until heaven and Earth pass away?

As we know from Revelation 21:1, there will be a time when heaven and Earth pass away and a new heaven and new Earth are created. Assuming that two times are given instead of two ways of referring to the same time creates confusion where no confusion exists. When Yeshua says *"it is finished"*, that's not the same thing as *"all having been accomplished"*. After all, we know a vital part of Yah's plan was Yeshua's resurrection, so it would be very strange if *"until all is accomplished"* comes when Yeshua died but before He rose again. This leaves us with no other choice but to reject this passage as proof that all was accomplished, and by extension Torah passed away, when Yeshua said *"it is finished"*.

Finally, in Matthew 5:19, Yeshua makes a distinction between those who will be called least and those who will be called greatest in heaven.

> [19] Whoever then annuls one of the least of these commandments, and teaches others to do the same, shall be called least in the kingdom of heaven; but whoever keeps and teaches them, he shall be called great in the kingdom of heaven.

Question 7: The distinction hinges on whether one practiced Torah and taught others to do the same or didn't obey and taught others that they also didn't have to obey. What are we to do with this verse if Torah was about to be abolished upon Yeshua's death and resurrection?

Question 8: What is the "word of God" Yeshua is referring to in Luke 11:28 if not Torah?

> [27] While Yeshua was saying these things, one of the women in the crowd raised her voice and said to Him, "Blessed is the womb that bore You and the breasts at which You nursed." [28] But He said, "On the contrary, blessed are those who hear the word of God and observe it."

As with the passage from John 14, it's important to keep in mind Yeshua's assertions that his words were not his own, but Yah's. Also remember that at this time, there was no New Testament that He could be referring to.

At this point you may be thinking, well this is all a bit of a moot point because all of these are references to points in time before Yeshua's death and resurrection and that's when Torah was abolished. Aside from the *"it is finished"* topic we just covered, does it make sense that Yeshua would promote Torah for the short time he was to remain alive even though He would have known it would be irrelevant in a matter of months and thus not at all applicable to future readers of Scripture? Additionally, as an aside, why did He never actually tell anyone the significant change of Torah's being abolished was coming?

Just to cover my bases though, let's move on to examples from after Yeshua's death. For those who teach that Torah observance is no longer necessary, every scriptural example cited comes from Paul's writings. There are zero proof-texts drawn from any other authors of New Testament texts (a fact which, on its own, should make us suspicious) . For this reason, I'll start with a few questions about Paul's beliefs.

Question 9: When Paul is accused of teaching that Torah has been abolished, why does he defend his belief in and observance of Torah in Acts 24 instead of simply explaining that the accusations are accurate; that Torah has, in fact, been abolished?

Paul is first informed of the false accusations against him in Acts 21:20-21:

> [20] *"...You see, brother, how many myriads of Jews there are who have believed, and they are all zealous for the law;* [21] *but they have been informed about you that you teach all the Jews who are among the Gentiles to forsake Moses, saying that they ought not to circumcise their children nor to walk according to the customs.*

Then the formal accusation appears in Acts 21:27-29:

> [27] *Now when the seven days were almost ended, the Jews from Asia, seeing him in the temple, stirred up the whole crowd and laid hands on him,* [28] *crying out, "Men of Israel, help! This is the man who teaches all men everywhere against*

> the people, the law, and this place; and furthermore he also brought Greeks into the temple and has defiled this holy place." [29] (For they had previously seen Trophimus the Ephesian with him in the city, whom they supposed that Paul had brought into the temple.)

And finally, Paul's response in Acts 24:10-21:

> [10] When the governor had nodded for him to speak, Paul responded:
>
> "Knowing that for many years you have been a judge to this nation, I cheerfully make my defense, [11] since you can take note of the fact that no more than twelve days ago I went up to Jerusalem to worship. [12] Neither in the temple, nor in the synagogues, nor in the city itself did they find me carrying on a discussion with anyone or causing a riot. [13] Nor can they prove to you the charges of which they now accuse me. [14] But this I admit to you, that according to the Way which they call a sect I do serve the God of our fathers, believing everything that is in accordance with the Law and that is written in the Prophets; [15] having a hope in God, which these men cherish themselves, that there shall certainly be a resurrection of both the righteous and the wicked. [16] In view of this, I also do my best to maintain always a blameless conscience both before God and before men. [17] Now after several years I came to bring alms to my nation and to present offerings; [18] in which they found me occupied in the temple, having been purified, without any crowd or uproar. But there were some Jews from Asia— [19] who ought to have been present before you and to make accusation, if they should have anything against me. [20] Or else let these men themselves tell what misdeed they found when I stood before the Council, [21] other than for this one statement which I shouted out while standing among them, 'For the resurrection of the dead I am on trial before you today.'"

This is a fascinating part of Acts. Paul has been told about rumors of his teaching against Torah, then he's formally accused of teaching that obedience to Torah is no longer required and is subsequently brought before a court to answer for these charges. Instead of defending the idea that upon Yeshua's death and resurrection Torah was abolished, he asserts his own obedience to Torah! In verse 13 he explicitly states that his accusers cannot prove their complaint but goes further in verse 14 saying explicitly that he *"believes everything that is in accordance with the Law and that is written in the Prophets"*. He goes on to give specific examples of his Torah observance including bringing alms and offerings, his purification, and earlier in the passage, his time spent in devotion at the temple. It's interesting that today mainstream Christians insist Paul teaches the abolishment of Torah when we have a record of his own legal defense against this very accusation.

Question 10: Why does Paul explain that the problem of the carnal mind is that it isn't subject to the Law of God in Romans 8?

> *⁵ For those who are according to the flesh set their minds on the things of the flesh, but those who are according to the Spirit, the things of the Spirit. ⁶ For the mind set on the flesh is death, but the mind set on the Spirit is life and peace, ⁷ because the mind set on the flesh is hostile toward God; for it does not subject itself to the law of God, for it is not even able to do so, ⁸ and those who are in the flesh cannot please God.*

This is another passage to address with care because it's often used to assert the abolition of Torah. Paul uses the word "law" to describe three distinct laws so we need to be precise in our study of this passage. For the purposes of this chapter, focus on verse 7 where he describes the nature of *"the mind set on the flesh"*. Why does Paul say it's hostile toward God? Because it does not subject itself to the Law of God! If there is no longer a Law of God to subject itself to, this seems to be an odd statement.

Because Paul's writings are so complex and deserving of their own chapter I'll leave it at that for now and move on to another New Testament author, James. In James chapter 1, we find the following:

> *²² But prove yourselves doers of the word, and not merely hearers who delude themselves. ²³ For if anyone is a hearer of the word and not a doer, he is like a man who looks at his natural face in a mirror; ²⁴ for once he has looked at himself and gone away, he has immediately forgotten what kind of person he was. ²⁵ But one who looks intently at the perfect law, the law of liberty, and abides by it, not having become a forgetful hearer but an effectual doer, this man will be blessed in what he does.*

The crux of this passage is James' reference to what he means by being a *"doer of the word"* in verse 25. The KJV renders this verse:

> *"But whoso looketh into the perfect law of liberty, and continueth therein, he being not a forgetful hearer, but a doer of the work, this man shall be blessed in his deed."*

James defines *"the word"* he's referring to as *"the perfect law of liberty"*. This language is also used in the Psalms, specifically Psalm 19:7, where we see Torah described as the perfect Law:

> *The law of the LORD is perfect, restoring the soul; The testimony of the LORD is sure, making wise the simple.*

Concerning liberty, consider Psalm 119:44-45:

> *[44] So I will keep Your law continually,*
> *Forever and ever.*
> *[45] And I will walk at liberty,*
> *For I seek Your precepts.*

I don't think it's too much of a stretch to assume James would have been familiar with the Psalms and was appealing to an audience also familiar with the Psalms. It seems clear James is not describing a new concept or a new law, but rather a concept that was well understood using terms familiar to a Hebrew mind in his day in reference to Torah.

To further illustrate, it's important to note the basic principles James illustrates in his epistle. At the end of chapter 1, verse 27, he mentions visiting and caring for orphans and widows:

> *[27] Pure and undefiled religion in the sight of our God and Father is this: to visit orphans and widows in their distress, and to keep oneself unstained by the world.*

This is part of the wisdom of Torah. In Exodus 22 we find instruction concerning orphans and widows in the negative:

> *[22] You shall not afflict any widow or orphan. [23] If you afflict him at all, and if he does cry out to Me, I will surely hear his cry; [24] and My anger will be kindled, and I will kill you with the sword, and your wives shall become widows and your children fatherless.*

And in Deuteronomy 10 we're told Yah executes justice for the orphan and widow:

> ¹⁸ He executes justice for the orphan and the widow, and shows His love for the alien by giving him food and clothing.

In James chapter 2, while teaching not to favor a person based on station or wealth, James rests his case on another Torah concept; to love one's neighbor as oneself. This is of course the second of the instructions given in Exodus 20 and according to Yeshua in Matthew 22, one of the two commandments on which, as the NIV and KJV render verse 40, "*all of Torah and the prophets rest*".

> ³⁷ And He said to him, "'YOU SHALL LOVE THE LORD YOUR GOD WITH ALL YOUR HEART, AND WITH ALL YOUR SOUL, AND WITH ALL YOUR MIND.' ³⁸ *This is the great and foremost commandment.* ³⁹ *The second is like it,* 'YOU SHALL LOVE YOUR NEIGHBOR AS YOURSELF.' ⁴⁰ *On these two commandments depend the whole Law and the Prophets.*"

Question 11: If Torah has been abolished doesn't it seem odd for James to refer to it so frequently. And not just to refer to it, but in fact to use Torah as the basis for what he writes?

Moving on to Peter, we see similar references to Torah. In 1 Peter chapter 1, Peter advises soberness and obedience. Leaving aside what Peter might be saying we should be obedient to, let's look at why he's advising what he does, namely that we're to be holy because Yah is holy:

> ¹³ *Therefore, prepare your minds for action, keep sober* in spirit, *fix your hope completely on the grace to be brought to you at the revelation of Yeshua Christ.* ¹⁴ *As obedient children, do not be conformed to the former lusts* which were yours *in your ignorance,* ¹⁵ *but like the Holy One who called you, be holy yourselves also in all* your *behavior;* ¹⁶ *because it is written,* "YOU SHALL BE HOLY, FOR I AM HOLY."

Peter is quoting Torah, specifically the beginning of Leviticus 11:44:

> *For I am the* LORD *your God. Consecrate yourselves therefore, and be holy, for I am holy...*

and Leviticus 20:26:

> Thus you are to be holy to Me, for I the Lord am holy; and I have set you apart from the peoples to be Mine.

In Chapter 4, Peter warns against a series of particular behaviors:

> ¹⁵ Make sure that none of you suffers as a murderer, or thief, or evildoer, or a troublesome meddler;

The KJV renders this verse:

> ¹⁵ But let none of you suffer as a murderer, or as a thief, or as an evildoer, or as a busybody in other men's matters.

In this one statement, we see commandments six and eight from Exodus 20 (Exodus 20:13 and 15) as well as the prohibition against slander or gossip (Leviticus 19:16), what the NASB calls a troublesome meddler and what the King James calls a busybody.

In Peter's second epistle there's an interesting phrase used in the context of his warning against false teaching. In chapter 2 we read:

> ¹ But false prophets also arose among the people, just as there will also be false teachers among you, who will secretly introduce destructive heresies, even denying the Master who bought them, bringing swift destruction upon themselves. ² Many will follow their sensuality, and because of them the way of the truth will be maligned; ³ and in their greed they will exploit you with false words; their judgment from long ago is not idle, and their destruction is not asleep.

I'd like to draw your attention specifically to verse 2, and what Peter calls *"the way of truth"*, which will be maligned by false teachers. Psalm 119:142 says:

> ¹⁴² Your righteousness is an everlasting righteousness,
> And Your law is truth.

In the King James, in Malachi 2, we find the following:

> [6] *The law of truth was in his mouth, and iniquity was not found in his lips: he walked with me in peace and equity, and did turn many away from iniquity. (KJV)*

In fact, if we keep going to Malachi 2:8, we see the prophet saying to false teachers of his day almost exactly what Peter foretells about false teachers to come (also note that Malachi refers to Yah's instruction as "the way", the same phrase Paul used in the passage I referenced from Acts as part of question 9):

> [8] *But as for you, you have turned aside from the way; you have caused many to stumble by the instruction; you have corrupted the covenant of Levi," says the* LORD *of hosts.*

Although the NASB, NIV, and ESV start with *"true instruction"* instead of *"the law of truth"*, the Hebrew word translated law or instruction in both Psalm 119:142 and Malachi 2:6 (as well as Malachi 2:8) is Torah. Regardless of how it's rendered in any given translation we're left with the *"true {Torah}"* or *"the {Torah} of truth"*, respectively.

Question 12: Isn't it reasonable to conclude that when Peter refers to the *"way of truth"* he's referring to Torah? If he is referring to Torah, does it not also raise serious questions about the validity of the teaching that Torah has been abolished when Peter warns here that Torah will be maligned by false teachers?

Question 13: Why does Peter, much like James, spend so much time warning readers not to turn from "the way" if it's irrelevant having been abolished?

Finally, we come to the letters of John. Right out of the gate John elicits language from several Old Testament sources. In the very first chapter of 1 John we read these words:

> [5] *This is the message we have heard from Him and announce to you, that God is Light, and in Him there is no darkness at all.* [6] *If we say that we have fellowship with Him and yet walk in the darkness, we lie and do not practice the truth;* [7] *but if we walk in the Light as He Himself is in the Light, we have fellowship with one another, and the blood of Yeshua His Son cleanses us from all sin.*

Consider the following:

> Proverbs 6:23 - "For the commandment is a lamp and the teaching is light; And reproofs for discipline are the way of life."
>
> Psalm 119:105-106 - "Your word is a lamp to my feet and a light to my path. I have sworn and I will confirm it, that I will keep Your righteous ordinances."
>
> Isaiah 2:3-5 - "And many peoples will come and say, **"Come, let us go up to the mountain of the LORD, to the house of the God of Jacob; That He may teach us concerning His ways and that we may walk in His paths." For the law will go forth from Zion and the word of the LORD from Jerusalem.** And He will judge between the nations, and will render decisions for many peoples; and they will hammer their swords into plowshares and their spears into pruning hooks. Nation will not lift up sword against nation, and never again will they learn war. **Come, house of Jacob, and let us walk in the light of the LORD.**"
>
> Isaiah 8:20 - "To the law and to the testimony: if they speak not according to this word, it is because there is no light in them." (KJV)

Question 14: Considering all these passages refer to obeying Torah as walking in the light, is it reasonable to believe that in 1 John 1:7 the author would use the exact same language to refer to something other than Torah?

We find additional supporting evidence in the second chapter of 1 John where John writes:

> ³ By this we know that we have come to know Him, if we keep His commandments. ⁴ The one who says, "I have come to know Him," and does not keep His commandments, is a liar, and the truth is not in him; ⁵ but whoever keeps His word, in him the love of God has truly been perfected. By this we know that we are in Him: ⁶ the one who says he abides in Him ought himself to walk in the same manner as He walked.

Some will insist that *"His commandments"* in this passage is referring to things Yeshua said or referenced directly, and while this view deserves a deeper analysis than I will give it in this chapter, it's important to look at this passage as a whole. John describes the same thing, namely *"abiding in Him"* in two ways. He describes it in verses 3 and 4 as *"keeping His commandments"* and in verse 6 as *"walking in the same manner as He walked"*. It's important to understand that these are not two different things being described but two ways of describing the same thing. Since we know that Yeshua was without sin, and we know that Torah is the standard by which any action or behavior is judged sinful or righteous, we know without question how he walked. To be judged sinless, He had to have walked in perfect Torah obedience.

Question 15: If the manner in which He walked (and by extension the manner in which he who abides in Him ought to walk) is in obedience to Torah, is it reasonable to believe that the statements in verses 3 and 4 are referring to some set of commandments other than Torah?

Question 16: Even if John is describing two different things, it stands to reason that one of those two is the manner in which He walked which was according to Torah. If Torah has been abolished, are we to simply accept that verse 3 and 4 are referring to some new set of commandments and ignore verse 6 entirely?

Some may suggest verse 6 isn't talking about Torah either, that perhaps Yeshua walked according to his own "New Testament commandments", rather than Torah. If we skip ahead briefly to 1 John 5:1-3 that becomes a problematic position:

> *[1] Whoever believes that Yeshua is the Christ is born of God, and whoever loves the Father loves the child born of Him. [2] By this we know that we love the children of God, when we love God and observe His commandments. [3] For this is the love of God, that we keep His commandments; and His commandments are not burdensome.*

Verses 2 and 3 refer to the commandments of God in no uncertain terms. Theologically, the Son and the Father are both "God", but in this passage, it's clear that the word "God" is referencing the Father as distinct from Yeshua, the Son, a fact that's established by verse 1. There's simply no room to argue that John's reference to God's commandments are somehow intended to mean new commandments that Yeshua established apart from Torah.

Further evidence that John is referring to Torah can be found in a passage I cited in the "Givens" chapter to define the word "sin". In 1 John 3 we find this passage (I've used the KJV here because the way the sentences are structured makes this illustration a bit clearer, but comparing other translations will yield the same results):

> ⁴ *Whosoever committeth sin transgresseth also the law: for **sin is the transgression of the law**. ⁵ And ye know that he was manifested to take away our sins; and in him is no sin. ⁶ Whosoever abideth in him sinneth not: whosoever sinneth hath not seen him, neither known him.*

In verse four John says clearly, sin is the transgression of the law. If we play a simple game of word replacement, writing "transgression of the law" wherever we see the word "sin" to see if this definition holds true, the verse becomes quite interesting and further proves my point:

> ⁴ *Whosoever committeth sin transgresseth also the law: for sin is the transgression of the law. ⁵ And ye know that he was manifested to take away our **{transgressions of the law}**; and in him is no **{transgression of the law}**. ⁶ Whosoever abideth in him **{transgresses the law}** not: whosoever **{transgresses the law}** hath not seen him, neither known him.*

Just for grins, let's go one step forward replacing the word law with the word Torah:

> ⁴ *Whosoever committeth sin transgresseth also **{Torah}**: for sin is the transgression of **{Torah}**. ⁵ And ye know that he was manifested to take away our **{transgressions of the Torah}**; and in him is no **{transgression of the Torah}**. ⁶ Whosoever abideth in him **{transgresses the Torah}** not: whosoever **{transgresses the Torah}** hath not seen him, neither known him.*

Question 17: Knowing that Yeshua's sinlessness and His perfect obedience to Torah are one and the same, and seeing that in verse 5 this word replacement exercise paints an accurate picture of our salvation through Yeshua, are we to believe that this understanding of John's definition of sin refers to Torah in verse 5 but something different in verse 6, or does it make more sense to assume the whole passage refers to Torah?

This leads us to the second epistle of John which provides a nice segue from direct questions about specific verses to a handful of thematic questions. Back in the discussion around questions 2, 3, and 4, I talked about how Yeshua explained that the things He came to say weren't His own but were His Father's – that what He taught wasn't new. There's a running theme throughout the New Testament that includes those passages in the gospel of John and picks up again in 2 John 4.

> ⁴ I was very glad to find some of your children walking in truth, just as we have received commandment to do from the Father. ⁵ Now I ask you, lady, not as though I were writing to you a new commandment, but the one which we have had from the beginning, that we love one another. ⁶ And this is love, that we walk according to His commandments. This is the commandment, just as you have heard from the beginning, that you should walk in it.

Some argue that here, as in 1 John 2:7, when John refers to *"the beginning"* he means since the start of Yeshua's ministry or from the beginning of the spread of Christianity; perhaps since the first gospel accounts. Different theories interpret different events as the beginning, but they all rely on the simple fact that the beginning can't mean way back in the Old Testament, because of course the Law has been done away with so that can't be the commandment in view here. Essentially the idea that John is referring to Torah is eliminated on the basis of the pre-conception that he can't be referring to Torah. As we've already seen, the instruction to love one another goes back much further than Yeshua's ministry. We've also already seen that Yeshua himself refers to Torah when he says, love of Yah and love of others are the greatest commandments.

Question 18: If the beginning in 2 John 4 refers to some point in time relatively close to Yeshua's life on earth, how do we interpret 1 John 3:11-17?

> ¹¹ For this is the message which you have heard from the beginning, that we should love one another; ¹² not as Cain, who was of the evil one and slew his brother. And for what reason did he slay him? Because his deeds were evil, and his brother's were righteous. ¹³ Do not be surprised, brethren, if the world hates you. ¹⁴ We know that we have passed out of death into life, because we love the brethren. He who does not love abides in death. ¹⁵ Everyone who hates his brother is a murderer; and you know that no murderer has eternal life abiding in him. ¹⁶ We know love by this, that He laid down His life for us; and we ought to lay down our lives for the brethren. ¹⁷ But whoever has the world's goods, and sees his brother in need and closes his heart against him, how does the love of God abide in him? ¹⁸ Little children, let us not love with word or with

> tongue, but in deed and truth. [19] We will know by this that we are of the truth, and will assure our heart before Him [20] in whatever our heart condemns us; for God is greater than our heart and knows all things. [21] Beloved, if our heart does not condemn us, we have confidence before God; [22] and whatever we ask we receive from Him, because we keep His commandments and do the things that are pleasing in His sight.

In these verses John begins by referencing *"the message that you heard from the beginning"*, takes the idea asserted by Yeshua, that if one is angry with one's brother that person has murdered his brother in his heart, as being originally illustrated way back in the account of Cain and Abel and ties it in with the nature of love itself. But wait! I thought the idea that anger in the heart being the same as murder was a New Testament idea? Apparently, John disagrees and makes a clear case that this was, if I may borrow the phrase, a *"message that was heard from the beginning"*. Does it make sense that in some places when John refers to *"commandments known from the beginning"* he's talking about relatively new ideas, i.e. contemporary to the life of Yeshua, even though they aren't new ideas, while in other places *"commandments known from the beginning"* refers to the origin of these supposedly new ideas, namely Torah?

Over and over again we see this concept that what is being taught is not new. That there is, in Yeshua, a new demonstration of the Father's wisdom and instruction to be sure, but the wisdom and instruction itself was shared long before Yah became man in the person of Yeshua.

Another thematic idea found in modern Christianity is that there is an opposition between Torah and grace. Some even go so far as to say that you undercut or insult Yeshua's sacrifice on our behalf by even attempting Torah obedience. For years this concept seemed to make sense. I was taught there was a sort of scale. On one end is the Law and on the other is grace; two polar opposite ideas that cannot co-exist. To put it another way, one can either follow the commandments of Yah, or claim the testimony of Yeshua. I was taught that it was either-or but cannot be both.

In Revelation, there are two verses that deserve consideration in light of the teaching I've just described. In Revelation 12, the apostle John describes the dragon making war with the remnant of believers saying:

> [17] So the dragon was enraged with the woman, and went off to make war with the rest of her children, who keep the commandments of God and hold to the testimony of Yeshua.

Later, in chapter 14, John talks about two groups. Those who take the mark of the beast and the saints. In verse 12 he describes *"the perseverance of the saints"* saying:

> [12] Here is the perseverance of the saints who keep the commandments of God and their faith in Yeshua.

This is another place where I think the KJV is a more consistent rendering:

> [12] Here is the patience of the saints: here are they that keep the commandments of God, and the faith of Yeshua.

Question 19: If the commandments of God, aka Torah, are distinct from and opposed to faith in Christ why does John not once but twice combine them? Why does he describe the remnant not as those who keep Torah *or* those who believe in Yeshua, but as those who do/have both?

In addition to my assertions that Yeshua's teaching referred to Torah principals established in the past, we also see references to Torah in the future. For this I'll have to dip into the Old Testament but I'll ask for a bit of latitude as each passage quoted in this section speaks prophetically of a time after Yeshua's death and resurrection, most referring to a time after His second coming. For instance, in reference to the millennial reign of Yeshua, Isaiah writes the following:

> [2] Now it will come about that
> In the last days
> The mountain of the house of the LORD
> Will be established as the chief of the mountains,
> And will be raised above the hills;
> And all the nations will stream to it.
> [3] And many peoples will come and say,
> "Come, let us go up to the mountain of the LORD,
> To the house of the God of Jacob;

> *That He may teach us concerning His ways*
> *And that we may walk in His paths."*
> *For the law will go forth from Zion*
> *And the word of the LORD from Jerusalem.*

The word translated as "law" at the end of verse 3 is the word Torah, which means this passage is inarguably saying that in the last days people, in fact all nations, will travel to Zion to learn Torah. Micah serves as a second witness in chapter 4 of his prophecy:

> *[1] And it will come about in the last days*
> *That the mountain of the house of the LORD*
> *Will be established as the chief of the mountains.*
> *It will be raised above the hills,*
> *And the peoples will stream to it.*
> *[2] Many nations will come and say,*
> *"Come and let us go up to the mountain of the LORD*
> *And to the house of the God of Jacob,*
> *That He may teach us about His ways*
> *And that we may walk in His paths."*
> *For from Zion will go forth the law,*
> *Even the word of the LORD from Jerusalem.*

The language is strikingly similar in these two passages; so similar that one might conclude one prophet is simply quoting the other. I suppose that could be true, although I highly doubt it because of the way each book begins. Isaiah chapter two begins with *"The word which Isaiah the son of Amoz saw concerning Judah and Jerusalem..."*, while the book of Micah starts with *"The word of the Lord which came to Micah...."*

This indicates Yah delivered the same prophecy to two prophets individually, not that one is quoting or borrowing from the other. It's beyond the scope of this book to go into detail on this, but the Biblical significance of two (or more) witnesses cannot be understated in establishing truth and here we have two witnesses to the fact that after Yeshua's return, Torah will *"go out from Zion"* to all nations.

In Ezekiel's prophecies, there are several similar prognostications indicating Torah's relevance in the days to come. For instance, in chapter 37, Ezekiel tells of the future reunion of the divided kingdom saying:

> ²¹ *Say to them, 'Thus says the Lord GOD, "Behold, I will take the sons of Israel from among the nations where they have gone, and I will gather them from every side and bring them into their own land;* ²² *and I will make them one nation in the land, on the mountains of Israel; and one king will be king for all of them; and they will no longer be two nations and no longer be divided into two kingdoms.* ²³ *They will no longer defile themselves with their idols, or with their detestable things, or with any of their transgressions; but I will deliver them from all their dwelling places in which they have sinned, and will cleanse them. And they will be My people, and I will be their God.* ²⁴ **"My servant David will be king over them, and they will all have one shepherd; and they will walk in My ordinances and keep My statutes and observe them.**

Later, in Chapter 43, Ezekiel recounts a vision where he sees the future kingdom of Yah. Interestingly, this vision shares significant similarities with John's visions related in Revelation, but specifically Ezekiel is asked to tell the people how things work in Yah's kingdom, saying:

> ¹⁰ *"As for you, son of man, describe the temple to the house of Israel, that they may be ashamed of their iniquities; and let them measure the plan.* ¹¹ *If they are ashamed of all that they have done, make known to them the design of the house, its structure, its exits, its entrances, all its designs, all its statutes, and all its laws. And write it in their sight, so that they may observe its whole design and all its statutes and do them.* ¹² *This is the law of the house: its entire area on the top of the mountain all around shall be most holy. Behold, this is the law of the house.*

It's interesting that Ezekiel is instructed to relate the *"law of the house"* so that *"they may observe its whole design and all its statutes and do them"*. As has been mentioned before regarding Yeshua's words (see question 1), it seems odd to instruct the people to obey Torah on the grounds that it will be part of the design of Yah's kingdom in the distant future (post second coming) but abolished in the near future (Yeshua's first coming). Are we to believe Torah was relevant, then not relevant, but will become relevant again?

We see similar advice in the fourth chapter of Malachi where the prophet is relating Yah's advice for those who wish to be prepared for Yeshua's second coming:

> [1] "For behold, the day is coming, burning like a furnace; and all the arrogant and every evildoer will be chaff; and the day that is coming will set them ablaze," says the Lord of hosts, "so that it will leave them neither root nor branch." [2] "But for you who fear My name, the sun of righteousness will rise with healing in its wings; and you will go forth and skip about like calves from the stall. [3] You will tread down the wicked, for they will be ashes under the soles of your feet on the day which I am preparing," says the Lord of hosts. [4] "Remember the law of Moses My servant, even the statutes and ordinances which I commanded him in Horeb for all Israel. [5] "Behold, I am going to send you Elijah the prophet before the coming of the great and terrible day of the Lord. [6] He will restore the hearts of the fathers to their children and the hearts of the children to their fathers, so that I will not come and smite the land with a curse."

Since these are all broad references to Torah, and because some will suggest that he's foretelling not of Old Testament law, but of some new law of Christ, it's helpful to illustrate specific examples from Torah which indicate in the future kingdom, the Millennial Kingdom that Yeshua will establish upon His return, Torah, in unaltered form, will remain. In Ezekiel 44 the prophet records a future when the Levitical priesthood will resume its temple duties. While this entire section is peppered with references to Torah from Leviticus, I'd like to focus on a few specifics: the separation between clean and unclean, the exercise of Torah judgments and statutes, and the keeping of the Sabbath:

> [23] Moreover, they shall teach My people the difference between the holy and the profane, and cause them to discern between the unclean and the clean. [24] In a dispute they shall take their stand to judge; they shall judge it according to My ordinances. They shall also keep My laws and My statutes in all My appointed feasts and sanctify My sabbaths.

Isaiah also refers to the Sabbath and the lunar calendar in 66:22-23:

> [22] "For just as the new heavens and the new earth
> Which I make will endure before Me," declares the Lord,
> "So your offspring and your name will endure.
> [23] "And it shall be from new moon to new moon
> And from sabbath to sabbath,
> All mankind will come to bow down before Me," says the Lord.

Moreover, we see Yah's holy days being kept. For instance, in Ezekiel 46:9 there's a reference to Yah's "appointed feasts" generally:

> [8] When the prince enters, he shall go in by way of the porch of the gate and go out by the same way. [9] But when the people of the land come before the LORD at the appointed feasts, he who enters by way of the north gate to worship shall go out by way of the south gate. And he who enters by way of the south gate shall go out by way of the north gate.

In Ezekiel 45 we see specific references to the Passover and the Feast of Unleavened Bread being kept:

> [21] "In the first month, on the fourteenth day of the month, you shall have the Passover, a feast of seven days; unleavened bread shall be eaten.

Finally, in Zechariah 14:16 we're told that the Feast of Tabernacles (here called the Feast of Booths) will be observed by all nations. In fact, a curse is levied on those who don't observe this feast in the future kingdom:

> [16] Then it will come about that any who are left of all the nations that went against Jerusalem will go up from year to year to worship the King, the LORD of hosts, and to celebrate the Feast of Booths. [17] And it will be that whichever of the families of the earth does not go up to Jerusalem to worship the King, the LORD of hosts, there will be no rain on them. [18] If the family of Egypt does not go up or enter, then no rain will fall on them; it will be the plague with which the LORD smites the nations who do not go up to celebrate the Feast of Booths. [19] This will be the punishment of Egypt, and the punishment of all the nations who do not go up to celebrate the Feast of Booths.

Perhaps most astonishing are all the references to sacrifices in the future kingdom. For instance, Ezekiel 43:18-27:

> [18] And He said to me, "Son of man, thus says the Lord GOD, 'These are the statutes for the altar on the day it is built, to offer burnt offerings on it and to sprinkle blood on it. [19] You shall give to the Levitical priests who are from the offspring of Zadok, who draw near to Me to minister to Me,' declares the Lord GOD, 'a young bull for a sin offering. [20] You shall take some of its blood and put it on its four horns and on the four corners of the ledge and on the border round about; thus you shall cleanse it and make atonement for it. [21] You shall also take the bull for the sin offering, and it shall be burned in the appointed place of the house, outside the sanctuary.

> ²² 'On the second day you shall offer a male goat without blemish for a sin offering, and they shall cleanse the altar as they cleansed it with the bull. ²³ When you have finished cleansing it, you shall present a young bull without blemish and a ram without blemish from the flock. ²⁴ You shall present them before the LORD, and the priests shall throw salt on them, and they shall offer them up as a burnt offering to the LORD. ²⁵ For seven days you shall prepare daily a goat for a sin offering; also a young bull and a ram from the flock, without blemish, shall be prepared. ²⁶ For seven days they shall make atonement for the altar and purify it; so shall they consecrate it. ²⁷ When they have completed the days, it shall be that on the eighth day and onward, the priests shall offer your burnt offerings on the altar, and your peace offerings; and I will accept you,' declares the Lord GOD."

Ezekiel 44:11:

> ¹¹ Yet they shall be ministers in My sanctuary, having oversight at the gates of the house and ministering in the house; they shall slaughter the burnt offering and the sacrifice for the people, and they shall stand before them to minister to them.

Ezekiel 46:1-8, which also mentions the Sabbath:

> ¹ 'Thus says the Lord GOD, "The gate of the inner court facing east shall be shut the six working days; but it shall be opened on the sabbath day and opened on the day of the new moon. ² The prince shall enter by way of the porch of the gate from outside and stand by the post of the gate. Then the priests shall provide his burnt offering and his peace offerings, and he shall worship at the threshold of the gate and then go out; but the gate shall not be shut until the evening. ³ The people of the land shall also worship at the doorway of that gate before the LORD on the sabbaths and on the new moons. ⁴ The burnt offering which the prince shall offer to the LORD on the sabbath day shall be six lambs without blemish and a ram without blemish; ⁵ and the grain offering shall be an ephah with the ram, and the grain offering with the lambs as much as he is able to give, and a hin of oil with an ephah. ⁶ On the day of the new moon he shall offer a young bull without blemish, also six lambs and a ram, which shall be without blemish. ⁷ And he shall provide a grain offering, an ephah with the bull and an ephah with the ram, and with the lambs as much as he is able, and a hin of oil with an ephah.

Isaiah also mentions sacrifices in the future kingdom in chapter 56:

> ⁷ Even those I will bring to My holy mountain
> And make them joyful in My house of prayer.

> Their burnt offerings and their sacrifices will be acceptable on My altar;
> For My house will be called a house of prayer for all the peoples."

Perhaps equally surprising are the prophecies about the criteria by which an individual will be included or excluded from the future kingdom. In Isaiah 56 particular and repeated emphasis is placed on the importance of keeping the Sabbath:

> Thus says the LORD,
> "Preserve justice and do righteousness,
> For My salvation is about to come
> And My righteousness to be revealed.
> ² "How blessed is the man who does this,
> And the son of man who takes hold of it;
> Who keeps from profaning the sabbath,
> And keeps his hand from doing any evil."
> ³ Let not the foreigner who has joined himself to the LORD say,
> "The LORD will surely separate me from His people."
> Nor let the eunuch say, "Behold, I am a dry tree."
>
> ⁴ For thus says the LORD,
>
> "To the eunuchs who keep My sabbaths,
> And choose what pleases Me,
> And hold fast My covenant,
> ⁵ To them I will give in My house and within My walls a memorial,
> And a name better than that of sons and daughters;
> I will give them an everlasting name which will not be cut off.
>
> ⁶ "Also the foreigners who join themselves to the LORD,
> To minister to Him, and to love the name of the LORD,
> To be His servants, every one who keeps from profaning the sabbath
> And holds fast My covenant;
> ⁷ Even those I will bring to My holy mountain
> And make them joyful in My house of prayer.
> Their burnt offerings and their sacrifices will be acceptable on My altar;
> For My house will be called a house of prayer for all the peoples."

According to Ezekiel 44:9, excluded are not just those who are uncircumcised in the heart but also those who are uncircumcised in the flesh:

> [9] 'Thus says the Lord GOD, "No foreigner uncircumcised in heart and uncircumcised in flesh, of all the foreigners who are among the sons of Israel, shall enter My sanctuary."

And we find a reference to those against whom Yah will execute judgment, which includes those who ignore Yah's dietary instructions in Isaiah 66:

> [16] *For the* LORD *will execute judgment by fire*
> *And by His sword on all flesh,*
> *And those slain by the* LORD *will be many.*
> [17] *"Those who sanctify and purify themselves* to go to the gardens,
> *Following one in the center,*
> *Who eat swine's flesh, detestable things and mice,*
> *Will come to an end altogether," declares the* LORD.

Question 20: Does it make sense that Torah would be suspended for the relatively short amount of time between Yeshua's first and second coming; that Torah would be in place from the beginning until Yeshua's death and resurrection, re-introduced upon his return, but somehow done away with in the span of time between those events?

Finally, I'll share one last piece of prophecy. Many readers will be familiar with Yeshua's promise to His disciples that a helper would be sent to them when He returns to His Father. This is recounted in John 14:16 and 14:25-26:

> [16] *I will ask the Father, and He will give you another Helper, that He may be with you forever;* [17] *that is the Spirit of truth, whom the world cannot receive, because it does not see Him or know Him, but you know Him because He abides with you and will be in you.*
>
> [25] *"These things I have spoken to you while abiding with you.* [26] *But the Helper, the Holy Spirit, whom the Father will send in My name, He will teach you all things, and bring to your remembrance all that I said to you.*

And again, in John 16:

> [12] *"I have many more things to say to you, but you cannot bear them now.* [13] *But when He, the Spirit of truth, comes, He will guide you into all the truth;*

> for He will not speak on His own initiative, but whatever He hears, He will speak; and He will disclose to you what is to come.

Yeshua is quite clear that the Holy Spirit will be sent to teach (14:26) and to guide in all truth (16:13), but what is it the Holy Spirit will teach and in what truth will the Holy Spirit guide us? I'll remind you at this point of previous references I've made to Psalm 119:142 *"Your righteousness is an everlasting righteousness, and Your law is truth"* and Malachi 2:6 *"The law of truth was in his mouth, and iniquity was not found in his lips: he walked with me in peace and equity, and did turn many away from iniquity." (KJV)*

This leads me to a final, bonus question. What is the work the Holy Spirit does in us?

To answer that question, we must again turn to prophecy, this time prophecy that has been fulfilled. Ezekiel talks about the concept of circumcision of the heart – that process by which our hearts of stone are replaced with hearts of flesh – in the eleventh Chapter. Relating what has been told him by Yah, Ezekiel writes:

> [19] **And I will give them one heart, and put a new spirit within them.** And I will take the heart of stone out of their flesh and give them a heart of flesh, [20] **that they may walk in My statutes and keep My ordinances and do them.** Then they will be My people, and I shall be their God.

And again, in Ezekiel 36:

> [24] For I will take you from the nations, gather you from all the lands and bring you into your own land. [25] Then I will sprinkle clean water on you, and you will be clean; I will cleanse you from all your filthiness and from all your idols. [26] Moreover, I will give you a new heart and put a new spirit within you; and I will remove the heart of stone from your flesh and give you a heart of flesh. [27] **I will put My Spirit within you and cause you to walk in My statutes, and you will be careful to observe My ordinances.**

Jeremiah refers to this same promise in chapter 31 of his book saying:

> [31] "Behold, days are coming," declares the Lord, "when I will make a new covenant with the house of Israel and with the house of Judah, [32] not like the covenant which I made with their fathers in the day I took them by the hand to

> bring them out of the land of Egypt, My covenant which they broke, although I was a husband to them," declares the LORD. ³³ "But this is the covenant which I will make with the house of Israel after those days," declares the LORD, **"I will put My law within them and on their heart I will write it**; and I will be their God, and they shall be My people.

Many refer to this passage as proof the covenant was going to change, and then use other passages to support the idea that the change would be such that grace would displace Torah. That is clearly not the difference in covenant Jeremiah describes here. The prophet doesn't say Torah will no longer apply or that the instructions provided by Torah will be nullified or superseded; he says that Torah will be written on our hearts instead of being written on tablets of stone. In a sense, he's saying it will apply more personally and intimately than ever before. It seems very strange that Yah planned to write Torah on our hearts, revealed that plan through the prophets, promised to send us the Spirit to help us walk out Torah, and sent Yeshua to demonstrate living Yah's way, only to pivot and abolish Torah instead without any prophecy or warning. What would be the point of writing on our hearts an obsolete set of instructions we no longer need to consider?

With that final question, I'll bring this chapter to a close by returning briefly to where I began; that great scene in the Lord of the Rings and the idea of developing deep roots so that we might stand against floods of misconceptions and false teaching. Isn't it interesting that the Psalms open with similar imagery, tying roots that provide stability and long life to obedience to the Law. From Psalm 1:

> ¹ How blessed is the man who does not walk in the counsel of the wicked,
> Nor stand in the path of sinners,
> Nor sit in the seat of scoffers!
> ² But his delight is in the law of the Lord,
> And in His law he meditates day and night.
> ³ He will be like a tree firmly planted by streams of water,
> Which yields its fruit in its season
> And its leaf does not wither;
> And in whatever he does, he prospers.

Although I've tried to explain the foundations of my questions, you'll notice, as I forewarned, I haven't really answered any of them. For answers, I encourage you to keep reading. It's also likely for some of you that, as you've read through these questions, you've thought of verses or concepts you've been taught that you'd submit as responses to these questions. Again, I'd encourage you to keep reading as I've hopefully addressed those responses in the following chapters. Finally, it's quite possible you've felt uncomfortable. You may see in these questions a challenge to things you've been taught or have believed are true for years, maybe decades. Trust me when I tell you I understand the feeling. It has not been easy for me to wrestle with these topics, nor has it been easy for me to admit that men and women who I long considered trustworthy, reputable and well educated in such matters may have taught me in error, though they may not have been aware of it themselves. The truth is though, I believe the Bible has no contradictions and, if it's true that Torah has been done away with, these questions illustrate an awful lot of confusing contradictions. On the other hand, as I'll use the rest of this book to prove, if we put this teaching to the test and find that Torah has NOT been altered or abolished, these perceived contradictions go away.

Whatever conclusions you reach, please know it is not my goal to prove that I'm right and others are wrong. My goal is to illustrate my own journey and realizations through these matters. I pray that by reasoning through these things we might all come to a better understanding of God's word, and most importantly, a closer relationship with the Father through our relationship with the Messiah, Yeshua.

Section II

Torah, Obedience, and Salvation

CHAPTER 4

The Truth About Torah

As was discussed at length in the first chapter, meaning and purpose is important. To this end, it's beneficial to establish what Torah is, what it isn't, what it was intended to do, and what it was never intended to do. Western Christianity tells us that Torah has come to an end; that it has been rendered void of purpose by the death and resurrection of Yeshua, but is that true? At the outset, I'd like to essentially give away what should probably be the surprise ending of this chapter. All the tension I've seen between Torah and grace stems from the simple idea that one can pursue salvation through one or the other. One can submit his or her record of obedience and hope to gain salvation, or one can rest his or her case on the grace of Yah through Yeshua. If this dichotomy were accurate, then I wouldn't be writing any of this because clearly salvation is by grace through faith in Yeshua and there is no other way. This indisputable fact is all over the Bible, including Yeshua's own teaching. In fact, the entire book of Galatians is a treatise on this topic and nothing else.

So why are we here? Because by and large the case that Torah obedience has no place in our lives rests on the idea that it was once the way of salvation but now Yeshua is the way; the former has been replaced by the latter; once by law, now by grace. This is one hundred percent false and the reality is, all of us who have been raised, theologically, on mainstream Western Christian doctrine have been fooled into a false dilemma. The surprising truth is, Torah was never related to salvation. It wasn't given as a means by which one might attain salvation and nowhere in the Old Testament will you find any indication that it had anything to do with salvation except as a response to one's salvation.

Although I'll go into much more depth as this chapter progresses, by way of proof of my assertion, we need look no further than the account of the Exodus. Most of us with a Christian background understand that there are parallels between the Exodus story and the future to which it points. The most well-known is the Passover lamb, a shadow of the reality that Yeshua would one day be offered as our Passover lamb. Just as the population of Egypt was under judgement, and only by the blood of a spotless lamb would a house be passed over, so too the entire world is under judgement and only by the blood of the perfect Son can any of us be passed over. It seems that almost every mature Christian knows this relationship and understands the nature of the shadow and reality juxtaposition of this story in Exodus, by which I mean, the shadow of the Exodus points us to certain realities regarding Yeshua. Unfortunately, it seems very few are familiar with the equally important parallels of the rest of the story and, for the purposes of my premise, the larger truth illustrated by the order of these events. In short, we see in the narrative of the Exodus the full framework that describes what Christian's would call New Testament salvation. To explain, I'll focus on four primary stages of the Exodus story: The initial state of Yah's people, the sacrifice of the lamb, the peoples' passing through the Red Sea, and the recording of Torah at Mt. Sinai.

I won't delve into the details of each of these stages but, as it relates to Torah's place in relation to salvation, the sequence of events is important. Yah's people found themselves suffering in their bondage to Egyptian masters, just as we, who are saved, were once in bondage to sin. Next, there is the sacrifice of the lamb and the use of its blood as a covering, just as Yeshua's blood served as a covering for our sins so that we would be passed over in judgment. Once the Israelites were delivered from judgment and subsequently freed from their bondage, they passed through the waters of the Red Sea just as we, having been delivered from judgment and freed from the power of sin in our lives, pass through the waters of baptism. How interesting that twice in the book of Joshua, the Israelites' passing through the Red Sea is used as evidence of Yah's being with them (Joshua 2:10-11 and Joshua 4:23-24), just as baptism for us doesn't save us but serves as evidence to the world of the relationship between us and Yeshua. This brings us, chronologically, to the giving of Torah to the mixed multitude that left Egypt. After being delivered out of bondage, saved through the blood of the lamb, and led through the waters, the people are given a set of instructions. The most important word in the previous sentence is the first word, "after". The people were not given Torah first and then once they perfectly obeyed it were redeemed out of Egypt and called Yah's people. The people were redeemed first, called Yah's people next, and then, having been saved, were given instruction regarding how saved people should live. I can't possibly stress this enough because it speaks directly to Torah's place in the lives of believers today. The assertion that stands at the center of this book is that, just as it was in the days of Moses, although obedience to Torah is not a way to be saved, it is a valid and proper response to having been saved.

What is the purpose of Torah then, if not for salvation? The answer can be summarized by three characteristics. One characteristic is related to intent and the other two describe relational outcome, by which I mean the outcome we can expect based on how we relate to Torah. First, the intent of Torah is simply to contrast sin and righteousness. Torah cannot save anyone from the *"wages of sin"*, but it does draw a distinction between right and wrong behavior as defined by Yah. As we've already seen, 1 John 3:4 defines sin as *"transgression of the law"*, and Romans 6:23 explains that the price of sin is death. We see sin and death on one side of the Torah spectrum and on the other, righteousness and life. This is no different than how Torah was described when it was initially presented. Consider, for example, the correlation between obedience and the outcome of obedience – righteousness and life – in this passage from Deuteronomy 6:

> [24] So the Lord commanded us to observe all these statutes, to fear the Lord our God for our good always and for our survival, as it is today. [25] **It will be righteousness for us if we are careful to observe all this commandment before the Lord our God, just as He commanded us.**

And in Ezekiel 18:

> [5] "But if a man is righteous and practices justice and righteousness, [6] and does not eat at the mountain shrines or lift up his eyes to the idols of the house of Israel, or defile his neighbor's wife or approach a woman during her menstrual period— [7] if a man does not oppress anyone, but restores to the debtor his pledge, does not commit robbery, but gives his bread to the hungry and covers the naked with clothing, [8] if he does not lend money on interest or take increase, if he keeps his hand from iniquity and executes true justice between man and man, [9] **if he walks in My statutes and My ordinances so as to deal faithfully—he is righteous and will surely live**," declares the Lord God.

The intent of Torah, to divide between right and wrong behavior, is inseparable from the two possible outcomes in relation to Torah. In Deuteronomy 11 we see both outcomes clearly illustrated:

> [26] "See, I am setting before you today a blessing and a curse: [27] the blessing, if you listen to the commandments of the Lord your God, which I am commanding you today; [28] and the curse, if you do not listen to the commandments of the Lord your God, but turn aside from the way which I am commanding you today, by following other gods which you have not known.

This idea is restated in Deuteronomy 30:15-20 where Moses again ties obedience to life and disobedience to death:

> [15] "See, I have set before you today life and prosperity, and death and adversity; [16] in that I command you today to love the Lord your God, to walk in His ways and to keep His commandments and His statutes and His judgments, that you may live and multiply, and that the Lord your God may bless you in the land where you are entering to possess it. [17] But if your heart turns away and you will not obey, but are drawn away and worship other gods and serve them, [18] I declare to you today that you shall surely perish. You will not prolong your days in the land where you are crossing the Jordan to enter and possess it. [19] I call heaven and earth to witness against you today, that I have set before you life and death, the blessing and the curse. So choose life in order that you may live, you and your descendants, [20] by loving the Lord your God, by obeying His voice, and by holding fast to Him; for this is your life and the length of your days, that you may live in the land which the Lord swore to your fathers, to Abraham, Isaac, and Jacob, to give them."

To summarize, two outcomes are possible in relation to Torah. One can obey, which is called righteousness, and enjoy blessing and life, or one can disobey, which is called sin, the price of which is cursing and death, but there's an obvious problem here. As a result of original sin, our hearts are bent toward disobedience. A study of the remainder of the Old Testament or, more personally, an examination of our own lives makes it clear that we are not born with the ability to avoid sin and by extension death. So, did Yah make a mistake? Was His intention for man to obey and achieve righteousness of his own efforts but discovering Torah's inadequacy He sent His son as an alternative? Absolutely not. Yah understood well the problem in the human heart and knew that, despite our desire to obey, the heart problem we inherited from Adam so long ago would not allow us to obey. Consider the exchange recorded in Deuteronomy 5:

> [27] Go near and hear all that the Lord our God says; then speak to us all that the Lord our God speaks to you, and we will hear and do it.'
>
> [28] "The Lord heard the voice of your words when you spoke to me, and the Lord said to me, 'I have heard the voice of the words of this people which they have spoken to you. They have done well in all that they have spoken. [29] **Oh that they had such a heart in them, that they would fear Me and keep all My commandments always, that it may be well with them and with their sons forever!** [30] Go, say to them, "Return to your tents." [31] But as for you, stand here by Me, that I may speak to you all the commandments and the statutes and the judgments which you shall teach them, that they may observe them in the land which I give them to possess.' [32] So you shall observe to do just as the Lord your God has commanded you; you shall not turn aside to the right or to the left. [33] You shall walk in all the way which the Lord your God has commanded you, that you may live and that it may be well with you, and that you may prolong your days in the land which you will possess.

In verse 27, the Israelites implore Moses to be their intermediary, that he might discover what Yah desires of them, and they promise to obey. In verse 28, Yah acknowledges and affirms their heartfelt desire to do as they're instructed, but in verse 29 we find a change in tone. Yah knows the disobedience that will permeate their future out of the corruption of their flesh. *"Oh that they had such a heart in them"*, Yah laments. They're saying they will hear and obey, but Yah knows they won't. It's also true, though, that without a standard, they will never know they've fallen short, so He continues by giving them instruction He knows full well they don't have the heart to follow because, as we'll see Paul saying later, *"sin is not imputed when there is no law"* (Romans 5:13).

Yah is perfectly merciful but He's also perfectly just and it would be decidedly unjust to condemn without first establishing the standard by which obedience and disobedience would be determined. As an aside that will become important later, does this point to a problem or deficiency with Torah? No, the problem is clearly not with the standard but with the human heart. Returning to my original point, this is further evidence that Torah was never given as a means of salvation, but to illustrate our need for a savior by defining holy and forbidden behavior. It has been this way since the beginning and will be until the end; *"until heaven and Earth pass away"*.

Understanding all of this helps us address questions 5 and 6 from chapter 3 by making sense of Yeshua's words in Matthew 5. As a reminder, those questions were, "In verse 17, are we to believe that the word abolish and fulfill have the same practical affect?" and "...in verse 18 Yeshua states clearly that nothing from Torah will pass away until heaven and Earth pass away. Since that hasn't happened, how can the entire Torah have been abolished let alone *'the smallest letter or stroke'*?" From Matthew 5:17-19:

> [17] *"Do not think that I came to abolish the Law or the Prophets; I did not come to abolish but to fulfill.* [18] *For truly I say to you, until heaven and earth pass away, not the smallest letter or stroke shall pass from the Law until all is accomplished.* [19] *Whoever then annuls one of the least of these commandments, and teaches others to do the same, shall be called least in the kingdom of heaven; but whoever keeps and teaches them, he shall be called great in the kingdom of heaven.*

If we believe that Torah has been abolished, or that it no longer stands as Yah's instruction, there seems to be an obvious problem with Yeshua's statement here. Some try to argue that abolishing the Law is different than His having fulfilled the requirement of the Law but if both equate to Torah having no place in our lives, does any distinction matter, practically? They essentially lead to the same conclusion and that understanding still leaves the question of verse 19. Follow me down this train of thought for a moment. If I stipulate that Torah was not done away with because it was abolished, but was done away with because it was fulfilled, why is Yeshua making a distinction between those who annul these commandments and teach others to, and those who keep them and teach others to keep them?

There are few who would argue with the principal that, among other things, Yeshua provided us with an example to follow. In this sense, doesn't it make much more sense that when Yeshua says He didn't come to abolish but to fulfill Torah, He's saying He didn't come to do away with it, but to give us a perfect example of what obedience looks like? If we want to get very geeky about it, it's worth looking at the underlying Greek word translated as "fulfill" which is "pleroo". Thayer's Greek Lexicon defines this as "to make full, to fill up, to fill to the full" as a primary definition but also includes, "to cause to abound", "to fill to the top", "to render perfect". What's being extolled in Matthew 5:17 is that Yeshua followed Yah's instruction flawlessly, perfectly – fully! Going further into the Greek, Thayer's defines "pleroo" specifically as it relates to matters of duty as "to perform" and "to execute", and, interestingly, even includes (and this is a direct quote from the Lexicon including the parenthetical statements) "to fulfil, i.e. to cause God's will (as made known in the law) to be obeyed as it should be, and God's promises (given through the prophets) to receive fulfillment".

All these definitions have the same connotation as it relates to the passage at issue in Matthew 5; that Jesus walked in perfect obedience to Yah's instructions. Fulfill does not mean complete in the sense that it no longer applies. While "to complete" and "to accomplish" are among the meanings of the word pleroo, to assert that these translations somehow stray from the intent behind every other definition of the word is quite a stretch. To put it another way, every other definition/translation of this word has the sense of doing something without leaving anything out, but we're supposed to believe that, in this case, the word means that an end has been brought to the thing being filled? Think of it this way: As husband to my wife, I have a responsibility to remain faithful to her. The fact that I "pleroo" or "fulfill" that responsibility today doesn't mean I've completed it and no longer need to remain faithful tomorrow. This is exactly what's being taught about Yeshua's words here though. Modern Christianity teaches that since the "obey the Law" box has been checked off there's no more law. Of course, this understanding also goes against what we've already seen in the history of Torah. We'd have to believe that Torah wasn't given to show mankind the difference between the holy and the profane, nor to give us instructions that will lead to blessing if we heed them but was simply a checklist that would no longer apply as soon as a single person did all of it even though Yah would have known no one would be capable of checking all the boxes until Yeshua. That contradicts everything the Old Testament teaches about Torah.

On the other hand, if we understand that in Matthew 5 Yeshua is saying He came not to do away with Torah but to follow every bit of its instruction, we see a message consistent with the rest of Scripture, and His contrast in verse 19 between those who disobey and teach others that the Law was annulled and those who obey and teach others to also obey makes much more sense. More importantly, it doesn't require that we ignore everything the Old Testament says about Torah. Let's take a closer look at that last part of the Matthew 5 passage:

> [19] Whoever then annuls one of the least of these commandments, and teaches others to do the same, shall be called least in the kingdom of heaven; but whoever keeps and teaches them, he shall be called great in the kingdom of heaven.

If we pay attention to where the two groups Yeshua refers to are located we see that both groups are in heaven and, by extension, we can conclude both groups are saved. This helps expand on a comment I made in the second chapter of this book. Our obedience can't save us anymore than our disobedience can rob us of salvation, but our response to salvation can absolutely affect our closeness with the Son and the Father. Just as we saw in the Exodus where a group of people were saved, then given instructions for life and told that there are specific outcomes based on whether they did or did not heed the instructions, we see the same kind of mechanism here where there's a distinction between those who *"annul the least of these commandments"* on one end of the spectrum and those who *"keep and teach them"* on the other.

We shouldn't be surprised to see the same kind of distinction being made by Yeshua that's made by Yah in the Old Testament. In Yeshua's own words, He didn't come with His own words but with the Father's. Yeshua says in John 12:48-49:

> ⁴⁸ He who rejects Me and does not receive My sayings, has one who judges him; the word I spoke is what will judge him at the last day. ⁴⁹ For I did not speak on My own initiative, but the Father Himself who sent Me has given Me a commandment as to what to say and what to speak.

This is a fulfillment of what Yah said would happen in Deuteronomy 18:18-20:

> ¹⁸ I will raise up a prophet from among their countrymen like you, and I will put My words in his mouth, and he shall speak to them all that I command him. ¹⁹ It shall come about that whoever will not listen to My words which he shall speak in My name, I Myself will require it of him.

What would be surprising would be to see the Father and the Son, who are indivisibly one, giving, not just different, but opposing instruction as we're expected to accept according to the abolished Law belief. If we test that teaching against everything I've explained from the Old Testament, suddenly Yeshua's statement makes much more sense and becomes much more consistent. What about the rest of the New Testament?

We could look to 1 John, which says in chapter 2:

> ³ By this we know that we have come to know Him, if we keep His commandments. ⁴ The one who says, "I have come to know Him," and does not keep His commandments, is a liar, and the truth is not in him; ⁵ but whoever keeps His word, in him the love of God has truly been perfected. By this we know that we are in Him: ⁶ the one who says he abides in Him ought himself to walk in the same manner as He walked.

Some might argue that in verse 3 John is talking about Yeshua's commandments as distinct from Torah but this cannot be. Let us remember that when this was written there was no New Testament so there wasn't a codified set of rules that could be called New Testament laws. But, perhaps some would say, surely the teachings of Yeshua would have been well known so that's what John means when he says, *"His commandments"*. Setting aside what we already discussed about Yeshua not coming with His own words but with the words of the Father, we can know for sure that John can't be referring to some new set of Jesus commandments because of the clarifying statement in verse 6, that the one who *"abides in Him ought himself to walk in the same manner as He walked"*. How did He walk if not in obedience to Torah?

Perhaps we could look at something we've probably all heard; the idea that Yah will give us whatever we ask. Funny how no one ever seems to finish the verse, which we also find in 1 John, this time in chapter 3:

> *22 and whatever we ask we receive from Him,* **because we keep His commandments and do the things that are pleasing in His sight.**
>
> *23 This is His commandment, that we believe in the name of His Son Jesus Christ, and love one another, just as He commanded us. 24 The one who keeps His commandments abides in Him, and He in him. We know by this that He abides in us, by the Spirit whom He has given us.*

Let me remind you that in the Hebrew mindset the word "name" above is the word "shem" and means reputation/authority. We are not being told to believe the word Jesus as a sort of magic word, we are being told to believe in Yeshua's reputation and authority and on that basis to love one another.

Torah is, as I have demonstrated, Yah's guidance for how we should live, or, as John puts it in verse 22 above, *"the things that are pleasing in His sight"*. Also notice the relationship between blessing (receiving from Him whatever we ask) and keeping His commandments. It sounds remarkably similar to the passages in Deuteronomy, does it not? Further, in verse 23-24 we see the same foundation of Torah that Yeshua pointed out. Yeshua said that loving Yah and loving one another was the foundation of all of Torah (Matthew 22:36-40) and we find that same theme here. These facts combined makes the commandments John is talking about an unmistakable reference to Torah.

We could also turn to James 1:22-25:

> *22 But prove yourselves doers of the word, and not merely hearers who delude themselves. 23 For if anyone is a hearer of the word and not a doer, he is like a*

> man who looks at his natural face in a mirror; ²⁴ for once he has looked at himself and gone away, he has immediately forgotten what kind of person he was. ²⁵ But one who looks intently at the perfect law, the law of liberty, and abides by it, not having become a forgetful hearer but an effectual doer, this man will be blessed in what he does.

Aside from an obvious encouragement to heed the word, James makes the distinction in verse 25 that he's talking about the perfect law of liberty an overt reference to Torah (Psalm 19:7, Psalm 119:45), and further relates what he's saying to Torah concepts saying that the doer will be blessed in what he does. It's not a coincidence that this is the exact language used to describe the expected result of Torah obedience throughout the Old Testament. These are just a few examples of New Testament passages that refer to Torah favorably but the topic of the purpose of Torah deserves a much deeper New Testament analysis by examining Paul's letter to the Romans.

Although I cover a lot of what Paul says regarding Torah in several chapters, for now I'll focus on the book of Romans for two reasons. First, all the concepts about the purpose of Torah as defined by the Scripture referenced thus far are reiterated and affirmed by Paul. Secondly, and equally important, is the fact that a lot of the arguments that Torah in its entirety has been abolished come from Romans. Armed with the information I've outlined up to this point, we should be able to navigate through Romans and see how Paul never taught against Torah and certainly never taught that it had been brought to an end; on the contrary, the letter to the Romans has been misunderstood and misinterpreted. Upon careful review of Romans, it becomes obvious that what Paul actually teaches is that a person redeemed by grace through Yeshua will respond in obedience compelled by the indwelling Spirit. Far from teaching that Torah has been abolished, he says throughout Romans that the heart, having been transformed, will finally be free to enjoy the blessings promised in Torah through obedience to the instruction provided by Torah, not for salvation but as a response to salvation.

It's important to keep in mind when approaching any of Paul's letters that Paul is exceedingly well educated and as a result he writes about complex ideas using complex language and sentence structure. Because of the complexity of what He wrote, it's easy to twist his words and end up in error so we need to be very careful in our approach to what he's written. This warning isn't my own but comes from none other than the Apostle Peter. In 2 Peter 3, Peter writes:

> [14] Therefore, beloved, since you look for these things, be diligent to be found by Him in peace, spotless and blameless, [15] and regard the patience of our Lord as salvation; just as also our beloved brother Paul, according to the wisdom given him, wrote to you, [16] as also in all his letters, speaking in them of these things, in which are some things hard to understand, which the untaught and unstable distort, as they do also the rest of the Scriptures, to their own destruction. [17] You therefore, beloved, knowing this beforehand, be on your guard so that you are not carried away by the error of unprincipled men and fall from your own steadfastness, [18] but grow in the grace and knowledge of our Lord and Savior Jesus Christ. To Him be the glory, both now and to the day of eternity. Amen.

I won't go into detail at this time about the two contrasting ways of life Peter talks about in chapters 1 and 2, but by way of context Peter is talking about the way followers of Yeshua are to live, namely in such a way, as it says in verse 14, that they would be found upon His return spotless and blameless, and says that Paul also wrote about how to live in this way, but warns us that some things in his letters are hard to understand and the *"untaught and unstable"* will distort them. He further says to be careful not to be carried away by the error of those who misunderstand and misinterpret Paul. In fact, where the NASB uses the word "unprincipled" to describe those who misunderstand and misinterpret, this is another case where the translators are a little off in my opinion. The NIV, ESV, HCSB, ISV and others translate the original Greek word here, "athesmon", as "lawless". Strong's defines this word as, "lawless, unrestrained, licentious". Peter is literally warning readers to be careful not to misunderstand Paul, because misunderstanding or misinterpreting Paul will leave one vulnerable to *"being carried away by the error of lawlessness"*. Although I believe this error is exactly the error I'm pointing out in writing this book, I bring this passage up now only to illustrate that all of Paul's letters should be approached with great caution and care. If Peter himself found some of what Paul wrote difficult to understand, that should make us pay close attention. Anyone who wants to refer to a single verse of Paul here or a single verse there to prove a point is very likely missing something *"to their own destruction"*, so without further ado, let us dive into Romans and find out what Paul has to say about the place and purpose of Torah, obedience and salvation.

CHAPTER 5

Obedience: Requirement or Response?

There are two ideas that really strike at the heart of my purpose in this chapter. One is that Torah was given so that we might know what sin is and that we might understand that we've all disobeyed and are in need of salvation. The other is that the reality of our righteousness through Yeshua does not eliminate Torah. These two ideas are described, among other places, in Romans 3:20 and 3:31, but because of the complexity of Paul's letters, it's not appropriate to pull these two verses out without explaining the context and other statements he makes that lead to these two conclusions.

In the first chapter of Romans, Paul starts by pointing out what we're facing in an effort to establish our need for a savior and that is the wrath of God, as he puts it:

> 18 For the wrath of God is revealed from heaven against all ungodliness and unrighteousness of men who suppress the truth in unrighteousness, 19 because that which is known about God is evident within them; for God made it evident to them.

As has been previously established, Yah's standard for righteousness and unrighteousness is defined by Torah and right from the start Paul tells us we're due wrath because of our disobedience, disobedience being synonymous with unrighteousness. Lest we think there is some other New Testament standard he's referring to, he goes on to describe particular behaviors in verses 22-32:

> [22] Professing to be wise, they became fools, [23] and exchanged the glory of the incorruptible God for an image in the form of corruptible man and of birds and four-footed animals and crawling creatures.
>
> [24] Therefore God gave them over in the lusts of their hearts to impurity, so that their bodies would be dishonored among them. [25] For they exchanged the truth of God for a lie, and worshiped and served the creature rather than the Creator, who is blessed forever. Amen.
>
> [26] For this reason God gave them over to degrading passions; for their women exchanged the natural function for that which is unnatural, [27] and in the same way also the men abandoned the natural function of the woman and burned in their desire toward one another, men with men committing indecent acts and receiving in their own persons the due penalty of their error.
>
> [28] And just as they did not see fit to acknowledge God any longer, God gave them over to a depraved mind, to do those things which are not proper, [29] being filled with all unrighteousness, wickedness, greed, evil; full of envy, murder, strife, deceit, malice; they are gossips, [30] slanderers, haters of God, insolent, arrogant, boastful, inventors of evil, disobedient to parents, [31] without understanding, untrustworthy, unloving, unmerciful; [32] and although they know the ordinance of God, that those who practice such things are worthy of death, they not only do the same, but also give hearty approval to those who practice them.

Verse 22 refers to the Torah prohibition against idolatry and making an image of anything (Exodus 20:4, Deuteronomy 5:8). Verse 25 says *"they exchanged the truth of God for a lie"*, so what is the truth of God? If we let the Bible define the Bible, that's Torah.

> *Psalm 119:142 - Your righteousness is an everlasting righteousness, and Your law is truth.*
>
> *Malachi 2:6-7 - True instruction was in his mouth and unrighteousness was not found on his lips; he walked with Me in peace and uprightness, and he turned many back from iniquity. For the lips of a priest should preserve knowledge, and men should seek instruction from his mouth; for he is the messenger of the Lord of hosts.*

In verse 6, let us recognize that iniquity is nothing more than a fancy word for lawlessness. Later in Romans we find this:

> Romans 2:20 - *a corrector of the foolish, a teacher of the immature, having in the Law the embodiment of knowledge and of the truth.*

Throughout the Bible, Torah is described as Yah's truth and Paul himself describes it as the very embodiment of truth, so it's reasonable to conclude that in verse 25 he's referring to Torah as *"the truth of God"* which has been traded for a lie.

Continuing to verses 26-32 we see one of what theologians refer to as vice lists. Another of these lists appears in Romans 12:9-21 to which what I'm about to say also applies. It's commonly and erroneously taught that right and wrong is no longer defined by Torah but by, among other things, the virtue and vice lists scattered throughout Paul's letters. This is utter foolishness. What we have in this list and similar lists elsewhere aren't simply vices to be avoided, but are the fruits that are the natural result of disobeying Torah. In verse 29, for example, greed is the result of disobeying Torah's prohibition against coveting as is being *"full of envy"*. One who is *"full of murder"* has obviously made a practice of disobeying Torah's commandment against it. The same holds true for gossips and slanderers in verse 30. Disobedience to parents is an infraction of Torah and disobedience to Torah's instruction toward honesty, lovingkindness, and mercy will result in the qualities that round out verse 31. Finally, in verse 32 we see what I pointed out earlier; that disobedience is sin, the price of which is death.

Admittedly, none of this explicitly means Torah is still binding in any way today, but it's important to understand the context as we move on to the next two chapters of Romans. Paul is standing unmistakably on Torah's instruction to make his points. These vice lists aren't describing disobedience but the fruits of disobedience – the externally visible signs of a disobedient life.

As we move to Romans 2, Paul begins to switch gears a bit and address the danger of hypocrisy, something that Yeshua also warned against repeatedly.

> ¹ Therefore you have no excuse, everyone of you who passes judgment, for in that which you judge another, you condemn yourself; for you who judge practice the same things. ² And we know that the judgment of God rightly falls upon those who practice such things.³ But do you suppose this, O man, when you pass judgment on those who practice such things and do the same yourself, that you will escape the judgment of God? ⁴ Or do you think lightly of the riches of His kindness and tolerance and patience, not knowing that the kindness of God leads you to repentance? ⁵ But because of your stubbornness and unrepentant heart you are storing up wrath for yourself in the day of wrath and revelation of the righteous judgment of God, ⁶ who will render to each person according to his deeds: ⁷ to those who by perseverance in doing good seek for glory and honor and immortality, eternal life; ⁸ but to those who are selfishly ambitious and do not obey the truth, but obey unrighteousness, wrath and indignation. ⁹ There will be tribulation and distress for every soul of man who does evil, of the Jew first and also of the Greek, ¹⁰ but glory and honor and peace to everyone who does good, to the Jew first and also to the Greek. ¹¹ For there is no partiality with God.

There's a critical break in Paul's train of thought between verses 3 and 4. In verses 1-3 Paul is addressing humility; let's not judge others for their disobedience because we've all disobeyed and we'll all be judged by Yah one day, Paul says, but in verse 4 there's a pivot where he's no longer talking strictly about us in our unsaved state but brings us to the choice we face in Yah's offer of salvation. Verse 4 is explaining that Yah's patience with us is what has allowed us time to come to repentance. This calls to mind the popular unattributed quote, "Sin wouldn't be so attractive if the wages were paid immediately". Yah did not deliver the wrath we deserve but was patient with us so that we might come to know Him through His Son and have a chance at salvation. In the context of verses 1-3 Paul is expressing the idea that just as we've been shown patience we should be patient with others.

What's interesting to the topic at hand is what Paul says in verses 5-8. He says that once you've come to the point of being offered salvation, if you continue in your disobedience, you're just storing up wrath for yourself. Throughout this passage, we also see the same two outcomes that we saw with Torah; blessing for those who obey and wrath for those who persist in their disobedience. Paul illustrates the difference between the one who has repented and the one who hasn't, saying in verse 7 that those who are genuinely repentant persevere in doing good, seeking for glory and honor and immortality, and are granted eternal life. Conversely in verse 8 he defines those who are inwardly unrepentant as those who *"do not obey the truth"* and are rendered unto wrath. Paul is clearly making a distinction between those who respond to an offer of repentance and salvation by turning from their disobedience, and those who continue in their disobedience. He points out that it does not matter if you're Jew or Gentile, what matters are the deeds that stand as evidence of salvation. As he says in verse 6, Yah *"will render unto each person according to his deeds"*!

For fear of being accused of misinterpreting Paul for my own ends, ask yourself if this isn't exactly the summary Paul gives in the next two verses:

> *12 For all who have sinned without the Law will also perish without the Law, and all who have sinned under the Law will be judged by the Law; 13 for it is not the hearers of the Law who are just before God, but the doers of the Law will be justified.*

The first thing I'd like to mention is that for some, the phrase, *"under the Law"* will trigger a learned response which compels one to immediately recall the teaching that, *"under the Law"* has been replaced by *"under grace"*. I will address this later as it comes up again in Romans 3, so I'd ask that you bear with me and allow me to skip over it for now. That said, it's important to point out here that Paul is definitely NOT saying Torah obedience is required for salvation, but it's equally clear that he's saying one who is truly saved will respond by turning from disobedience and will start to follow Torah (becoming a doer). He goes on to say even if the person who is saved doesn't know Torah, they'll instinctively begin to obey because it will be written on their hearts. Romans 2:14-16:

> *14 For when Gentiles who do not have the Law do instinctively the things of the Law, these, not having the Law, are a law to themselves, 15 in that they show the work of the Law written in their hearts, their conscience bearing witness and their thoughts alternately accusing or else defending them, 16 on the day when, according to my gospel, God will judge the secrets of men through Christ Jesus.*

This falls precisely in line with the prophecies from Jeremiah 31:33:

> "But this is the covenant which I will make with the house of Israel after those days," declares the Lord, "I will put My law within them and on their heart I will write it; and I will be their God, and they shall be My people."

and Ezekiel 36:27:

> "I will put My Spirit within you and cause you to walk in My statutes, and you will be careful to observe My ordinances."

and is further underpinned by what is recorded in James 2:18-23:

> [18] But someone may well say, "You have faith and I have works; show me your faith without the works, and I will show you my faith by my works." [19] You believe that God is one. You do well; the demons also believe, and shudder. [20] But are you willing to recognize, you foolish fellow, that faith without works is useless? [21] Was not Abraham our father justified by works when he offered up Isaac his son on the altar? [22] You see that faith was working with his works, and as a result of the works, faith was perfected; [23] and the Scripture was fulfilled which says, "And Abraham believed God, and it was reckoned to him as righteousness," and he was called the friend of God.

At this point, some will focus only on the last verse and say, see, it says Abraham's faith, not his obedience, was counted as righteousness. That's true, Abraham's salvation was by faith, but what was his response to salvation if not obedience as James points out in verse 21. Everyone seems to know, and often quotes, that Abraham's faith was counted as righteousness, however, as I've said previously, obedience doesn't secure salvation, a response of obedience to salvation secures blessing. As it relates to Abraham, I'd direct you to the lesser known statement about why the blessing promised to Abraham was reiterated to Isaac from Genesis 26:

> [4] I will multiply your descendants as the stars of heaven, and will give your descendants all these lands; and by your descendants all the nations of the earth shall be blessed; [5] because Abraham obeyed Me and kept My charge, My commandments, My statutes and My laws."

Even Abraham, though he was saved through faith, was granted the blessing not because of his faith, but because of the obedience that was compelled by his faith.

Returning to Romans, let us move on to the last half of chapter 2. I'll mostly skip over verses 17-29 as they aren't directly related to the subject of this chapter, except to point out a few broad concepts, and encourage you to read it on your own. Verses 17-24 are talking mostly about Jews who proclaim the Law but aren't keeping it themselves and the poor witness that serves to Gentiles. Isn't it interesting that by contrast Paul asserts that if they actually practiced the Torah obedience they were preaching it would be beneficial? Remember in Matthew 23:3 where Yeshua says, *"therefore all that they tell you, do and observe, but do not do according to their deeds; for they say things and do not do them."* Paul, in Romans, is saying the exact same thing from the opposite angle. He's addressing the pride of the Jews and their reliance on external displays of, and strict adherence to, rules and traditions which they've added to Torah as proof of their righteousness. This is something Yeshua spoke a lot about. For instance, in Matthew 23:5, Yeshua calls the Jewish leaders out for trying to impress everyone with the size of their phylacteries (a small leather box containing Hebrew Scriptures, used during morning prayers by orthodox Jewish men) and the length of their tzitzits (the tassels worn on the corners of one's garments). Also, consider the relationship between this section and what Paul talked about back in Romans 2:1-4.

Paul continues in Romans 2:26-29 to address another topic that comes up throughout his letters; the distinction between circumcision and uncircumcision. He's making the point that circumcision is an external sign of an internal state. He's not saying one shouldn't be circumcised, nor is he saying there's no longer any value in circumcision. He's simply saying if you're circumcised and haven't repented in faith through Yeshua, your circumcision is not actually a sign of anything. This goes all the way back to Abraham and, like the Exodus, the order of events is important. First Abraham's faith was counted as righteousness, then out of obedience he was circumcised as an outward sign of his inward transformation. The opposite, and what Paul is describing, is similar to one being baptized but not believing Yeshua is the

Messiah. The external symbol would be of no value because it's not actually symbolizing anything. You can do it, but there's no significance to it.

Think of it like wearing a wedding band. Nothing says an unmarried man can't wear a ring on his left ring finger, but for that man it isn't a symbol of anything the way it is for the married man. The external meaning of the ring worn by the unmarried man does not relate to any internal truth of his being married. This is important because some will pull verse 29 out of context and determine that Paul is saying it's the spirit of the Law not obeying it to the letter that's important. The problem is, that's not at all what this section is about. It's saying the outward signs of obedience don't matter if you're not actually obedient. That's very different than saying there's no need to be obedient to anything anymore because the Law is done away with. In fact, the very next verses underpin the importance of circumcision and bolster the case for the Law. Chapter 3 begins:

> [1] Then what advantage has the Jew? Or what is the benefit of circumcision? [2] Great in every respect. First of all, that they were entrusted with the oracles of God. [3] What then? If some did not believe, their unbelief will not nullify the faithfulness of God, will it? [4] May it never be! Rather, let God be found true, though every man be found a liar, as it is written,
>
> > "That You may be justified in Your words,
> > And prevail when You are judged."
>
> [5] But if our unrighteousness demonstrates the righteousness of God, what shall we say? The God who inflicts wrath is not unrighteous, is He? (I am speaking in human terms.) [6] May it never be! For otherwise, how will God judge the world? [7] But if through my lie the truth of God abounded to His glory, why am I also still being judged as a sinner?

Verse 2 points out that even though the Jews did not obey the Law perfectly, it was presented in written form to the world through them which Paul says is a great thing. Verse 3 expresses that their lack of belief did not mean Torah itself was untrue or deficient. In verses 5-7, Paul makes an interesting point. He says the disobedience of the Jews and the consequences of their disobedience serve as an example to the world of the price of straying from Torah's boundaries. Since, by seeing that example, many might understand the price of disobedience and repent, isn't their disobedience a good thing in a way, and if so, is it unrighteous for God to still judge them for it? Paul restates this point in verse 7 basically asking the reader, if I lie and that lie leads you to God is it unjust for God to judge me a sinner for that lie? In other words, isn't my lying a good thing? The answer is back in verse 6, "God forbid!" You can't disobey and get away with it, even if Yah does have the ability to take what is meant for evil and turn it to good. What's truly interesting is the parenthetical statement in verse eight:

> *⁷ But if through my lie the truth of God abounded to His glory, why am I also still being judged as a sinner? ⁸ And why not say (as we are slanderously reported and as some claim that we say), "Let us do evil that good may come"? Their condemnation is just.*

As he did in verse 7, in verse 8 Paul reiterates the point he's making a third time saying, if disobedience shows others the price and leads them to obedience why not disobey more so that more will be encouraged to obedience *("let us do evil that good may come")*? Of course, that's a terrible idea. Paul says that the condemnation of anyone who thinks and behaves that way is just. Interestingly, the parenthetical statement in verse 8 above, makes clear they are being falsely accused of teaching that it would be good to do evil that good may come! There is an assertion made by many Christian teachers, pastors, and theologians that Paul teaches Torah obedience is no longer important. This is evidence that even in Paul's day people were making the same assertion. Paul says it's a slanderous report. Just as it was a false accusation then, it must be false today.

Concerning chapter 3, verse 9-20, it's expedient at this point to address what it means to be under something. In verse 9 Paul refers to all being *"under sin"* and in verse 19 he refers to those who are *"under law"*. This relates to the popular assertion that we are no longer under law but are under grace as a statement of the Law having been abolished. As with other supposed proofs of Torah's abolishment this is really just a misunderstanding of the concept of being under something. The meaning of being under something is that of being covered by something or something providing a covering over us. This goes all the way back to Genesis and the garden of Eden when man first fell and became aware of his own nakedness. We're told Adam and Eve covered themselves with leaves and that this covering was insufficient, so God provided animal skins for them. There is much truth about salvation packed into this. Among other things, it teaches that man cannot provide a covering for himself (the leaves gathered through their own efforts, symbolically the works of man, were insufficient), and that God must provide the covering (the animal skins). In addition, the covering that God provided required blood (the skins from the animals stand as the first occurrence in the Bible of something sacrificed for man). In this small section of Genesis, we see a foreshadowing of the entire salvation story, but what's relevant at the moment is man needs a covering. He needs to be under something. With that in mind, when Paul says in verse 9 that all are under sin, he's simply restating what we've established; everyone has disobeyed and, being covered by sin, we will be judged unrighteous before a holy God. Verses 10-18 are entirely comprised of quotes from various old testament sources (Psalm 14:1-3, Psalm 5:9, Jeremiah 5:16, Psalm 140:3, Psalm 10:7, Proverbs 1:16, Isaiah 59:7-8 and Psalm 36:1) which hammer home with no uncertainty the assertion made in verse 9, which brings us to verses 19-20:

> [19] Now we know that whatever the Law says, it speaks to those who are under the Law, so that every mouth may be closed and all the world may become accountable to God; [20] because by the works of the Law no flesh will be justified in His sight; for through the Law comes the knowledge of sin.

Paul is not saying the Law no longer applies. What he IS saying is, just as the fig leaves were an insufficient covering for Adam and Eve, Torah is an insufficient covering for us, not because Torah is insufficient but because we've failed to obey it. He's saying that anyone who wants to use Torah as a covering before Yah, would be wise not to mention his record according to Torah because nobody's record is good. In verse 20 Paul reiterates that Torah is not intended for salvation, it merely shows us the difference between righteousness and sin and time and time again we have all chosen sin. When the time comes we can rely on the covering that comes of our own works (our record of obedience according to Torah) or we can accept the covering

Yah provided through the sacrifice of His son (Yeshua's record of obedience according to Torah). This is the essence of verses 21-30:

> [21] But now apart from the Law the righteousness of God has been manifested, being witnessed by the Law and the Prophets, [22] even the righteousness of God through faith in Jesus Christ for all those who believe; for there is no distinction; [23] for all have sinned and fall short of the glory of God, [24] being justified as a gift by His grace through the redemption which is in Christ Jesus; [25] whom God displayed publicly as a propitiation in His blood through faith. This was to demonstrate His righteousness, because in the forbearance of God He passed over the sins previously committed; [26] for the demonstration, I say, of His righteousness at the present time, so that He would be just and the justifier of the one who has faith in Jesus.
>
> [27] Where then is boasting? It is excluded. By what kind of law? Of works? No, but by a law of faith. [28] For we maintain that a man is justified by faith apart from works of the Law. [29] Or is God the God of Jews only? Is He not the God of Gentiles also? Yes, of Gentiles also, [30] since indeed God who will justify the circumcised by faith and the uncircumcised through faith is one.

This entire section is about justification by faith, not by obedience. Of course, justification is by faith and not works, but one goes too far and reads into the text something that isn't there if one tries to say that since one is not justified by obedience, there is no need for obedience once justified. As it says in verse 21, the righteousness of God has been manifested apart from Torah, but that can't and shouldn't be extended to mean Torah is no longer relevant. In other words, if obedience was always described as a response to salvation, not a means to salvation, the revelation of salvation by grace through Yeshua has no effect on the value of obedience for the saved.

By way of analogy let's say I've stolen a car. According to the law I'm guilty and due punishment for my crime. Now let's imagine the governor grants me a pardon. My pardon didn't come through the law, it came through the governor. Does that mean there's no longer a law against stealing cars that applies to me? Obviously, that would be a silly conclusion yet that's exactly what is proposed by those who use this passage and others like it to claim Torah has been abolished. In our imaginary scenario, the law against stealing cars still applies, only now, having been pardoned, I'm wise enough to obey rather than disobey the law because I recognize the penalty

I was facing for my disobedience just as Yeshua's horrific punishment and death on the cross has left the whole world with an illustration of the wrath we were headed for. Once saved by our faith, we would be wise to avoid the way of disobedience again because we've seen the awful price of it. This is Paul's conclusion in Romans 3:31:

> *Do we then nullify the Law through faith? May it never be! On the contrary, we establish the Law.*

"Establish" means, "to found, institute, build or bring into being on a firm or stable basis". Paul is saying once we are saved by faith in Yeshua, we respond with obedience to the Law written on our hearts; to Torah. We bring Torah "into being on a firm and stable basis"; not on the basis of the efforts of our flesh as a means to salvation, but on the basis of the work of the indwelling Spirit as a result of our salvation. We did not have the heart to obey before, but through Yeshua we've been given a new heart. One that opens up to us the beautiful possibility of realizing the wonderful blessings that result from obedience.

On the contrary, contemporary Christians insist that because our pardon came through Yeshua and not through the Law, there simply are no more instructions to obey and in doing so arrive at a conclusion that's no less misguided than my grand theft auto scenario. The only reason it doesn't seem misguided is because the error has been repeated for so long it has become traditional doctrine, but an error long held is an error nonetheless.

Romans chapter 4 restates many of the points already discussed; that salvation is by faith and it is imputed to all, not just Jews but also Gentiles, groups Paul refers to here, and elsewhere in his writing, as the circumcision and the uncircumcision, respectively. Paul talks a lot about Abraham and again makes the case for salvation by faith, but by doing so it doesn't mean he's making a case against Torah obedience. Looking specifically at verses 10-15 we see that salvation through faith and obedience as a response are placed side by side.

> [9] *Is this blessing then on the circumcised, or on the uncircumcised also? For we say, "Faith was credited to Abraham as righteousness."* [10] *How then was it*

> credited? While he was circumcised, or uncircumcised? Not while circumcised, but while uncircumcised; ¹¹ and he received the sign of circumcision, a seal of the righteousness of the faith which he had while uncircumcised, so that he might be the father of all who believe without being circumcised, that righteousness might be credited to them, ¹² and the father of circumcision to those who not only are of the circumcision, but who also follow in the steps of the faith of our father Abraham which he had while uncircumcised.
>
> ¹³ For the promise to Abraham or to his descendants that he would be heir of the world was not through the Law, but through the righteousness of faith. ¹⁴ For if those who are of the Law are heirs, faith is made void and the promise is nullified; ¹⁵ for the Law brings about wrath, but where there is no law, there also is no violation.

In verse 9 and 10, talking about Yah's forgiveness of sin, Paul points out that righteousness was credited to Abraham before Abraham was circumcised. This underscores the event timeline addressed previously, but let's not forget, after being counted righteous Abraham responded to Yah's instruction with obedience and received the sign of his righteousness – circumcision. This falls squarely in line with the verse in Genesis 26 that we looked at earlier:

> ⁴ I will multiply your descendants as the stars of heaven, and will give your descendants all these lands; and by your descendants all the nations of the earth shall be blessed; ⁵ because Abraham obeyed Me and kept My charge, My commandments, My statutes and My laws."

In verse 11 Paul says he obeyed so he might be the father of all who believe, and the passage in Genesis says he was the father of all who will believe because he obeyed. This is not the same as what's taught when we are told that grace stands on one side and obedience on the other, but throughout Scripture faith and obedience stand together. Consider James' comment on this same subject in James 2:

> ²⁰ But are you willing to recognize, you foolish fellow, that faith without works is useless? ²¹ Was not Abraham our father justified by works when he offered up Isaac his son on the altar? ²² You see that faith was working with his works, and as a result of the works, faith was perfected; ²³ and the Scripture was fulfilled which says, "And Abraham believed God, and it was reckoned to him as righteousness," and he was called the friend of God. ²⁴ You see that a man is

> justified by works and not by faith alone. ²⁵ In the same way, was not Rahab the harlot also justified by works when she received the messengers and sent them out by another way? ²⁶ For just as the body without the spirit is dead, so also faith without works is dead.

The generally held doctrine of western Christianity seems to be this idea of a single event and I'm done kind of approach – saying a prayer of salvation, inviting Jesus into your heart, answering an altar call, or some similar activity. Once saved there's nothing more to do but coast through life until heaven, or so they say. Dallas Willard famously coined the phrase "Vampire Christianity" saying:

> "Vampire Christianity is in essence when a person says to Jesus, 'I'd like a little of your blood, please. But I don't care to be your student (disciple) or have your character. In fact, won't you just excuse me while I get on with my life, and I'll see you in heaven'." (Willard, p. 1)

The Bible, on the other hand, paints a consistent picture whereby salvation is the beginning of a lifestyle of continued relationship development through obedience. While it's vaguely acknowledged in most Christian circles that there's still something left to do after being saved, most treat the meaning of these passages as a mystery. Some might say well, yes, James says there are works that result from our salvation and regenerate spirit but who knows what those works are? Or, yes, there seems to be a continued perfecting of faith that goes on, but who knows by what mechanism? Let me ruin the surprise for you. The works are obedience and the mechanism is Torah. By practicing obedience as a result of salvation, instead of practicing sin (or disobedience) as we did before we were saved, our faith enters the constant state of being perfected and the result is good fruit, as was promised of obedience from the beginning.

Paul drives this point home in verse 12 referring to Abraham being the father of those who *"follow in the steps of the faith"*. He doesn't say those who have the faith of Abraham but those who follow in the steps of that faith. In other words, those who respond the way Abraham responded. This fits very nicely with other passages like Philippians 2:12-13 when Paul talks about working out one's salvation:

> ¹² *So then, my beloved, just as you have always obeyed, not as in my presence only, but now much more in my absence, work out your salvation with fear and trembling;* ¹³ *for it is God who is at work in you, both to will and to work for His good pleasure.*

Finally, in Romans 4:14-15, there's something very interesting. Some use verse 14 to support the idea that the Law has been done away with. They conclude that *"those who are of the Law"* is referring to those who obey Torah and further assert that the rest of the passage is saying those who obey Torah make faith null and void.

> ¹⁴ *For if those who are of the Law are heirs, faith is made void and the promise is nullified;* ¹⁵ *for the Law brings about wrath, but where there is no law, there also is no violation.*

This is essentially where the idea comes from that if you try to obey Torah you're devaluing Yeshua's sacrifice and nullifying the gift of grace. This is not at all what Paul is saying. Just as Paul uses *"those who are of the circumcision"* as a euphemism for Jews, he's using *"those who are of the Law"* to mean Jews. He's saying, consistently with the rest of this section of Romans, and further illustrated in verse 16, that Jews aren't automatically saved just because they were given Torah, nor could they have been saved even if they had been obedient, because that's not what Torah was for. Paul is saying that if there was a way to be saved by obedience, there truly would be no need for faith. We could do it of our own effort and wouldn't need Yeshua, which would indeed make salvation by faith null and void. What would be the point of Yeshua's death and resurrection if man could gain salvation by his own efforts and simply failed to do so? If that was what Torah was for, Yah would have provided a way and it would be up to us to obey or not and face the consequences of our choice.

Paul isn't saying obedience makes faith null and void, he's saying if there was a way to be saved through obedience, Yeshua's death and resurrection wouldn't have been necessary, and by extension, it was necessary because obedience wasn't intended as a way of salvation. Ever. Yeshua is and has always been the only way to salvation. Always.

CHAPTER 6

Life and Death

Since obedience and disobedience was measured by the Law, and because everyone has disobeyed, Torah brought wrath as Paul says in Romans 4:15 but he doesn't stop there. He also says without law there is no violation. He repeats this idea in chapter 5 verse 13:

> ...for until the Law sin was in the world, but sin is not imputed when there is no law.

If you'll allow me the philosophical latitude to go on another brief tangent (too late, some of you might be thinking), I'd like to raise a question about the nature of sin in the life of the believer. If I am saved, sin is not imputed to me, but I am still able to sin, agreed? By the blood of Yeshua, we have been freed from the power and penalty of sin but not from the presence of sin, and although my faith is being perfected, it is not perfect. This means that although the regenerate man will not make a practice of sin, he will occasionally sin.

What then are we to make of Paul's final statement if we believe that the Law has been done away with? He doesn't say through grace there is no violation, he says without law there is no violation. This is a vital distinction because through grace there is no penalty for violation to be sure, but that's very different than saying there is no violation. To begin with, if there is no violation without a standard, but we know that sin IS a violation, mustn't there still be a standard by which to judge something a violation? By what standard are we to determine the difference between righteous and sinful behavior? There is no evidence of a new standard, which leaves the only standard the Bible describes, namely Torah. This very small statement has big implications for those who would believe there is no law.

We find more evidence for the distinction between righteousness and obedience on one side and sin and disobedience on the other toward the end of chapter 5 and into chapter 6. Let's look at Romans 5:17-19:

> *[17] For if by the transgression of the one, death reigned through the one, much more those who receive the abundance of grace and of the gift of righteousness will reign in life through the One, Jesus Christ. [18] So then as through one transgression there resulted condemnation to all men, even so through one act of righteousness there resulted justification of life to all men. [19] For as through the one man's disobedience the many were made sinners, even so through the obedience of the One the many will be made righteous.*

In these verses, we can establish the language Paul uses to describe transgression, righteousness, disobedience, and obedience. In verse 17, Paul describes Adam's transgression which led to death for himself and, by extension, all of us. In verse 19, Paul calls this same thing disobedience and draws an equivalence between the terms disobedience and sinner. Likewise, Paul describes Yeshua's death and resurrection as an act of righteousness that led to life in verse 18 which is reiterated in verse 19 as *"obedience of the one"* that makes all who believe righteous. I point this out to strengthen the case that where you see righteousness and life, it's related to obedience and where you see sin and death it's related to disobedience. This is so well matched to the language we saw in Deuteronomy that it's reasonable to believe Torah is what stands between the two, dividing one from the other.

Recall Deuteronomy 6:25:

> *[25] It will be righteousness for us if we are careful to observe all this commandment before the Lord our God, just as He commanded us.*

and Deuteronomy 30:19-20:

> [19] I call heaven and earth to witness against you today, that I have set before you life and death, the blessing and the curse. So choose life in order that you may live, you and your descendants, [20] by loving the Lord your God, by obeying His voice, and by holding fast to Him; for this is your life and the length of your days, that you may live in the land which the Lord swore to your fathers, to Abraham, Isaac, and Jacob, to give them."

To be fair, this particular section of Romans is talking about Yeshua's obedience and doesn't specifically speak to the relevance of obedience in our lives. Continuing into Chapter 6 though, Paul addresses this. In verse 1, Paul asks if we should continue in sin, aka disobedience, and his answer is, "God forbid". In verse 4, Paul says that being raised with Christ we should walk in newness of life. How interesting that in Deuteronomy 30:19, after Yah says He has set before us in Torah life and death, He implores us to choose life which means to walk according to His instruction. Romans 6:12-19 provides further evidence:

> [12] Therefore do not let sin reign in your mortal body so that you obey its lusts, [13] and do not go on presenting the members of your body to sin as instruments of unrighteousness; but present yourselves to God as those alive from the dead, and your members as instruments of righteousness to God. [14] For sin shall not be master over you, for you are not under law but under grace. [15] What then? Shall we sin because we are not under law but under grace? May it never be! [16] Do you not know that when you present yourselves to someone as slaves for obedience, you are slaves of the one whom you obey, either of sin resulting in death, or of obedience resulting in righteousness? [17] But thanks be to God that though you were slaves of sin, you became obedient from the heart to that form of teaching to which you were committed, [18] and having been freed from sin, you became slaves of righteousness. [19] I am speaking in human terms because of the weakness of your flesh. For just as you presented your members as slaves to impurity and to lawlessness, resulting in further lawlessness, so now present your members as slaves to righteousness, resulting in sanctification.

If we keep in mind Paul's establishment of disobedience as synonymous with sin, and righteousness as synonymous with obedience, this passage makes my case for me. In verse 12, Paul recommends NOT obeying sin, which is another way of recommending against disobedience or presenting yourself as an instrument of wickedness but asks his readers to present themselves as instruments of righteousness. Regarding the concept of being under grace rather than law, this is another passage where Paul's words are misconstrued by some as meaning we needn't obey Torah. Being under law does not mean being obedient to the Law, rather it has everything to do with what covers us as people who have already broken Yah's laws. Paul is saying our disobedience cannot be held against us because we don't claim our obedience to Torah as our covering, we claim the blood of Yeshua's record of obedience in place of our own as our covering. This is why, in verse 15, Paul adds that we should not sin (disobey) just because we don't claim our obedience to Torah as our covering.

Let's look at this another way. The common teaching is that there's no longer a need to obey because Yeshua paid the price of our disobedience. If this is true, then why would Paul write verse 15?

> [15] *What then? Shall we sin because we are not under law but under grace? May it never be!*

He's specifically addressing this idea and saying it's wrong and should never be. It's as if Paul understood that one day people would think that because Torah can't save them there's no point in obeying it and he's telling us that's a false conclusion. He makes this point clear again in verse 16 where he states unequivocally that every one of us is a slave to the choice we make. We are either a slave to sin resulting in death or a slave to obedience leading to life. If Torah has been done away with, or if Paul is talking about some new, undefined New Testament law, why is Paul using the same language used throughout the Old Testament to describe Torah's purpose and possible outcomes to make the distinctions he's making here? He continues in verse 17 saying that even though we were disobedient, slaves of sin, we became obedient *"from the heart to that form of teaching to which you were committed"*. What form of teaching is that if not Torah? Paul is saying, using identical language, that what was prophesied by Ezekiel and Jeremiah, has come to pass. Remember Ezekiel 36:26-27:

> [26] *Moreover, I will give you a new heart and put a new spirit within you; and I will remove the heart of stone from your flesh and give you a heart of flesh.* [27] *I*

> will put My Spirit within you and cause you to walk in My statutes, and you will be careful to observe My ordinances.

And Jeremiah 31:33:

> "But this is the covenant which I will make with the house of Israel after those days," declares the Lord, "I will put My law within them and on their heart I will write it; and I will be their God, and they shall be My people.

Paul is saying, in verse 17, that what the prophets said would happen has happened and says we should be thankful for it. Paul puts this idea in simple terms in verse 19 saying that being saved, we should present ourselves to righteousness, just as we were once lost in lawlessness. To put it another way using Paul's own definitions, now that we're saved we should practice obedience just as we once practiced disobedience.

This leads us into another part of Romans that gets a bit complicated and unfortunately can't just be discussed in summary. Many individual verses in chapters 7 and 8 have been pulled out of context and misinterpreted so while this review is a bit tangential to the main point, it's important to untangle the mess that's been made of some of these passages and sort through the confusion that has resulted. As we've seen, there's a running theme throughout Romans of the disobedience that marked our unsaved life and the obedience that serves as evidence of our salvation. Obedience is not the means by which we're saved but stands as a sign of our having been saved and that theme continues in the next few chapters.

It behooves us to pay attention to Paul's parenthetical statement in verse 1 of chapter 7. Paul explicitly says he's speaking in this next section to *"them that know the law"*. What I take this to mean is, if we don't know Torah with a decent level of familiarity we'd better be very careful about our conclusions. In short, he's not talking to those who don't know Torah, and this unfortunately includes many Christian pastors, leaders, and teachers over the last 2000 years. I mention this only to say, be cautious of what is taught from this section of Romans by those who don't know Torah well. The difficulty is Paul doesn't always explain concepts before making his points. He expects his audience to be familiar enough with Torah that certain points don't need explanation, but elsewhere, when making a different but related point he provides more detail for context. As a result, it's necessary to bounce around a bit more than in other portions of Paul's letters. While I try hard not to do that for fear of being accused of leaving the context of a passage, it's somewhat unavoidable here because Paul brings up points that he had already explained in letters he had written previously. As a result, to explain things Paul summarizes in one letter, one often has to refer to another letter for additional details. Hopefully you'll see that these thoughts remain cohesive even though there's some separation between certain concepts and their definitions.

Paul's expectation that his audience would know Torah is immediately evident in verses 2-6:

> *¹ Or do you not know, brethren (for I am speaking to those who know the law), that the law has jurisdiction over a person as long as he lives? ² For the married woman is bound by law to her husband while he is living; but if her husband dies, she is released from the law concerning the husband. ³ So then, if while her husband is living she is joined to another man, she shall be called an adulteress; but if her husband dies, she is free from the law, so that she is not an adulteress though she is joined to another man. ⁴ Therefore, my brethren, you also were made to die to the Law through the body of Christ, so that you might be joined to another, to Him who was raised from the dead, in order that we might bear fruit for God. ⁵ For while we were in the flesh, the sinful passions, which were aroused by the Law, were at work in the members of our body to bear fruit for death. ⁶ But now we have been released from the Law, having died to that by which we were bound, so that we serve in newness of the Spirit and not in oldness of the letter.*

Some teach the analogy presented here is evidence of Torah having been done away with. After all, does verse 4 not say *"you also were made to die to the Law through the body of Christ"*? The problem is one of misunderstanding the analogy Paul's describing as it relates to Torah. The misinterpretation essentially says Torah is the husband in this passage, and just as the husband passed away leaving the wife free, so too has Torah passed away, leaving us free from having to practice obedience. Armed with an understanding of Torah, this interpretation can easily be shown false.

By Torah law, a woman who was married could not "join" to another man. This would be disobedience, which we know is sin, specifically the sin of adultery. This is what's being described in verses 2-3. It's important to understand this isn't talking about Torah in general, but one specific instruction from Torah. That's why Paul says at the end of verse 2 that if the husband dies, she is released from *"the law concerning her husband"*. He's not saying she's released from all the instruction of Torah, simply that she's released from this one instruction that concerns her being bound to her husband. According to that one instruction, the binding concludes upon the death of either spouse. This is important to understand when we get to verse 3 where Paul says, *"if her husband dies, she is free from the law"*. He's not saying she's free from the whole of Torah, he's saying she's free from the specific, single instruction established in verse 2 as the object of these statements. Because this rule is no longer binding, being joined to another man is no longer disobedience; it's no longer sin. This analogy is then used to describe our pre-salvation and post-salvation states. Paul is saying that before we were saved, we were "married" to sin, and being "married" to sin we could not join ourselves to Yah. To borrow the language at the end of verse 4, we could not *"bear fruit for God"* because we were joined to sin. But, as Paul wrote in Romans 6:5-11 we, through faith, have shared in Christ's death and, according to Paul's analogy, our "marriage" to disobedience according to Torah has ended. At last we are free to join ourselves to another; as Paul says in the last half of verse 4, *"to Him who was raised from the dead"*. In verse 5, Paul says before we were saved, sinful passions were at work to bear fruit unto death. As we've seen, this is the language of disobedience, the fruit of which was described in the vice list of Romans 1:28-32.

This leaves us with Romans 7:6 where, once more, popular Christian teaching will contend, "see, it says we've been released from the law". To take this to mean Torah is no longer relevant is to rip this single verse from the context of the analogy Paul is making. As I've stated, Paul is assuming the reader's familiarity with Torah marriage instruction and is leveraging that familiarity to describe the nature of our relationship with sin. We were once "married" to it and by analogy could not join ourselves to Christ. In other words, we couldn't save ourselves, but, having shared in Christ's death, we're no longer "married" to sin. We've been released. This isn't meant to say we can ignore Torah. It means we're freed from serving disobedience as Paul explained at the end of Romans 6 in verses 16-18, and by extension are finally free to obey.

It's a shame that translators chose to put a break between Romans 6 and 7 (and 8 for that matter). All three chapters stand as one continuous thought and it relates to the same ideas throughout. We were once lost in our disobedience but now we have new life and through the Spirit are free to enjoy the blessings of obedience in response to our salvation.

I'd like to pause for a moment in my analysis as there are some points Paul makes in verses 5 and 6 that deserve some further explanation.

> [5] *For while we were in the flesh, the sinful passions, which were aroused by the Law, were at work in the members of our body to bear fruit for death.* [6] *But now we have been released from the Law, having died to that by which we were bound, so that we serve in newness of the Spirit and not in oldness of the letter.*

First, in verse 5 what does Paul mean when he says that these *"sinful passions"* were *"aroused by the Law"*? And second, what does he mean in verse 6 when he says we serve in newness of Spirit not in the oldness of the letter?

The statement in verse 5 makes Torah sound like a bad thing, does it not? Fortunately, we don't have to go far for Paul's clarification in verses 7-12:

> [7] *What shall we say then? Is the Law sin? May it never be! On the contrary, I would not have come to know sin except through the Law; for I would not have known about coveting if the Law had not said, "You shall not covet."* [8] *But sin, taking opportunity through the commandment, produced in me coveting of every kind; for apart from the Law sin is dead.* [9] *I was once alive apart from the Law; but when the commandment came, sin became alive and I died;* [10] *and this commandment, which was to result in life, proved to result in death for me;* [11] *for sin, taking an opportunity through the commandment, deceived me and through it killed me.* [12] *So then, the Law is holy, and the commandment is holy and righteous and good.*

Lest we think that Paul is saying Torah is sin, causes sin, or promotes sin, Paul specifically says in verse 7 that's not the case so we can be certain that's not what he's saying in verse 5. He explains that Torah defines that behavior which is sinful. He wouldn't even have known he was disobedient if not for Torah providing a definition of right and wrong behavior. In verse 8-9 he reiterates what he said in Romans 4:15 and 5:13. When he says he was alive apart from the Law, it's simply another way of saying that when there is no law there is no condemnation. When he says he died when the commandment came, he's saying that Torah, being Yah's standard for judgement, made him aware of his disobedience and by extension he became aware of the penalty due him. Furthermore, he understood through Torah that the wages of sin is death. But was the intention of Torah simply to condemn? Of course not. Torah merely defined sin while life and death is determined by whether we followed or strayed from its instruction. We saw in Deuteronomy 5:29 that Yah's intention was that we would have the heart to obey and enjoy blessing as a result:

> [29] Oh that they had such a heart in them, that they would fear Me and keep all My commandments always, that it may be well with them and with their sons forever!

This is exactly what Paul means in verse 10 when he says, *"this commandment, that was to result in life, resulted in death for me"*. It wasn't Torah itself that resulted in death instead of life. It was his own, and by extension, our own disobedience that results in death. In this way, to answer the initial question of whether Torah is good or bad, Paul concludes in verse 12 that the Law is holy, righteous and good.

As for the explanation of verse 6, Paul expands on this in verse 13. To restate the question, what does Paul mean when he says in 7:6 that we should serve in newness of Spirit and not oldness of letter? First, we need to understand that throughout Romans, Paul has expressed the idea that Jews following the letter of Torah are not guaranteed salvation because they too have disobeyed. We also need to remember the context of the gospels wherein Yeshua consistently talked about the Pharisees and Sadducees strictly following traditional practices and neglecting the purpose of the Torah commands to which they had added so much man-made doctrine. This is what Paul is talking about when he refers to the oldness of the letter of the Law. As an example, consider Matthew 23:23 where Yeshua says:

> *"Woe to you, scribes and Pharisees, hypocrites! For you tithe mint and dill and cummin, and have neglected the weightier provisions of the law: justice and mercy and faithfulness; but these are the things you should have done without neglecting the others."*

He's referring to the fact that they were following the letter, in this case tithing, but were ignoring the underlying purpose of the Torah instructions, simply put, love. For us it would be like giving to the poor because we believe we have to out of obedience, or because it would make us a good person, not because we have a genuine heart for the poor and a desire to help those in need. Notice that Yeshua does NOT say you should have done the *"weightier"* things not the *"letter of the Law"* things. He says you should have done both. You should have observed *"the letter of the Law"*, without neglecting the *"spirit of the Law"*.

Returning to Romans, let's move on to *"serving in newness of Spirit"*. I've discussed at length the relationship between what Paul says here and elsewhere in Romans to what the prophets Isaiah and Ezekiel said about the work the Spirit would do in us; that He would write Torah on our hearts and cause us to walk in it, but let's look to Paul's own definitions. To understand what Paul thinks, we need look no further than the rest of Romans 7, specifically verses 14 and 22:

> [14] **For we know that the Law is spiritual, but I am of flesh, sold into bondage to sin.** [15] For what I am doing, I do not understand; for I am not practicing what I would like to do, but I am doing the very thing I hate. [16] But if I do the very thing I do not want to do, I agree with the Law, confessing that the Law is good. [17] So now, no longer am I the one doing it, but sin which dwells in me. [18] For I know that nothing good dwells in me, that is, in my flesh; for the willing is present in me, but the doing of the good is not. [19] For the good that I want, I do not do, but I practice the very evil that I do not want. [20] But if I am doing the very thing I do not want, I am no longer the one doing it, but sin which dwells in me.
>
> [21] I find then the principle that evil is present in me, the one who wants to do good. [22] **For I joyfully concur with the law of God in the inner man,** [23] but I see a different law in the members of my body, waging war against the law of my mind and making me a prisoner of the law of sin which is in my members. [24] Wretched man that I am! Who will set me free from the body of this death? [25] Thanks be to God through Jesus Christ our Lord! So then, on the

> one hand I myself with my mind am serving the law of God, but on the other, with my flesh the law of sin.

Right from the start we see a shocking statement from Paul. The Law is spiritual! He says he is of flesh and sold into bondage to sin, and this is contrasted with Torah, which is of the Spirit. Can it be that to serve in newness of Spirit is to walk according to the Law; to obey Torah? I submit the answer is yes. Knowing that Torah is spiritual we see this interesting and, to most, familiar, if not somewhat confusing, passage about doing what he doesn't want to do and not doing what he does want to do. I won't go into the details of 15-20 except to touch briefly on verse 16. Paul makes the point that he does do what he doesn't want to do, a feeling I'm sure we've all had when we've sinned since being saved. He's explaining that though he stumbles in sin he doesn't want to, and his desire not to sin is evidence that he agrees with Torah and thinks it good. I sincerely believe this is true of all of us who are saved and enjoy a relationship with Yeshua.

There was a time in my life where sin appeared fun and seemed satisfying, but it was only satisfying to the flesh. Since being saved there's a grievousness and bitterness to sin that wasn't apparent in my unregenerate state. Even before I followed Torah, in my spirit – what Paul calls the inner man in verse 22 – my discomfort toward sin proved my agreement with Torah's distinction between righteous and sinful behavior. So, what we find in verses 21-25 is Paul's distinction between two "laws", one related to the flesh and the other to the Spirit. He says in verse 22 that he joyfully agrees with Torah in spirit but says in verse 23 there's a law of sin in his flesh and asks in verse 24 who will set him free from this body of death. We find his conclusion in verse 25 – Thanks be to Yah who, through Yeshua, no longer holds him, or us, accountable for the sins of the flesh but has freed him to serve *"the Law of God"*. Throughout this passage, what we have is Paul's explanation that in Spirit he obeys Torah even though his flesh still struggles with sin.

Paul summarizes all of this in chapter 8 verses 1-8:

> [1] *Therefore there is now no condemnation for those who are in Christ Jesus.* [2] *For the law of the Spirit of life in Christ Jesus has set you free from the law*

> of sin and of death. ³ For what the Law could not do, weak as it was through the flesh, God did: sending His own Son in the likeness of sinful flesh and as an offering for sin, He condemned sin in the flesh, ⁴ so that the requirement of the Law might be fulfilled in us, who do not walk according to the flesh but according to the Spirit. ⁵ For those who are according to the flesh set their minds on the things of the flesh, but those who are according to the Spirit, the things of the Spirit. ⁶ For the mind set on the flesh is death, but the mind set on the Spirit is life and peace, ⁷ because the mind set on the flesh is hostile toward God; for it does not subject itself to the law of God, for it is not even able to do so, ⁸ and those who are in the flesh cannot please God.

In verse 1, Paul says even though we now practice obedience, there is no condemnation when we stumble. Knowing what we know about Torah and the fruits of obedience and disobedience we can better understand the two "laws" Paul is referring to in verse 2. He's not using law here in the sense of Torah but in the sense of, say, the law of gravity. It's simply an immutable fact. There's the fact of the Spirit of life in Christ Jesus, and the fact of sin and death. In other words, the fact of our having disobeyed Torah is called sin, and the price is death, but we're free from that penalty because of the fact that we have life in Yeshua and, because of this new life, are indwelt by the Spirit. In verse 3 Paul says again that Torah could not save us, not because of Torah's weakness but because of the weakness of the flesh that meant we couldn't obey. What the Law could not do is give us a new heart; a heart that could obey, but that's exactly what Yeshua's death and resurrection does for any who would believe on Him. The word gospel means "good news" and this is good news, indeed!

In verse 4 we see the astonishing statement that Yah, having sent His own Son, condemned sin in the flesh so *"the requirement of the Law might be fulfilled in us"*. What was the requirement of the Torah? Was it not that we obey? And now we can in a way that wasn't possible before the Spirit was sent after Yeshua's departure to the Kingdom. Paul further explains saying we who are saved *"do not walk according to the flesh"*.

In other words, we don't walk in disobedience, but according to the Spirit, or, in obedience, just as the prophets said we would. Lest someone say I'm making too much of the relationship between "serving in Spirit" being synonymous with obeying Torah, continue to verse 5 where Paul explicitly separates those who *"set their minds on things of the flesh"* and those who set their minds on things of the Spirit. Then, in verse 6, Paul describes the mind set on the flesh as death, the result Yah said would come from disobeying Torah, while he says the mind set on the Spirit is life and peace, the exact blessings promised to those who obey Torah (for instance, Deuteronomy 30:15-20). Paul doesn't stop there though. He specifically says in verse 7 that the mind set on the flesh is hostile toward God. What reason does he give for this hostility? Because *"the mind set on the flesh does not subject itself to the Law of God, for it is not even able to do so"*!

By extrapolation, and by following the contrasts layered throughout this passage between the mind set on the flesh and the mind set on the Spirit it is reasonable to conclude that the opposite is true of the one *"serving in Spirit"*. Stated directly, the mind set on the Spirit is NOT hostile to God because it DOES subject itself to the Law of God. Paul isn't just encouraging believers to practice Torah obedience, he's stating outright that the natural result of setting one's mind on the Spirit is obedience, though it's not us that obeys but the Spirit within us, while disobedience is evidence of a mind set on the flesh. This is not my summary of what's being said. This is how Paul summarizes his own thoughts in verse 9-11:

> *⁹ However, you are not in the flesh but in the Spirit, if indeed the Spirit of God dwells in you. But if anyone does not have the Spirit of Christ, he does not belong to Him. ¹⁰ If Christ is in you, though the body is dead because of sin, yet the spirit is alive because of righteousness. ¹¹ But if the Spirit of Him who raised Jesus from the dead dwells in you, He who raised Christ Jesus from the dead will also give life to your mortal bodies through His Spirit who dwells in you.*

It's not simply that Yeshua's righteousness is imparted to our account, although that's true. Paul goes one step further in verse 11 and says, having been saved by the fact of Yeshua's righteousness being credited to us, the same Spirit who raised Jesus and now dwells in the saved will give life to our bodies. In other words, Paul is asserting the same truth he touched on in chapter 7 verses 22 and 25, saying the Spirit will lead us to obey the Torah now written on our hearts, the blessing of which is life.

From here, Paul leaves the subject of the obedience of those counted righteous in Christ and moves on to other important truths; the predestination of the elect, the tribulation that will face those who follow Yeshua, the concept of being spiritually Israelite, and Yah's authority to condemn or save whom He wills, to name a few. While these are important truths, they are topics for a different book, so I won't cover them here.

While I believe I've presented enough evidence in the first half of Romans to support the claim that Paul spoke favorably of Torah, promoted following its instruction, and stated repeatedly that obedience would be the natural state of anyone redeemed by Yeshua, there's an important passage in chapter 13 that makes this absolutely inarguable. Up until now, I suppose one could still cling, albeit tenuously, to the idea that everything Paul is talking about is referring to some other, newer, or perhaps changed Law of God other than Torah. Romans 13:8-10 really blows this argument out of the water:

> [8] *Owe nothing to anyone except to love one another; for he who loves his neighbor has fulfilled the law.* [9] *For this, "You shall not commit adultery, You shall not murder, You shall not steal, You shall not covet," and if there is any other commandment, it is summed up in this saying, "You shall love your neighbor as yourself."* [10] *Love does no wrong to a neighbor; therefore love is the fulfillment of the law.*

There can be no question that Paul is talking about Torah here and more than that, he's echoing exactly what Yeshua said when He was asked what the greatest commandment was in Matthew 22:

> [36] *"Teacher, which is the great commandment in the Law?"* [37] *And He said to him, "'You shall love the Lord your God with all your heart, and with all your soul, and with all your mind.'* [38] *This is the great and foremost commandment.* [39] *The second is like it, 'You shall love your neighbor as yourself.'* [40] *On these two commandments depend the whole Law and the Prophets."*

Having provided evidence for Paul's support for and encouragement toward obeying Torah instruction and having addressed the passages people mistakenly use to claim Torah has been done away with, either by taking Paul's words out of context or by simply misunderstanding the core concepts Paul refers to, there are a few points in the last half of Romans that bear mentioning. While they aren't directly related to Torah's purpose and the question of obedience, I feel it's better to address them here rather than making a small number of additional comments about Romans in a later chapter.

The first thing I'd like to address is another supposed proof text for the end of Torah. In Romans 10, we find the following verses:

> *¹ Brethren, my heart's desire and my prayer to God for them is for their salvation. ² For I testify about them that they have a zeal for God, but not in accordance with knowledge. ³ For not knowing about God's righteousness and seeking to establish their own, they did not subject themselves to the righteousness of God. ⁴ For Christ is the end of the law for righteousness to everyone who believes. ⁵ For Moses writes that the man who practices the righteousness which is based on law shall live by that righteousness.*

Of course, for most Christians verse 4 will stand out as it seems to clearly say Torah has ended and verse 5 could be taken as support for verse 4. The problem is, this is just a terrible translation and sadly it's the way these verses are translated in most English Bibles. Alongside the NASB, ESV, KJV, HCSB and several others all use the word "end" in verse 4 and it's an unfortunate word to use as it doesn't mean "end" in the common meaning, as in the opposite of beginning, it means end in the sense of a phrase like, "to that end, I will do such and such". The original Greek word used is the word "telos" which means object or aim. The NIV is the lone popular version that gets this right, saying:

> *Christ is the culmination of the law so that there may be righteousness for everyone who believes.*

In the context of verses 1-3, Paul is talking about his Jewish brethren who were trying to earn their salvation through Torah obedience not understanding that only the covering provided by Yah, His son Yeshua, was sufficient (verse 3). Also remember that the purpose of Torah was to establish our need for a savior by showing us that we have all disobeyed as a result of the bondage of sin. This is what Paul means when he says Christ is the "telos" or "aim" of Torah. Torah points us to Yeshua because it shows us our inability to save ourselves. Incidentally, being alive at a point in history after Yeshua's death and resurrection, Torah also provides the foundation to describe how He walked so that we might live as He did as it says in 1 John 2:6. Verse 5 of Romans 10 is simply supporting this from a different angle by saying exactly what Moses himself said in Deuteronomy: That the man who practices obedience to Torah will live. Of course, no one, prior to being saved practices righteousness, which brings us right back to our need for a savior. The point is, although this passage uses the English word "end", Paul is definitely not saying Torah has ended. He's simply saying what he's said throughout Romans, that Torah isn't meant for salvation, but is meant to show us that we cannot save ourselves and point us to the one who can, a fact he wishes was understood by his fellow Jews.

As an aside, with all the evidence I've presented that providing a mechanism for salvation was never the purpose of Torah, the New Living Translation (NLT) does the worst job possible with verse 4:

> *For Christ has already accomplished the purpose for which the law was given. As a result, all who believe in him are made right with God. (NLT)*

If Yeshua accomplished the purpose for which Torah was given (and having proven the purpose of Torah wasn't to save us) we'd all be in trouble because that would mean Yeshua pointed out our need for a savior without providing a mechanism by which to be saved. This is not just a bad translation, this demonstrates a fundamental ignorance of everything the Old Testament teaches about Torah and illustrates a shocking lack of theological understanding on the part of the translators. Regardless of how you feel about the thesis of this book, please consider a different translation if you use an NLT Bible. Differences in translation, like using "end" rather than "culmination" or "aim" for the word "telos" is one thing but what we have here in the NLT isn't simply an ambiguous word choice, it's undeniably incorrect and if its incorrect here, I'd be very concerned about what else they've gotten flat out wrong.

Finally, I'll wrap up my review of Torah, obedience, and salvation by jumping to the end of Romans. At the conclusion of Paul's letter, in chapter 16, he leaves his audience with one final bit of advice in verses 17-21:

> *17 Now I urge you, brethren, keep your eye on those who cause dissensions and hindrances contrary to the teaching which you learned, and turn away from them. 18 For such men are slaves, not of our Lord Christ but of their own appetites; and by their smooth and flattering speech they deceive the hearts of the unsuspecting. 19 For the report of your obedience has reached to all; therefore I am rejoicing over you, but I want you to be wise in what is good and innocent in what is evil. 20 The God of peace will soon crush Satan under your feet. The grace of our Lord Jesus be with you.*

If you recall from the beginning of this journey through Romans, I quoted Peter's warning that Paul's writing was complicated and was being twisted by false teachers even then. Peter said that by doing so, people would be led into lawlessness. It's interesting that Paul gives his audience basically the same warning. In verse 17 he's telling believers to beware of those who would teach things contrary to what they had already learned because such men are not slaves of Christ. We've seen that Paul distinguishes between "slaves of sin" and "slaves of Christ" based on their disobedience or obedience, respectively. This is further established by the reason Paul gives for why he's warning them. In verse 19 we read that he's warning them because the report of their obedience *"has reached to all"* and he doesn't want them to stumble. To paraphrase, Paul is saying, "you have a reputation for obedience. Don't let flattering but deceptive men lead you into disobedience through their false teaching". If that was happening then, it shouldn't be a stretch for us to believe it continued, and continues, happening. My assertion is that what was false teaching in Peter and Paul's day is still false teaching today and, just as Peter warned, many of us have been led astray into lawlessness and are missing out on a profound level of blessing from and closeness with Yah that is opened up to those who live obedient lives as a result of and response to being saved.

In conclusion, allow me to restate the error Paul and Peter warned about, which goes something like this: There have been, throughout history, two paths to salvation. First was Torah which required obedience, and second, because obedience wasn't possible, the Son was given. As we now know this isn't the picture that the Bible paints. Both the Old and New Testaments present the same explanation of purpose for Torah. It was given so that we might benefit from Yah's instructions; that we might know, given

Yah's design for life in His creation, what is good and what is not, and that we might understand that there are consequences to our choices and behavior; blessing and life if we live according to Yah's instruction or sin and death if we live contrary to it.

Ultimately Torah was given so that we would recognize our need for salvation by illustrating to each of us that we have lived disobedient lives according to Yah's standard. These facts were recorded when Torah was given at Mt. Sinai, were repeated throughout the Old Testament, and were confirmed by several of the authors of New Testament books including Paul. With this preponderance of evidence, it's impossible to cling to the idea that Torah was given as a means of salvation, and if it wasn't, then it's equally impossible to support the idea that it stands at odds with salvation by grace. Torah and grace have always had distinctly different roles to play. If the latter didn't replace the former, one must reassess the idea that Torah has no place in the lives of believers in Yeshua today.

Section III

Liberty or Bondage

CHAPTER 7

The Pattern of Paul

In the last section, a lot of time was spent untangling the misinterpretations and misunderstandings of Paul's views of Torah in his letter to the Romans but a bit more inspection of Paul's life and words outside of the book of Romans is beneficial. As a starting point, let's look at an interesting statement Paul makes in Philippians chapter 3:

> [17] Brethren, join in following my example, and observe those who walk according to the pattern you have in us. [18] For many walk, of whom I often told you, and now tell you even weeping, that they are enemies of the cross of Christ, [19] whose end is destruction, whose god is their appetite, and whose glory is in their shame, who set their minds on earthly things. [20] For our citizenship is in heaven, from which also we eagerly wait for a Savior, the Lord Jesus Christ; [21] who will transform the body of our humble state into conformity with the body of His glory, by the exertion of the power that He has even to subject all things to Himself.

While we'll get to the topic of heavenly citizenship soon, for now focus on Paul's instruction in verse 17. He says that the brethren should follow his example and refers to a pattern of behavior. Acts has a lot to say about Paul's lifestyle so let's spend some time there.

Acts 18:20-21 says:

> [20] When they desired him to tarry longer time with them, he consented not; [21] But bade them farewell, saying, I must by all means keep this feast that cometh in Jerusalem: but I will return again unto you, if God will. And he sailed from Ephesus."(KJV).

In the interest of transparency, the phrase, *"I must by all means keep this feast that cometh in Jerusalem"* has been removed from many translations but his keeping of this feast (likely the feast of Tabernacles) is consistent with Acts 20:16 which says:

> *For Paul had decided to sail past Ephesus so that he would not have to spend time in Asia; for he was hurrying to be in Jerusalem, if possible, on the day of Pentecost.*

Pentecost is the Greek word for the Biblical holy day, Shavuot, otherwise known as the Feast of Weeks. While it's worth studying the parallels between the first Shavuot where Torah was written on stone 50 days after the first Passover, and later the Holy Spirit was poured out and Torah was written on our hearts on Shavuot (Pentecost) 50 days after Yeshua's death and resurrection (our Passover lamb), that's a bit beyond the scope of this book. The point is there are examples of Paul keeping the holy days included as part of Torah.

In addition to his observance of Yah's holy days, we see examples of Paul keeping the Sabbath. Like Yeshua, Paul was a rabbi, and where would a rabbi be on the Sabbath if not teaching in the synagogue? This is exactly what we see in Acts 13:13-15:

> [13] *Now Paul and his companions put out to sea from Paphos and came to Perga in Pamphylia; but John left them and returned to Jerusalem.* [14] *But going on from Perga, they arrived at Pisidian Antioch, and on the Sabbath day they went into the synagogue and sat down.* [15] *After the reading of the Law and the Prophets the synagogue officials sent to them, saying, "Brethren, if you have any word of exhortation for the people, say it."*

Paul goes on to preach the good news of salvation. Lest we believe this was an isolated incident, Acts 13:42 says:

> *As Paul and Barnabas were going out, the people kept begging that these things might be spoken to them the next Sabbath.*

And Paul did return on the next Sabbath (verse 44). In fact, Acts 17:2 says that it was Paul's custom to do this:

> And according to Paul's custom, he went to them, and for three Sabbaths reasoned with them from the Scriptures

Interestingly, this was Yeshua's custom as well, as it says in Luke 4:16:

> And He came to Nazareth, where He had been brought up; and as was His custom, He entered the synagogue on the Sabbath, and stood up to read.

At this point, you may be thinking Paul's presence in the Synagogue doesn't prove he was observing the Sabbath. Perhaps that's just a day he knew where he could find a captive audience. That the fourth commandment is a double commandment is often missed. It doesn't just instruct us to rest but also to work. It says six days we shall work and on the seventh we shall rest. With this in mind let's look at Acts 18:1-4:

> *1 After these things he left Athens and went to Corinth. 2 And he found a Jew named Aquila, a native of Pontus, having recently come from Italy with his wife Priscilla, because Claudius had commanded all the Jews to leave Rome. He came to them, 3 and because he was of the same trade, he stayed with them and they were working, for by trade they were tent-makers. 4 And he was reasoning in the synagogue every Sabbath and trying to persuade Jews and Greeks.*

In verse 3, the writer talks about Paul staying with Aquila and Priscilla and working but says in verse 4 that he reasoned in the synagogue every Sabbath. There's clearly a distinction between days Paul worked and the Sabbath when he didn't work, satisfying both sides of the fourth commandment. It's also interesting to note that verse 4 says he reasoned in the synagogue every Sabbath when one considers the assertion of Acts 18:11:

> And he settled there a year and six months, teaching the word of God among them.

That's 18 months' worth of Sabbaths for those keeping score. That's a lot for a guy who we're told taught no one had to observe the Sabbath anymore. That would make Paul quite the hypocrite, no? Speaking of hypocrisy, many teach that Paul discouraged circumcision. Mostly this comes from another misunderstood passage, Galatians 5:2, which says, *"Behold I, Paul, say to you that if you receive circumcision, Christ will be of no benefit to you."* To understand the context of this verse we have to go all the way back to Galatians 2:

> *¹ Then after an interval of fourteen years I went up again to Jerusalem with Barnabas, taking Titus along also. ² It was because of a revelation that I went up; and I submitted to them the gospel which I preach among the Gentiles, but I did so in private to those who were of reputation, for fear that I might be running, or had run, in vain. ³ But not even Titus, who was with me, though he was a Greek, was compelled to be circumcised.*

What Paul is talking about here is a group of Jews who insisted that before a person could be saved that person had to be circumcised. Paul explains at length the place of Torah and in 5:2 says that if you get circumcised to be saved you've missed the point. I've touched on this elsewhere, but this has everything to do with the order of events. Like baptism, circumcision is an outward mark of an inward transformation. If the inward transformation hasn't happened, the mark means nothing, and if one takes the sign of the covenant, i.e. circumcision, in order to "earn" salvation he does, as Paul says, make Christ of no benefit. That person is trying to earn salvation on his own merits. That's quite different than a person who has been saved, and having been saved, is circumcised as a sign of the covenant he's been included in, having been grafted into Israel. As mentioned in a previous chapter, this is the pattern left by Abraham. Abraham was already counted righteous and as an outworking of that righteousness obeyed Yah's instruction to be circumcised.

What does all of this have to do with hypocrisy? If it's true that Paul was teaching against circumcision, why did Paul personally circumcise Timothy in Acts 16:

> *¹ Paul came also to Derbe and to Lystra. And a disciple was there, named Timothy, the son of a Jewish woman who was a believer, but his father was a Greek, ² and he was well spoken of by the brethren who were in Lystra and Iconium. ³ Paul wanted this man to go with him; and he took him and circumcised him because of the Jews who were in those parts, for they all knew that his father was a Greek.*

This would seem odd unless you understand that, in Galatians, Paul isn't condemning circumcision, he's condemning the belief that a person MUST be circumcised before he can be saved. As we've seen throughout Scripture, Paul is making the case that obedience is the fruit of salvation, not a prerequisite.

At this point we have feast days, Sabbaths, and circumcision on the list of Torah instruction that Paul supported and continued to observe and while actions speak louder than words, it's important to continue by looking at what Paul said about his view of Torah. To that end, there's no better place than the 21st and 22nd chapters of the book of Acts. In the 21st chapter, Paul is informed of accusations being leveled against him:

> [17] After we arrived in Jerusalem, the brethren received us gladly. [18] And the following day Paul went in with us to James, and all the elders were present. [19] After he had greeted them, he began to relate one by one the things which God had done among the Gentiles through his ministry. [20] And when they heard it they began glorifying God; and they said to him, "You see, brother, how many thousands there are among the Jews of those who have believed, and they are all zealous for the Law; [21] and they have been told about you, that you are teaching all the Jews who are among the Gentiles to forsake Moses, telling them not to circumcise their children nor to walk according to the customs.

As we've seen before, "Moses" is used as a reference to Torah so, at the end of this passage, to forsake Moses is to forsake Torah. The accusation articulated in verse 21 is that Paul is teaching that Torah need not be obeyed, that circumcision has no relevance, and that no one need *"walk according to the customs"* outlined in Torah: The Sabbath, the Holy Days, the food laws, etc. With this accusation in mind, the elders advised Paul saying:

> [22] What, then, is to be done? They will certainly hear that you have come. [23] Therefore do this that we tell you. We have four men who are under a vow; [24] take them and purify yourself along with them, and pay their expenses so that they may shave their heads; and all will know that there is nothing to the things which they have been told about you, but that you yourself also walk orderly, keeping the Law. [25] But concerning the Gentiles who have believed, we wrote, having decided that they should abstain from meat sacrificed to idols

> and from blood and from what is strangled and from fornication." ²⁶ Then Paul took the men, and the next day, purifying himself along with them, went into the temple giving notice of the completion of the days of purification, until the sacrifice was offered for each one of them.

The key phrase here is toward the end of verse 24. The elders mention that there is a certain group of men who have taken a vow and as part of that vow are going to shave their heads and purify themselves and they suggest that Paul should join them. Why do they give him this advice? So *"all will know that there is nothing to the things which they have been told about you"*; so everyone will know that Paul walks according to Torah and does NOT teach that Torah has been abolished. This seems like a perfect opportunity for Paul to make his case for abandoning Torah; for Paul to set the record straight and reason through the idea that through Yeshua's death and resurrection, Torah has been fulfilled and done away with. Instead, Paul does exactly as the elders advise. Either Paul followed their advice to accomplish exactly what they said, namely to prove his obedience to Torah and likewise to prove that the accusation that he taught against Torah was false, or he purposely acted out Torah obedience in some sort of rouse even though the accusations against him were true. Hopefully I don't have to explain why "deceitful Paul" would be a problem. It is far more reasonable to believe that Paul did what he did to prove the accusations against him were false because they were false. If the idea that Paul taught against Torah was false then, it cannot be true today.

Sadly, Paul's efforts did not have the intended effect:

> ²⁷ When the seven days were almost over, the Jews from Asia, upon seeing him in the temple, began to stir up all the crowd and laid hands on him, ²⁸ crying out, "Men of Israel, come to our aid! This is the man who preaches to all men everywhere against our people and the Law and this place; and besides he has even brought Greeks into the temple and has defiled this holy place."

Again, the same accusation is repeated: That Paul preaches against the Jews, against Torah and against the temple. Paul was dragged out of the temple and nearly beaten to death before Roman soldiers stopped the mob. Being unable to discern why the mob was beating Paul, they arrested him and started to lead him away when Paul, on the basis of his Roman citizenship, asked for and was granted the opportunity to address the crowd. Did Paul use this opportunity to explain why he was preaching against Torah? Did he seize the moment to make the case for a new kind of freedom in Yeshua; freedom from Torah? By now the answer shouldn't surprise you. He did not.

In Acts chapter 22, Paul begins to make his case by telling the people of his upbringing as a Pharisee of Pharisees, raised in Jerusalem, a student of Gamaliel. He tells them how he persecuted the followers of Yeshua with the endorsement of the Sanhedrin and how he was even happily present when Stephen was being stoned. He then describes his encounter with Yeshua on the road to Damascus, how it left him blind, and how he regained his sight and was sent to the Gentiles with a message of salvation; a message of Yeshua. At this point, the crowd is in a frenzy again, so the Romans take him away intending to scourge him to compel truthfulness. Thankfully, Paul's status as a Roman citizen prevents the torture and he's held in custody instead.

In chapter 23 we read of a plot to kill Paul and are told that, as a result, the Roman commander sends Paul to the governor in Caesarea with the following letter:

> [26] "Claudius Lysias, to the most excellent governor Felix, greetings.
>
> [27] "When this man was arrested by the Jews and was about to be slain by them, I came up to them with the troops and rescued him, having learned that he was a Roman. [28] "And wanting to ascertain the charge for which they were accusing him, I brought him down to their Council; [29] and I found him to be accused over questions about their Law, but under no accusation deserving death or imprisonment.
>
> [30] "When I was informed that there would be a plot against the man, I sent him to you at once, also instructing his accusers to bring charges against him before you."

Essentially, Paul gets passed up the chain of command and the Governor Felix, agrees to allow both sides of the case to be heard. Chapter 24 starts with the High Priest's accusations:

> ¹ After five days the high priest Ananias came down with some elders, with an attorney named Tertullus, and they brought charges to the governor against Paul. ² After Paul had been summoned, Tertullus began to accuse him, saying to the governor,
>
> "Since we have through you attained much peace, and since by your providence reforms are being carried out for this nation, ³ we acknowledge this in every way and everywhere, most excellent Felix, with all thankfulness. ⁴ But, that I may not weary you any further, I beg you to grant us, by your kindness, a brief hearing.⁵ For we have found this man a real pest and a fellow who stirs up dissension among all the Jews throughout the world, and a ringleader of the sect of the Nazarenes. ⁶ And he even tried to desecrate the temple; and then we arrested him. We wanted to judge him according to our own Law. ⁷ But Lysias the commander came along, and with much violence took him out of our hands,⁸ ordering his accusers to come before you. By examining him yourself concerning all these matters you will be able to ascertain the things of which we accuse him." ⁹ The Jews also joined in the attack, asserting that these things were so.

The primary accusations here are in verse 5. Paul is accused of being a pest, one who stirs up dissension, and a ringleader of the Nazarenes. Of the first two, Paul flatly denies the charges and challenges the accusation asserting that his accusers cannot prove their claim. Of the latter, Paul proudly acknowledges that he is a follower of Yeshua but includes some aspects of that "Way" that may surprise you:

> ¹⁰ When the governor had nodded for him to speak, Paul responded:
>
> "Knowing that for many years you have been a judge to this nation, I cheerfully make my defense, ¹¹ since you can take note of the fact that no more than twelve days ago I went up to Jerusalem to worship. ¹² Neither in the temple, nor in the synagogues, nor in the city itself did they find me carrying on a discussion with anyone or causing a riot. ¹³ Nor can they prove to you the charges of which they now accuse me. ¹⁴ But this I admit to you, that according to the Way which they call a sect I do serve the God of our fathers, believing everything that is in accordance with the Law and that is written in the Prophets; ¹⁵ having a hope in God, which these men cherish themselves, that there shall certainly be a resurrection of both the righteous and the wicked. ¹⁶ In view of this, I also do my best to maintain always a blameless conscience both before God and before men.¹⁷ Now after several years I came to bring alms to my nation and to present offerings; ¹⁸ in which they found me occupied in the temple, having been purified, without any crowd or uproar. But there were some Jews from Asia— ¹⁹ who ought to have been present be-

> fore you and to make accusation, if they should have anything against me. [20] Or else let these men themselves tell what misdeed they found when I stood before the Council, [21] other than for this one statement which I shouted out while standing among them, 'For the resurrection of the dead I am on trial before you today.'"

In verse 12, Paul basically says, not only was I not a pest, I didn't even talk to anyone. In verse 13, Paul asserts that the prosecution can't prove the charges, and then admits to following Yeshua saying *"I do serve the God of our fathers, believing everything that is in accordance with Torah and that is written in the Prophets"*. That's a very strange statement for a man who believes Torah has been abolished and obedience isn't required of those who follow *"the Way"*. Finally, in verses 18-20, Paul makes the observation that the only problem was with a small group of Jews from Asia who, if they had an accusation, should have come to make it themselves. Paul is saying his real accusers didn't even show up and the men that did show up weren't present for the initial altercation and cannot act as witnesses to those complaints. He says they were only present at the council trial that followed and are really just angry about what he said regarding the resurrection of the dead.

At the conclusion of this hearing there was still no evidence of or merit to the case being brought against him, so Felix ordered him kept under house arrest until he decided the case. Two years later the case was still undecided, and Paul was still under house arrest. Again, it seems like at some point during this ordeal Paul would just come clean and say, yes, I teach against Torah because there's this new thing called Christianity and Torah has been abolished. Especially if, as we're taught today, Torah is bondage, you'd think Paul would be eager to share the good news of freedom from Yah's instruction rather than sit under house arrest for two years proving that accusations against him were false when the accusations were actually true. Perhaps I'm simply not giving Paul the Machiavellian credit he's due, but the simpler explanation is he endured the trials and imprisonment because what he was being accused of simply wasn't true. It wasn't true then and isn't true today.

Next, in Chapter 25, Felix's successor, Festus, takes up Paul's case in an effort to get to the bottom of the matter. At the new tribunal, Paul continues to maintain his innocence:

> *7 After Paul arrived, the Jews who had come down from Jerusalem stood around him, bringing many and serious charges against him which they could not prove, 8 while Paul said in his own defense, "I have committed no offense either against the Law of the Jews or against the temple or against Caesar."*

It's interesting that Paul says directly that he's committed no offense against Torah, but more interestingly is that in verse 7 it's specifically noted that the Jews in attendance brought charges they could not prove. At the close of the tribunal, Paul gets passed up the chain of command a third time and Felix notes that, after all this time, there still aren't any actual charges:

> *24 Festus said, "King Agrippa, and all you gentlemen here present with us, you see this man about whom all the people of the Jews appealed to me, both at Jerusalem and here, loudly declaring that he ought not to live any longer. 25 But I found that he had committed nothing worthy of death; and since he himself appealed to the Emperor, I decided to send him. 26 Yet I have nothing definite about him to write to my lord. Therefore I have brought him before you all and especially before you, King Agrippa, so that after the investigation has taken place, I may have something to write. 27 For it seems absurd to me in sending a prisoner, not to indicate also the charges against him."*

In Chapter 26 Paul makes his case again, this time before King Agrippa, and again no merit is found to the accusations brought against him. Paul is passed up the chain of command once more and sent to Rome. Chapter 27 tells the story of Paul's harrowing journey to Rome, including a shipwreck, and in chapter 28 Paul takes up his defense again saying:

> *17"Brethren, though I had done nothing against our people or the customs of our fathers, yet I was delivered as a prisoner from Jerusalem into the hands of the Romans. 18 And when they had examined me, they were willing to release me because there was no ground for putting me to death.*

"I had done nothing against our people or the customs of our fathers", Paul said. If Paul had abandoned Torah and was teaching others to also abandon Torah, how could he say he had done nothing against his people or the customs of their fathers? It wouldn't just be untrue it would be provably untrue, yet time and time again no one can offer any proof at all.

Finally, the whole thing just fizzles out when the Jewish elders of Rome whom Paul is addressing basically say they've heard nothing from Judea, and they aren't aware of any accusations against Paul:

> [21] They said to him, "We have neither received letters from Judea concerning you, nor have any of the brethren come here and reported or spoken anything bad about you. [22] But we desire to hear from you what your views are; for concerning this sect, it is known to us that it is spoken against everywhere."

While the charges against Paul are dropped, Paul had taken the opportunity at each step to make a "case for Christ", so to speak, and his most recent self-defense had piqued the curiosity of Roman Jews. When they came to hear Paul's views, his testimony was grounded in, you guessed it, Torah!

> [23] When they had set a day for Paul, they came to him at his lodging in large numbers; and he was explaining to them by solemnly testifying about the kingdom of God and trying to persuade them concerning Jesus, from both the Law of Moses and from the Prophets, from morning until evening.

Today, we're expected to believe that Paul teaches that Torah was abolished, that the Holy Days are no longer important, that the Sabbath has been done away with, that food laws are no longer relevant, and so on. In contrast to this teaching we have the record of Scripture. We've already looked at Romans and several other letters where Paul makes comments in support of Torah as a whole or in defense of specific portions of Torah, we've seen instances where Paul walked according to Torah, and now, in Acts we have a historical record of legal proceedings where Paul, speaking in his own defense, asserts his obedience to Torah and denies accusations that he has abandoned, or teaches others to abandon, Torah. In every case, what the Bible actually says should take precedence over of what mainstream Christian tradition teaches the Bible says. This is especially true considering

Christian tradition perfectly echoes assertions the legal proceedings recorded in Acts repeatedly label as baseless and false accusations.

CHAPTER 8

Three Torah Tests

I've previously addressed a fundamentally flawed concept that seems to underpin a lot of the "Torah is done away with" teaching, which is that Torah was given as a means of salvation. Knowing that this isn't the case doesn't fully address the misinformation and objections that, paradoxically, both spring from and feed into this abolished Torah doctrine. In my personal experience discussing Torah and its applicability in the Christian life with Christian friends and family, there appears an almost knee-jerk reaction that Torah is inherently bad. I believe this reaction stems from one aspect I touched on in the last section; the false choice between Torah and grace. The simplest expression of this idea is that if grace is good, then Torah must be bad. For one to accept that Torah is little more than a failed means of self-earned salvation one must be given an explanation for its insufficiency, so we've been taught things like "the Law is bondage", and "obedience is impossible". I'd like to spend some time addressing a host of perceptions Christians have toward Torah – perceptions I held as true myself for many years for no other reason than I was told they were true – and point out that it's quite inconsistent with the way the Bible portrays Torah. More than this, in some cases what we've been taught about Torah specifically contradicts what the Bible describes.

To start with, I'd like to point out the high regard Scripture places on Torah. We've seen that Paul called Torah good in Romans 7:16, and in 7:12 he says, *"the Law is holy, and the commandment is holy and righteous and* good". In Luke 11:28, Yeshua says, *"blessed are those who hear the word of God and observe it"*. James echoes these sentiments in James 1:25 calling Torah perfect, and the man who continues in it, blessed. Regarding Yeshua's statement, let's remember that to the audience hearing His words there was no New Testament. They would have understood *"the word of God"* to mean Torah. No matter how much one searches the New Testament there isn't a single negative reference to Torah to be found. There are plenty of passages that are twisted and misrepresented in a way that makes it sound like Yah's instructions are painted in a negative light but every one of these instances including several I've discussed in previous chapters can be shown to have been taken out of context and misconstrued. For instance, some may try to argue that Torah is called a curse in Galatians 3:13 which says, *"Christ redeemed us from the curse of the Law, having become a curse for us"*, but since we already know from previous chapters that Torah was a blessing and a curse depending on our obedience or disobedience we know this verse isn't saying Torah itself is a curse. Rather, we fell on the "curse side" of Torah through our own disobedience. Yeshua did not redeem us from the Law, He redeemed us from the penalty, or the curse, due us for disobeying the Law, so even this verse doesn't say anything negative about Torah.

One would assume that if there was anything negative to be said about the Law surely it would be recorded in the Old Testament. After all, if Torah is bondage, the Old Testament Israelites would be the ones under this bondage and the best witnesses to its burdens. What we find instead is constant praise for and delight in Torah. In one of Moses' encouragements to the people to keep Torah in Deuteronomy 4 he says the nations they encounter will be envious of them because of the wisdom and righteousness of Torah.

> [5] *"See, I have taught you statutes and judgments just as the Lord my God commanded me, that you should do thus in the land where you are entering to possess it.* [6] *So keep and do them, for that is your wisdom and your understanding in the sight of the peoples who will hear all these statutes and say, 'Surely this great nation is a wise and understanding people.'* [7] *For what great nation is there that has a god so near to it as is the Lord our God whenever we call on*

> Him? *⁸ Or what great nation is there that has statutes and judgments as righteous as this whole law which I am setting before you today?*

In Kings and Chronicles observance of Torah is linked to success in life:

> *1 Kings 2:3 - Keep the charge of the Lord your God, to walk in His ways, to keep His statutes, His commandments, His ordinances, and His testimonies, according to what is written in the Law of Moses, that you may succeed in all that you do and wherever you turn.*
>
> *2 Chronicles 31:20-21 - Thus Hezekiah did throughout all Judah; and he did what was good, right and true before the Lord his God. Every work which he began in the service of the house of God in law and in commandment, seeking his God, he did with all his heart and prospered.*

Keep in mind this passage in Chronicles refers to a time when Torah instruction had been abandoned and Hezekiah, having witnessed the effect this had on the culture and the people, brought the people back to Torah to benefit from its blessing and liberty!

Please don't misunderstand me. Torah obedience is not a secret to a trouble-free life, nor do I hold to any kind of prosperity gospel. The concept is simply this: Yah created the universe and knows better than any of us how it works. He's left instructions for us by way of Torah so that we might navigate the world He created in the way we were intended to navigate it and by following the instructions things will go more smoothly than when the instructions are ignored. Think of something simple like making toast. You can use a toaster any way you like, but it's likely that you'll get the best results by following the instructions. Not by just reading the instructions, mind you, but by following the instructions. It doesn't mean you'll never burn some toast, but you'll be far less likely to by using the toaster the way it was designed to be used. A.W. Tozer hit this particular nail on the head when he said, "To be entirely safe from the devil's snares, the child of God must be completely obedient to the word of the Lord. The driver on the highway is safe, not when he reads the signs; but when he obeys them."

In Proverbs 8 we find the following:

> ³² "Now therefore, O sons, listen to me,
> For blessed are they who keep my ways.
> ³³ "Heed instruction and be wise,
> And do not neglect it.

Furthermore, the Psalms are full of glowing evaluations of the Law:

> Psalm 1:1-2 - How blessed is the man who does not walk in the counsel of the wicked, nor stand in the path of sinners, nor sit in the seat of scoffers! But his delight is in the law of the Lord, and in His law he meditates day and night.
>
> Psalm 19:7-8 - The law of the Lord is perfect, restoring the soul; The testimony of the Lord is sure, making wise the simple. The precepts of the Lord are right, rejoicing the heart; The commandment of the Lord is pure, enlightening the eyes.
>
> Psalm 37:30-31 - The mouth of the righteous utters wisdom, and his tongue speaks justice. The law of his God is in his heart; His steps do not slip.
>
> Psalm 40:8 - I delight to do Your will, O my God; Your Law is within my heart.
>
> Psalm 111:10 - The fear of the Lord is the beginning of wisdom; A good understanding have all those who do His commandments; His praise endures forever.
>
> Psalm 112:1 - Praise the Lord! How blessed is the man who fears the Lord, who greatly delights in His commandments.
>
> Psalm 128:1 - How blessed is everyone who fears the Lord, who walks in His ways.

And of course, there's Psalm 119, possibly the most interesting of the Psalms because each of the 22 eight verse stanzas is an acrostic that walks through the Hebrew alphabet. In the original Hebrew, each of the first eight verses starts with the first Hebrew letter, aleph, each of the second group of eight verses starts with the second Hebrew letter, bet, and so on. That it's the longest chapter in the Bible means I won't quote the entire thing but I encourage you to read it because the whole thing refers to Torah in consistently glowing terms, with, what I believe, is some of the most beautiful prose in the entire Bible. As Yeshua is referred to in Revelation as the Alpha and the Omega or, in Hebrew, the Aleph and the Tav, I would like to quote the first and last sections, the Aleph and Tav sections, of Psalm 119 to illustrate my point:

> ¹ How blessed are those whose way is blameless,
> Who walk in the law of the Lord.
> ² How blessed are those who observe His testimonies,
> Who seek Him with all their heart.
> ³ They also do no unrighteousness;
> They walk in His ways.
> ⁴ You have ordained Your precepts,
> That we should keep them diligently.
> ⁵ Oh that my ways may be established
> To keep Your statutes!
> ⁶ Then I shall not be ashamed
> When I look upon all Your commandments.
> ⁷ I shall give thanks to You with uprightness of heart,
> When I learn Your righteous judgments.
> ⁸ I shall keep Your statutes;
> Do not forsake me utterly!
>
> ¹⁶⁹ Let my cry come before You, O Lord;
> Give me understanding according to Your word.
> ¹⁷⁰ Let my supplication come before You;
> Deliver me according to Your word.
> ¹⁷¹ Let my lips utter praise,
> For You teach me Your statutes.
> ¹⁷² Let my tongue sing of Your word,
> For all Your commandments are righteousness.
> ¹⁷³ Let Your hand be ready to help me,
> For I have chosen Your precepts.
> ¹⁷⁴ I long for Your salvation, O Lord,
> And Your law is my delight.
> ¹⁷⁵ Let my soul live that it may praise You,
> And let Your ordinances help me.
> ¹⁷⁶ I have gone astray like a lost sheep; seek Your servant,
> For I do not forget Your commandments.

This is a small list compared to the total number of passages that speak favorably of Torah throughout Scripture; there are so many it would take an entire chapter to include them all.

For something that I was taught to view as archaic, insufficient, and contrary to the goodness and blessing of grace, Scripture doesn't seem to portray it that way. That's not to say that grace and one's salvation by grace isn't a wonderful blessing and an entirely good and positive thing. The point is, there is a flaw in the assertion that Torah is somehow bad or has a negative connotation about it. The goodness and blessing of grace isn't opposite to or at odds with Torah, they are both a wonderful blessing according to the Bible, but I'd go a step further and say that it is here where one can best draw a true distinction between license and legalism. License is nothing more than grace without Torah while Torah without grace is the very definition of legalism. Both operate in wonderful harmony, not in contrast to one another as many would have us believe.

Having established the Bible's high view of Torah, it's obvious that what many of us have been told doesn't square with what is written in the Bible. With that in mind, let's walk through a few other basic ideas that one must accept to believe Torah has been abolished and see how they stand up. There are three in particular which I believe deserve careful testing:

- The Law has been nailed to the cross.
- Torah was only for the Jews.
- Obedience is an impossible burden.

The first concept we'll put to the test is the simple proof statement that says, "the Law has been nailed to the cross". This seems like an open and shut argument straight from Scripture, but it isn't. The idea that the Law has been nailed to the cross comes from a verse that says no such thing. The passage people are making reference to when they say this comes from Colossians 2 which says:

> [13] *When you were dead in your transgressions and the uncircumcision of your flesh, He made you alive together with Him, having forgiven us all our transgressions,* [14] *having canceled out the certificate of debt consisting of decrees against us, which was hostile to us; and He has taken it out of the way, having nailed it to the cross.*

I don't know where the idea came from that this was proof of Torah's being done away with, but how long ago this idea was first suggested, or by whom, doesn't matter. It has always been a mistake. Verse 13 sets the stage for verse 14 and clearly articulates that the object of this passage is our transgressions, not Torah itself. That verse 13 narrows our focus to our transgressions, which are further described as *"decrees against us"* in verse 14, should be enough for us to know that it's our transgressions that have been nailed to the cross in verse 14, not Torah. Let's take this a step further to be thorough.

This passage is talking about something we're likely all familiar with even if we don't know it. At the time this was written, when a criminal was crucified a placard was placed on the cross detailing the reason for the person's punishment. We see this done in Yeshua's case in John 19:19-22 where Pilate and the high priests argue about what should be written. That wasn't a practice unique to the crucifixion of the Messiah, it was just part of a person's execution and this practice is what Paul is describing in verse 14 of Colossians 2. The *"certificate of debt consisting of decrees against us"* isn't the Law in its entirety but is essentially a list of our infractions against the Law. In contemporary terms, it would be like our rap sheet; the criminal record for which we're being condemned. The picture Paul paints is beautiful and quite consistent with what we all understand Yeshua did for us. He took all those things we've done, all the ways we've disobeyed and incurred Yah's wrath, all the things that should be written on OUR sign and nailed to OUR cross and He had them nailed to HIS cross. They are no longer our transgressions, but they were ascribed to and paid by Him!

To say that this verse is talking about Torah being done away with, in my opinion, deeply undermines Yeshua's sacrifice in the sense that it would not make us right with Yah's judgement and leave justice satisfied. Instead it would nullify Yah's judgement and essentially let us "get away with it". Yeshua did not die so that there would no longer be a Law by which we'd be considered righteous or guilty, He died so that we wouldn't suffer the penalty for our transgressions against that Law. There's a big difference between those two ideas. The fact that we'd all agree that Yeshua died, not to invalidate justice but to pay the just price on our behalf so that we could be shown mercy illustrates that at some level we all concede that Torah could not have abolished. To put it another way, there are two ways our *"certificate of debt"* could have been cancelled. By getting rid of the standard by which we were deemed debtors, or by paying the debt for us. Paying the debt for us doesn't remove the standard by which we were judged debtors.

Perhaps it did both, you might say; Yeshua's death satisfied justice and subsequently did away with Torah. First, it's clear that this particular passage doesn't say anything about the state of Torah, only the state of our condemnation, and that being the case, there's a big problem with Torah having been abolished. By what standard is anyone judged righteous or guilty from the time of the resurrection forward? I was born in 1979. That's well after Yeshua's death and resurrection, so by what standard was I judged a sinner? To repeat what I quoted earlier, Paul wrote *"where there is no Law there is no transgression"* so what was I guilty of? Is the argument that Torah applies only to the unsaved and because they're unsaved, it exists only to condemn? That even though Yah said Torah was a blessing and a curse, upon Yeshua's sacrifice it became a curse only? Am I to believe that prior to my relationship with Yeshua I was guilty according to Torah but having been saved there is no Torah for me and, if so, doesn't that imply that Torah wasn't actually abolished upon Yeshua's sacrifice but becomes abolished for each sinner upon his or her salvation? None of these ideas are supported by Scripture. The idea that "the Law has been nailed to the cross" doesn't fit with Scripture any more than does a low view of Torah.

Let's turn to another common idea; that Torah was something for the Jews but, as Christians, doesn't apply to us. This seems to be more of a backup plan then a scripturally supportable doctrine. Sort of a catch all that says something like, "Torah was done away with, but, even if it wasn't, it was only for the Jews, so it doesn't apply to us Christians anyway." It's said that "necessity is the mother of all invention". If that's true, I'd ask why this idea was invented? If the Law was done away with, isn't for whom it was intended totally irrelevant? The doctrine is unnecessary unless perhaps the case for the abolishing of Torah isn't very convincing and a second line of defense is needed to convince us we don't need to hear or heed Yah's instructions. This view comes up often though, so let's test it.

First, since I'm very particular about clarity of meaning, I'd like to point out that the term Jew isn't really applied correctly when people say things like, "that was just for the Jews" or "isn't that a Jewish thing". The problem is it paints things in human terms instead of Yah's terms. We don't have Jewish feasts, we have Yah's feasts. We don't have a Jewish Sabbath, we have Yah's Sabbath, and so on. Jewish people are most commonly those who observe these things, but they aren't theirs in the sense that they weren't created by them. They were ordained by Yah and are intended for all those who follow Him. For these reasons, I'll refer to Israel in the analysis that follows because what follows refers to the whole nation of Israel and to things Yah established, not His people.

I'd like to start in Exodus again, at the original recording of the Law at Mt. Sinai and specifically look at who was there. When first leaving Egypt, we find this in Exodus 12:

> [37] Now the sons of Israel journeyed from Rameses to Succoth, about six hundred thousand men on foot, aside from children. [38] A mixed multitude also went up with them, along with flocks and herds, a very large number of livestock.

While there is a lot of conjecture about who this "mixed multitude" consisted of, what is never disputed is that the group as a whole was not just made up of the descendants of Jacob. Torah was given not just to Israel but to anyone who was willing to leave his or her own ways and follow Yah whether they were genetically Israelite or not. By now it shouldn't surprise us that this is yet another foreshadowing event pointing to Yeshua. As most Christians know, the offer of salvation by grace through faith in Yeshua is open to anyone, regardless of who they are, where they're from, or who their parents were. That's exactly how Yah shared Torah; not just to Israelites but to Gentiles as well who, having been brought into a covenant relationship with Yah, became part of Israel. To borrow from the New Testament, they were grafted in.

To set the stage, let's take a look at one of the metaphors Yeshua used to describe Himself in John 15:

> [1] "I am the true vine, and My Father is the vinedresser. [2] Every branch in Me that does not bear fruit, He takes away; and every branch that bears fruit, He prunes it so that it may bear more fruit. [3] You are already clean because of the word which I have spoken to you. [4] Abide in Me, and I in you. As the branch cannot bear fruit of itself unless it abides in the vine, so neither can you unless you abide in Me. [5] I am the vine, you are the branches; he who abides in Me and I in him, he bears much fruit, for apart from Me you can do nothing. [6] If anyone does not abide in Me, he is thrown away as a branch and dries up; and

> they gather them, and cast them into the fire and they are burned. ⁷ If you abide in Me, and My words abide in you, ask whatever you wish, and it will be done for you. ⁸ My Father is glorified by this, that you bear much fruit, and so prove to be My disciples. ⁹ Just as the Father has loved Me, I have also loved you; abide in My love. ¹⁰ If you keep My commandments, you will abide in My love; just as I have kept My Father's commandments and abide in His love.

Yeshua's repeated use of the word "abide" is particularly interesting. According to the Oxford English Dictionary, to abide means to "Accept or act in accordance with (a rule, decision, or recommendation)". A rule or recommendation? Sounds a lot like a law or instruction, doesn't it? Synonyms for abide include obey, observe, follow, conform to, adhere to, act in accordance with, and consent to. What is it we'd be observing, following, or conforming to if there were to be no instructions to observe, follow or conform to soon after Yeshua said this?

Returning to the topic of the vine and being grafted in, similar imagery is used throughout Scripture. In Psalm 80, the psalmist talks about the vine taken out of Egypt:

> ⁸ You removed a vine from Egypt; You drove out the nations and planted it. ⁹ You cleared the ground before it, And it took deep root and filled the land.

Clearly this is referring to Israel as the vine, a metaphor carried on by the prophets. In Jeremiah 2, we find commentary on the disobedience of Israel:

> ²¹ "Yet I planted you a choice vine, a completely faithful seed. How then have you turned yourself before Me into the degenerate shoots of a foreign vine?

Later, in Jeremiah chapter 11, the following is written about Israel:

> ¹⁶ The LORD called your name, "A green olive tree, beautiful in fruit and form"; With the noise of a great tumult He has kindled fire on it, and its branches are worthless.

Familiarizing ourselves with Yeshua's speaking of Himself as the vine and the prophets' use of the vine and the olive tree in relation to Israel prepares us to better understand what Paul describes in Romans chapter 11:

> [16] If the first piece of dough is holy, the lump is also; and if the root is holy, the branches are too. [17] But if some of the branches were broken off, and you, being a wild olive, were grafted in among them and became partaker with them of the rich root of the olive tree, [18] do not be arrogant toward the branches; but if you are arrogant, remember that it is not you who supports the root, but the root supports you. [19] You will say then, "Branches were broken off so that I might be grafted in." [20] Quite right, they were broken off for their unbelief, but you stand by your faith. Do not be conceited, but fear; [21] for if God did not spare the natural branches, He will not spare you, either. [22] Behold then the kindness and severity of God; to those who fell, severity, but to you, God's kindness, if you continue in His kindness; otherwise you also will be cut off. [23] And they also, if they do not continue in their unbelief, will be grafted in, for God is able to graft them in again. [24] For if you were cut off from what is by nature a wild olive tree, and were grafted contrary to nature into a cultivated olive tree, how much more will these who are the natural branches be grafted into their own olive tree?

In this passage, there are two types of olive branch, one that comes from the cultivated tree, in other words Israel, and one that comes from the wild olive tree, aka Gentiles. There really are no other options. To be blunt, there isn't a "Christian tree". The Bible consistently defines this as an Israelite tree so being grafted in literally means being counted as a citizen of Yah's nation; an Israelite. Knowing this, the case that Torah was "just for the Jews" doesn't stand up. According to what the Bible actually says, Torah was given as instruction for Yah's people, a nation called Israel that was made up of a "mixed multitude". A nation that followers of Yeshua are grafted into, whether of Israelite or Gentile descent.

A modern equivalent of this is citizenship. Israelites, as Yah's chosen people, are simply citizens of His kingdom. When someone accepts the free gift of grace through faith in Yeshua that person becomes a fellow citizen but what does that actually mean? Let's compare this idea to the concept of United States citizenship. When an immigrant becomes a naturalized citizen of the United States, there are two balancing truths. The citizen becomes a rightful participant in the freedoms and opportunities afforded to every citizen, whether born here or not. At the same time, the person agrees to abide by the laws and statutes that form the necessary boundaries of a free society. I've insisted throughout this book that Torah isn't just a set of legal codes so please forgive the imperfect analogy but there is a strong similarity. When Paul talks about a person being grafted in, he's talking about naturalization. He's talking about a person, who may not have been born an Israelite, becoming a part of Yah's nation of people. Paul makes this crystal clear in Ephesians chapter 2:

> [17] And He came and preached peace to you who were far away, and peace to those who were near; [18] for through Him we both have our access in one Spirit to the Father. [19] So then you are no longer strangers and aliens, but you are fellow citizens with the saints, and are of God's household...

Paul also makes mention of this idea in a passage we looked at in the previous chapter. As a reminder, Philippians 3:17-22 says:

> [17] Brethren, join in following my example, and observe those who walk according to the pattern you have in us. [18] For many walk, of whom I often told you, and now tell you even weeping, that they are enemies of the cross of Christ, [19] whose end is destruction, whose god is their appetite, and whose glory is in their shame, who set their minds on earthly things. [20] For our citizenship is in heaven, from which also we eagerly wait for a Savior, the Lord Jesus Christ; [21] who will transform the body of our humble state into conformity with the body of His glory, by the exertion of the power that He has even to subject all things to Himself.

In verse 20, Paul explicitly calls the regenerate person a citizen of heaven. As citizens of that kingdom we should walk according to the laws and instructions that govern that kingdom, just as we, being citizens of a particular city, state or nation abide by the rules and regulations of that city, state or nation. We've already established the example Paul set so when Paul says, *"citizens of the kingdom"* should follow his example, we know he meant they should remain obedient to Yah's instruction as he had remained obedient. As a result, we can conclude that since we, as believers, are grafted into Israel the concept that Torah was "just for the Jews" is false.

The third concept that needs testing is the idea that obedience is impossible. The way it was always related to me was something along the lines of "trying to obey Torah is impossible" or "only Jesus was able to perfectly obey", the unstated implication of the latter being, "so why even try". While I certainly agree that obeying Torah perfectly is not possible for us for the simple fact that we are still living in a fallen world, is the unspoken implication true? Should we refrain from anything we cannot do perfectly? I won't expand on that question as it strays from the primary point, but I will point out that if we only attempted those things we could do perfectly, none of us would do very much at all. Leaving that aside, what of the difficulty of obedience? In all my searching of the Bible I cannot find one passage that says Torah obedience is difficult, or impossible, or burdensome, or hard, or any other word or metaphor that indicates Torah obedience is a struggle. What I do find, on the other hand, are passages like Deuteronomy 30:11:

> "For this commandment which I command you today is not too difficult for you, nor is it out of reach."

And a very similar statement from Yeshua in Matthew 11:

> [28] "Come to Me, all who are weary and heavy-laden, and I will give you rest. [29] Take My yoke upon you and learn from Me, for I am gentle and humble in heart, and you will find rest for your souls. [30] For My yoke is easy and My burden is light."

For those who believe Torah was abolished so Yeshua couldn't have been talking about Torah, let's dig into this part of Matthew because it's really quite intriguing. The mention of the yoke invokes an obvious metaphor of a team of oxen which points us to the reality that when a new ox needs to learn how to do its work it's paired with an ox that knows what it's doing. What should occur to us is that just as the new ox will learn to walk the way the old ox does, so we, if we take Yeshua's yoke upon us, will learn to walk as He does. I challenge anyone who works with oxen or draft horses or other teams of animals to find me one example where the younger animal is yoked with the older animal and the younger animal is simply allowed to do as it pleases, dragging the experienced animal along for the aimless ride. Why, then, are we taught that we're yoked with Yeshua but don't have to live the way He did or at least are allowed to live in whatever way is deemed socially acceptable in the culture in which we find ourselves? This doesn't fit the illustration Yeshua is making. I've covered this already, but I'll at least pose the question again; how did Yeshua walk if not in obedience to Torah? If we assume being yoked with Yeshua means we will learn how to walk in obedience it makes sense that He would describe it as easy and light considering what we read in Deuteronomy, that it's not too difficult for us, so that seems to line up, but let's take it a step deeper.

Back in Matthew, at the end of verse 29, when Yeshua says *"you will find rest for your souls"*, many people don't know and sadly aren't taught that Yeshua is quoting the prophet Jeremiah, specifically chapter 6 verse 16:

> *Thus says the Lord,*
> *"Stand by the ways and see and ask for the ancient paths,*
> *Where the good way is, and walk in it;*
> *And you will find rest for your souls.*
> *But they said, 'We will not walk in it.'*

In inviting us to walk with Him and learn from Him that we might find rest, Yeshua quotes a passage spoken by Yah to Jeremiah imploring the people to return to Torah obedience. The people's response in Jeremiah's day was *"We will not walk in it"*. To put it bluntly, in Matthew 11:28-30, Yeshua is making the exact same offer to us. By quoting Jeremiah He is not hiding the fact that it's the same offer; to find rest for our souls by walking the way He did, and the way Yah asked His people to in Jeremiah's day. Yeshua is inviting us to walk in obedience to Yah's life-giving and wise instruction. Will we really respond the same way our Israelite forebears did saying, *"We will not walk in it"*? Perhaps if what we were taught were true, that it was difficult or impossible, I'd understand, but Scripture, both Old and New Testament, says it's light, easy, and within our reach. Between what I've been taught and what the word says, there's really no contest.

This leaves us with a single conclusion regarding the three concepts we set out to test. Has Torah been nailed to the cross? Is Torah only for the Jews? Isn't obedience an impossible burden? In all three cases, the answer

Scripture gives is no. Our transgressions were nailed to the cross, Torah is for all of Yah's people, whether of Israelite or Gentile descent, and what Yah has set before us in Torah is *"...not too difficult for you, nor is it out of reach..."* (Deuteronomy 30:11). All three concepts have failed to stand up to scriptural testing which leaves Torah on the table, so to speak, for contemporary Christians.

CHAPTER 9

A Philosophical Perspective

Seeing that, according to Scripture, Torah wasn't nailed to the cross, that Torah wasn't just meant for Jews, and that obedience is not too difficult, the case for Torah having been abolished is unraveling quickly. To expand on my case, I'd like to turn to a handful of rational problems or, to put it another way, problems that arise when one thinks through the implications of a belief or examines where a belief leads. These are concepts that, when reasoned through, either become problematic at best or downright frightening at worst if it's true that Torah has been abolished.

I'll start with the problematic idea of Christian freedom that bases itself on verses like Colossians 3:17:

> And whatever you do, whether in word or deed, do it all in the name of the Lord Jesus, giving thanks to God the Father through him.

Or 1 Corinthians 10:31:

> Whether, then, you eat or drink or whatever you do, do all to the glory of God.

I'm not saying these verses are problematic, but they have been ripped from their context and used as a foundation to support some problematic philosophies. The idea is that, since there is no Law anymore, we can sort of do whatever we want so long as we do it in the name of Yeshua and do it thankfully. The funniest example I've witnessed in my own experience is a

Deacon who was using the verses above to say it was okay that he occasionally smoked cigars because he smoked them thankfully and in the name of Jesus. Just to be clear, I'm not aware of any Torah prohibition against cigar smoking so don't think I'm denouncing cigars here, it just strikes me as humorous that there's someone out there smoking cigars in the name of Jesus because he believes that's what Scripture teaches. What's less funny is what happens when we try to reason through this concept of Christian liberty, because the way these verses are used doesn't articulate an assertion of Christian liberty, it describes an assertion of personal autonomy. The difference is this: the person who seeks true liberty understands that there must be boundaries that prevent that liberty from falling into chaos. Personal autonomy, on the other hand, says I must be able to do what I want with no limits. That kind of "freedom" can only ever end in anarchy.

Think of a train moving along its tracks. It can come and go as it pleases but to ensure its safety it must stay on its tracks. That's freedom. Autonomy is a train freed from its tracks. It's true that it is no longer "constrained" by the boundaries imposed by its tracks, but that kind of freedom ends in disaster, ends very quickly, and ends quite violently. Interestingly, this is what is illustrated time and time again with the nation of Israel in the Old Testament. They are obedient and humming along nicely, prosperously, and safely until they decide that Yah's instructions are too binding. They desire autonomy, and in "freeing" themselves from Torah, they wind up in disastrous ruin and bondage every time, only to find freedom again once they return to the boundaries of Torah.

If Paul is truly saying that we can do what we want as long as we do it *unto the Lord* are there boundaries? According to Scripture, the necessary constraints to liberty come from Yah's instruction – Torah. We're told that's no longer binding so are we left to guess what boundaries there might be? Can I commit adultery as long as I do it thankfully and unto the Lord? Can I steal? Can I murder? Of course, these are silly questions, but the root of the issue is quite serious. Hopefully, everyone reading this would acknowledge there are definitely still constraints but can anyone reading this clearly articulate those constraints? As I've said previously, this is where some would go to the virtue and vice lists of the New Testament. Others might say only the Old Testament ideas repeated in the New Testament count. Still others will start hedging their bets indicating the moral law still applies but nothing else. Put another way, the Ten commandments still apply, the unstated assumption being that nothing else does. Interestingly, when reasoning through this aspect of doctrine almost all Christians will back off from the position that Torah has been abolished and settle on a position whereby some of Torah is abolished but some of it still applies. Aside from the immediate problem of a doctrine people cling to so tightly but immediately dial back on when it comes to practical application, there are scriptural issues with both forms taken by this dialed back position.

Let's look at the idea of the moral law still being applicable but nothing else. This view takes Torah and splits it into three types of instruction: Ceremonial law, civil law and moral law. According to those who take this position to explain the boundaries of Christian liberty, Yah's instructions regarding civil and ceremonial matters no longer apply but where morality is concerned, Torah remains a guide for the lives of believers. The problem with this is no such division of Torah can be justified by Scripture. While one can academically categorize certain instructions into distinct groupings, the Bible itself makes no such distinctions. In Psalm 19:7, it says Torah is perfect. It does not say a part of Torah is perfect or that Torah is morally perfect but that Torah, in its entirety, is perfect. From the perspective of pure logic, if a thing is perfect and you divide it and remove from it, is it not, by definition, made less than perfect? Are we to believe that we were once the benefactors of something perfect but because of our lack of understanding and obedience Yah hacked out the bulk of it and we now live by a less perfect instruction? That would be strange indeed.

Even if we set aside the fact that the Bible never speaks of "parts of Torah" but only ever speaks of the whole Law, there's still the problem that such manipulation is explicitly against Torah. Deuteronomy 4:2 says clearly,

> "You shall not add to the word which I am commanding you, nor take away from it, that you may keep the commandments of the Lord your God which I command you."

Dividing Torah into categories and tossing two of the three categories seems like taking away from it, but let's not forget how we got to this issue. The idea, as it's taught, says that all of Torah has been abolished. Practically speaking, though, that can't be supported. For example, the assertion would include Deuteronomy 4:2 which would mean there's no longer a prohibition against adding to or subtracting from Yah's word. But of course, those of us who are Protestant believe in the inerrancy and total authority of Scripture. Timothy said all Scripture is God breathed and he wrote that before there was a New Testament so Timothy must have been talking about the Old Testament. But now we're back to being forced to consider that perhaps not all of Torah has been abolished so Torah is removed, divided, and a subset is added back.

As part of that subset, where does the prohibition against adding to or subtracting from the word of God fall? It's certainly not ceremonial or civil. Since adding to or removing from God's word has the potential to make Yah a liar, I'd suggest that it's most certainly a moral instruction (if I believed Torah could be divided as so many claim) and assert that it sits squarely on the foundation of the third commandment:

> "You shall not take the name of the Lord your God in vain, for the Lord will not leave him unpunished who takes His name in vain.

While some think this means you shouldn't say things like, "Oh my God", it's actually a commandment about truth. Simply put, don't swear in God's name that something that isn't true is true. For example, don't point to a dog and say, "By God, that's a cat". That leaves us with another circular problem though because if the moral law still applies and the prohibition against changing Yah's instruction is a matter of morality on the grounds that it's a matter of truth, and the moral aspects still apply, then we don't have the authority to change Yah's instruction. If we don't have the authority, then on what basis have we divided Torah and removed significant portions in the first place?

This leads us to the biggest problem with this position. Not only is there no support for a division of Torah in Scripture, and not only does such a division and the removal of portions of Torah, according to man's categorizations, violate Yah's instruction, this position violates its own truth statement to convince us it's true. This position breaks the moral law against tinkering with Yah's word and then tells us that, having tinkered with Yah's word in violation of a moral component, only the moral components still apply. That's a fascinating level of nonsense!

The simple explanation, that the ceremonial and civil law were done away with, but the moral law wasn't, doesn't stand up to scrutiny, nor does the explanation that Torah has been abolished except for the 10 commandments. Aside from the obvious similar problem of dividing and removing large portions of Yah's word, there's another problem no one seems to talk about. What about the fourth commandment? Don't murder, don't steal, don't have idols, don't covet your neighbor's wife; all of these stand with no opposition in the Christian ethos but if the 10 commandments still apply, why are there so few Christians that *"remember the Sabbath day, to keep it holy"*? Some may object at this point and say, "but wait, I go to church every Sunday". Well that's good but we don't get to redefine things that Yah has defined.

Sunday is, theologically speaking, quite different than the biblically defined Sabbath day. First and foremost, Sunday is the first day of the week, whereas Yah set apart the last day of the week as the Sabbath day. There were also specific instructions for how we're supposed to observe the Sabbath day; we're to rest and do no work and we're to make it a day set apart for Yah. A few hours at church and then on to our lives doesn't exactly fit what Yah described when He gave us the fourth commandment. There are probably some out there who refrain from work on Sunday but most of the Christian's I know go to church, maybe a little brunch and then it's business as usual. It's a day to get things done. One might mow the lawn, clean up a little, or perhaps get any work done or errands run that one was too busy during the week to attend to. That's not *"remembering the Sabbath day"* the way the Bible defines it.

It may seem like I'm clinging tightly to this Sabbath thing, and I am, but only to make evident the problem with teaching that Torah has been abolished, except for the 10 commandments. In practice those who subscribe to this idea don't really mean it. Just like with the "moral law" explanation there appear to be addendums, provisos, and exceptions to this explanation. More accurately stated one should say, "Torah has been abolished, except for the 10 commandments, which still apply, except for the fourth commandment" and then they'd hopefully offer an explanation why commandments 1-3 and 5-10 are still in but commandment 4 got the boot. Sadly, I've heard the explanations and they're unconvincing to say the least. Let me explain.

As mentioned previously, everyone should be very suspicious when someone uses a single verse from one of Paul's letters to support a point, but this is exactly what happens where the Sabbath is concerned. Even though, in my experience, very few actually observe the Sabbath according to the Bible's definition of observance, some will insist they do satisfy the fourth commandment by resting one day a week, asserting that it no longer matters which day this is done. Others will say we no longer have to observe the Sabbath at all. Intriguingly, both groups use Romans 14:5 to support their view. For the sake of discussion, I've included a larger portion of the passage that contains verse 5 so we can more closely evaluate the context.

Romans 14:3-6:

> [3] The one who eats is not to regard with contempt the one who does not eat, and the one who does not eat is not to judge the one who eats, for God has accepted him. [4] Who are you to judge the servant of another? To his own master he stands or falls; and he will stand, for the Lord is able to make him stand.
>
> [5] One person regards one day above another, another regards every day alike. Each person must be fully convinced in his own mind. [6] He who observes the day, observes it for the Lord, and he who eats, does so for the Lord, for he gives thanks to God; and he who eats not, for the Lord he does not eat, and gives thanks to God.

The first thing I'd like to draw your attention to is the fact that there is no mention of the Sabbath or a holy day anywhere in this passage. What is spoken of here are certain days, where some people eat and some people don't. In verse 3 we see this idea that one who eats shouldn't judge one who doesn't and vice versa, and in verse 6 this is linked to the days being discussed where one who observes the day is contrasted with one who eats. What Paul is saying is one who observes the day doesn't eat and one who eats doesn't observe the day.

The context of this passage is fast days, specifically four days that mark solemn events during Babylon's attack on Israel. These days are still observed as fast days by some today and are mentioned in Zechariah 8:19. Yah is explaining through prophecy that all sorrows will be turned to joy and says of these days:

> Thus says the Lord of hosts, 'The fast of the fourth, the fast of the fifth, the fast of the seventh and the fast of the tenth months will become joy, gladness, and cheerful feasts for the house of Judah; so love truth and peace.'

Described in chronological order, the fast of the tenth month is a reverence to a fast held on the 10th day of the 10th month on the Hebrew calendar, Tevet, which was the day on which Nebuchadnezzar set up a siege around Jerusalem. Details of this event are given in 2 Kings 25:1-4, the prophet Jeremiah writes about it in Jeremiah 52:4-6 and Ezekiel is given a prophecy to deliver to the people on this day in Ezekiel 24:1-2.

Next comes what Zechariah calls the feast of the fourth month, the month of Tammuz. This is known simply as the fast of Tammuz and marks the day that Nebuchadnezzar's army breached the walls of Jerusalem. We find references to this in Jeremiah 52:6-7 and Jeremiah 39:2.

The fifth month on the Hebrew calendar is called Av so the fast of the fifth month is simply known today as Tisha B'Av, meaning the 9th of Av, and has become a fast to remember many tragedies that have occurred on or around the 9th. Originally, the fast of the fifth month was set aside to remember the events between the 7th and 12th of Av when the first temple was looted and destroyed, Jerusalem burned, and the Israelites exiled beginning the Babylonian captivity. All of this is described in 2 Kings 25:8-21 and by Jeremiah starting with Jeremiah 52:12. The reason this is "officially" observed on the 9th is because of how many events in Israel's history have landed specifically on the 9th. So many that some believe this day is a day set aside for calamity. On this day in 70 CE the second temple was destroyed. In 135 a Judean revolt against Rome was defeated. In 1290, Jews were expelled from England on the 9th of Av and in 1941, Heinrich Himmler was given approval by Nazi leadership to implement "the final solution", starting the holocaust; this last event being the primary reason people fast on Tisha B'Av today.

The final event remembered by fasting is the fast of the seventh month, the month of Tishrei. It's known as the fast of Gedeliah because it marks the day when the Israelite governor, Gedeliah, appointed by the Babylonians to oversee those not taken into captivity (see Jeremiah 52:16), was assassinated by a band of Ammonites. The details of this assassination can be found in 2 Kings 25:22-26 and Jeremiah 41:1-3.

Not everyone observed these fast days. There was no Torah instruction that they must be observed, but there were some that believed since the prophets wrote about these events and acknowledged them as days of fasting, they should be treated with the same weight as Torah instruction. What Paul is doing is stating very clearly these are traditions not instructions. Each person should decide for him or herself whether to fast or not on these days and no one should judge another for their decision because fasting is a personal choice. That's it. That's all we have in view here. There is nothing about this passage that applies to the Sabbath (or to dietary instructions for that matter). Anyone suggesting Paul is declaring the fourth commandment abolished here has misunderstood the context, but this is the only Scripture anyone ever references to justify the idea that the fourth commandment no longer applies or that the Sabbath can be observed on any day.

Interestingly, the reason for these events remembered by fasting is given through prophecy in Ezekiel chapter 20. The Babylonian invasion and subsequent captivity was punishment for idol worship and breaking the Sabbath. It's a long section so I won't include it here, but I encourage you to pause here and read it. Notice how often the Sabbath is mentioned in Ezekiel 20. In verse 12, Yah reiterates that He gave His people the Sabbath as a sign between Him and them and charges His people with profaning His Sabbath in verses 13, 16, 21, and 24 and goes on to say that because of this, horrible punishment is coming.

Isn't it ironic that today this passage of Paul is used to encourage people to profane the Sabbath; the very thing that led to the terrible events commemorated through the fast days about which Paul is speaking!

As much as it's unwise to pull a single verse from any of Paul's letters without looking at the surrounding context, it's equally unwise to base an entire doctrinal belief on a single verse in all of Scripture. When it comes to things like snake handling or drinking poison most Christians acknowledge the danger of taking a single verse out of context, but no one seems to have a problem with the very same thing being done with Romans 14:5.

As with the moral law explanation, the 10 commandments explanation has some serious flaws. What they have in common is neither provides an explanation without massive holes. We have the idea that the moral law still applies, but not the whole moral law, or the idea that the 10 commandments still apply, but not all of the 10 commandments, and neither group can clearly articulate from Scripture the reasoning behind the exceptions. If we believe the Bible is true and without error, it should make us all very uncomfortable that there are so many exceptions given without convincing reasons. We're left with the following mess: Torah has been abolished, except for certain parts which still apply, and of the parts that still apply, there are portions which also don't apply. It's no wonder atheists accuse us of picking and choosing Bible verses that fit our own viewpoints or agenda.

Allow me to take this line of reasoning one step deeper to the bedrock of these two arguments. At their core, they're based on the idea that the nature of the old covenant was fundamentally different then the nature of the new covenant. The way it's usually explained is something along these lines: The old covenant was made with Israel and included Torah, but it was replaced by a new covenant. There isn't a ruleset, per se, that was given along with the new covenant, so we must glean the ruleset by careful study of the New Testament.

According to this idea, the parts of Torah that were repeated in the New Testament are part of the ruleset, but anything not repeated is no longer relevant. It sounds interesting, and there is no doubt there's a new covenant but according to Scripture it doesn't match the characterization that's been taught in mainstream Christianity. The nature of the new covenant is found as prophecy in Jeremiah 31:31-34:

> ³¹ *"Behold, days are coming,"* declares the Lord, *"when I will make a new covenant with the house of Israel and with the house of Judah,* ³² *not like the covenant which I made with their fathers in the day I took them by the hand to bring them out of the land of Egypt, My covenant which they broke, although I was a husband to them,"* declares the Lord. ³³ *"But this is the covenant which I will make with the house of Israel after those days,"* declares the Lord, *"I will put My law within them and on their heart I will write it; and I will be their God, and they shall be My people.* ³⁴ *They will not teach again, each man his neighbor and each man his brother, saying, 'Know the Lord,' for they will all know Me, from the least of them to the greatest of them,"* declares the Lord, *"for I will forgive their iniquity, and their sin I will remember no more."*

We're told, erroneously, that the new covenant abolished Torah and a new ruleset replaced it, but that's not at all what's recorded in Jeremiah. What was the difference between the old and new? How is it *"not like the covenant which {Yah} made with their fathers"*? The difference is Torah will be written on the heart instead of on tablets of stone. It doesn't say anywhere that Torah will be different, it says it will be internal rather than external. I've said this before, but it bears repeating here. The problem was never Torah. The problem was always the human heart and as such, it was never Yah's intention to change His instructions. It was always His intention to change the human heart.

The author of Hebrews, in quoting this passage from Jeremiah 31, makes the problem clear. In Hebrews 8:8 below, notice how the author says fault was found *"with them"*, not with Torah. The new covenant, which was not like the covenant made with *"their fathers"* in the sense that it was written on their hearts instead of on tablets, was made to fix the *"fault with them"*. There is no indication there was any change to the content of Yah's Guidance.

> ⁷ *For if that first covenant had been faultless, there would have been no occasion sought for a second.* ⁸ *For finding fault with them, He says,*
>
> *"Behold, days are coming, says the Lord,*
> *When I will effect a new covenant*

> With the house of Israel and with the house of Judah;
> ⁹ Not like the covenant which I made with their fathers
> On the day when I took them by the hand
> To lead them out of the land of Egypt;
> For they did not continue in My covenant,
> And I did not care for them, says the Lord.
> ¹⁰ "For this is the covenant that I will make with the house of Israel
> After those days, says the Lord:
> I will put My laws into their minds,
> And I will write them on their hearts.
> And I will be their God,
> And they shall be My people.
> ¹¹ "And they shall not teach everyone his fellow citizen,
> And everyone his brother, saying, 'Know the Lord,'
> For all will know Me,
> From the least to the greatest of them.
> ¹² "For I will be merciful to their iniquities,
> And I will remember their sins no more."
>
> ¹³ When He said, "A new covenant," He has made the first obsolete. But whatever is becoming obsolete and growing old is ready to disappear.

But wait, you might be saying, there in verse 13 it says the first covenant is obsolete. Doesn't that mean Torah is obsolete along with it? Not at all. The reason the first covenant is obsolete is that with Torah written on our hearts, according to the new covenant, we simply don't need it written on stone anymore. There is no evidence anywhere that what was written on our hearts is different than what was written on stone. On the contrary, there's every indication it's the same set of instructions; the same unaltered Torah.

We've discussed the way Scripture describes Torah. It's wise, good, and holy; a blessing to those who follow it. We've also tested the idea that Torah was nailed to the cross, the idea that Torah was just for the Jews, and the idea that obedience is too difficult for us. In doing so, we've found that all three fail to stand up to scrutiny and, more than that, stand in opposition to what Scripture says on these topics.

Furthermore, we've examined the conceptual issue of unrestrained Christian freedom and the unconvincing attempts that are made to resolve the problem of liberty without boundaries. It's at this point I'd like to turn to a deeper set of conceptual issues that necessarily result from the belief that

Torah has been abolished: The renunciation of Yah's inerrancy and immutability.

Remember, although the word Torah is translated as the word "law", that's not the best definition. There are legal components as part of Torah but the word "instruction" is more accurate; instruction in personal matters, legal matters, civil matters and so on; instruction that would help us to avoid certain pitfalls inherent to a fallen world. That's not to say obedience is a way to avoid problems or hardship, but Yah's plan and His will are what is best for us no matter what difficulties His will might lead us through for our good and His glory. The point is, by following Him obediently we avoid problems that result from asserting our will over His. To believe that Torah has been abolished is to believe that Yah's instructions have changed, or that Yah no longer has instructions to help guide us.

Yah is likened to a father throughout Scripture, for example Matthew 7:9-11:

> [9] Or what man is there among you who, when his son asks for a loaf, will give him a stone? [10] Or if he asks for a fish, he will not give him a snake, will he? [11] If you then, being evil, know how to give good gifts to your children, how much more will your Father who is in heaven give what is good to those who ask Him!

It's helpful to consider how and why a loving parent teaches and instructs his or her child. A loving parent gives instruction and guidance in the hopes that the child, having heard and followed that instruction, might avoid unnecessary struggles or pain in life. A parent doesn't set boundaries and express expectations to put their child in bondage or to prevent them from enjoying their life; boundaries and expectations along with clearly articulated consequences are shared with a child so they might avoid going off the rails and making a mess of their life. They're given out of love. So it is with Torah. Let's say a parent has a child that is rebellious and disobedient and winds up in serious trouble, but the parent finds a way to get that child out of trouble. Is it more likely that a parent would sit down with that child and explain that these were the consequences the child was warned about and plea for the child to heed the instruction that's been given now that the child has felt the consequences first hand, or is it more likely that the parent will simply say, "now that I've gotten you out of trouble, ignore all the guidance I gave you and live however you want and I promise you'll never get in trouble again"? Instead of asking which is more likely, perhaps it would be better to ask which is more loving.

This is exactly the state we're in. Yah, being a loving Father who wants what's best for all His children, left His instruction and guidance in Torah and, as we've seen, it was His desire that we'd have the heart to obey so that it would go well with us and with our children. But we rebelled and were subject to the consequences He warned us would result from going our own way. Now having pardoned us, does it make sense that He put His instruction in our very hearts as the prophets predicted, or does it make more sense that He would, in essence, say forget my guidance and live how you want? It's living how we wanted that got us in trouble in the first place!

What does all this have to do with Yah's inerrancy and immutability? It has to do with the language He used to express His instruction. If Torah has been abolished, we must believe that Yah wanted His people to live a certain way but then either changed His mind or knew all along that it wasn't going to last forever. If it was the first, then clearly, He's changed. His preferences aren't what they once were. If it's the second, then either Yah was mistaken or He lied. Both are obviously problematic.

There are a lot of people that seem to believe that Yah has changed. They talk about the wrathful God of the Old Testament as opposed to the merciful God of the New Testament, but this cannot be. In Malachi 3, Yah says explicitly that He *"changes not"*:

> [5] *"Then I will draw near to you for judgment; and I will be a swift witness against the sorcerers and against the adulterers and against those who swear falsely, and against those who oppress the wage earner in his wages, the widow and the orphan, and those who turn aside the alien and do not fear Me," says the Lord of hosts.* [6] *"For I, the Lord, do not change; therefore you, O sons of Jacob, are not consumed.*

How interesting that in verse 5, Yah is talking about judging those who are breaking Torah instruction. It's in that context that He says, *"I, the Lord, do not change"*, but because "early church fathers" said He actually did end up changing, contrary to His own words, we're supposed to believe it? I think not.

Along those same lines, let's look at the language Yah used to describe things like the feast days and the Sabbath.

First let's look at Deuteronomy 5:29 again:

> [29] Oh that they had such a heart in them, that they would fear Me and keep all My commandments **always**, that it may be well with them and with their sons **forever!**

Regarding the Sabbath consider Exodus 31:16-17:

> [16] So the sons of Israel shall observe the sabbath, to celebrate the sabbath **throughout their generations** as **a perpetual covenant.'** [17] It is a sign between Me and the sons of Israel **forever**; for in six days the Lord made heaven and earth, but on the seventh day He ceased from labor, and was refreshed."

Regarding Passover, Exodus 12:14 and 12:24

> [14] 'Now this day will be a memorial to you, and you shall celebrate it as a feast to the Lord; **throughout your generations** you are to celebrate it as **a permanent ordinance.**
>
> [24] And you shall observe this event as an ordinance for you and your children **forever.**

And the Feast of Unleavened Bread, Exodus 12:17:

> [17] You shall also observe the Feast of Unleavened Bread, for on this very day I brought your hosts out of the land of Egypt; therefore you shall observe this day **throughout your generations** as **a permanent ordinance.**

First Fruits, Leviticus 23:14 and 21:

> [14] Until this same day, until you have brought in the offering of your God, you shall eat neither bread nor roasted grain nor new growth. It is to be **a perpetual statute throughout your generations in all your dwelling places.**

> [21] On this same day you shall make a proclamation as well; you are to have a holy convocation. You shall do no laborious work. It is to be **a perpetual statute in all your dwelling places throughout your generations.**

The Day of Atonement, Leviticus 15:29-31 and 23:31

> [29] "This shall be **a permanent statute** for you: in the seventh month, on the tenth day of the month, you shall humble your souls and not do any work, whether the native, or the alien who sojourns among you; [30] for it is on this day that atonement shall be made for you to cleanse you; you will be clean from all your sins before the Lord. [31] It is to be a sabbath of solemn rest for you, that you may humble your souls; **it is a permanent statute**.

> [31] You shall do no work at all. It is to be **a perpetual statute throughout your generations in all your dwelling places.**

I could go on, but I believe you understand the pattern. Yah said these things, all of which modern Christianity tells us have been done away with, are forever, perpetual, everlasting, and should be observed throughout our generations regardless of where we live. Being omniscient, if He knew these things would one day come to an end, He could have simply said to do them without saying for how long. He could have explicitly said these things will be memorials until Messiah comes. He could have spoken through His prophets to indicate that changes were coming. None of this is found in the Bible. There are only a handful of options that can explain this. One option is Yah lied, or perhaps exaggerated, and they aren't actually perpetual and everlasting. Maybe He made a mistake and sort of pivoted when He realized Torah wasn't working, or He changed His mind? If one believes Yah simply lied, that opens up a can of worms I don't think anyone is prepared for. If we cannot know what in the Bible is true and what is a lie we need to throw the entire thing out, so let's set that aside as impossible. I also don't know anyone who would argue that Yah made a mistake or somehow had a plan but didn't foresee the problems in the plan and had to make some changes along the way. That would call into question Yah's infallibility and omniscience so that must also be ruled out as impossible.

Did Yah change? Well, in my opinion, that's the scariest option of them all for one simple fact. What if Torah obedience was the original plan and because it wasn't working Yah changed tactics and decided to send His son. Aside from the problem of the lamb being slain before the foundation of the world there's a deeper issue. What would prevent Yah from seeing that more and more people are rejecting Yeshua as time goes by? Could He not change His mind again and decide Yeshua isn't working so a third way should be tried? How can we be secure in our salvation through faith in Yeshua if we believe we have a record of Yah changing the method of salvation once already? This cannot be.

The other option, of course, is that what we've been taught isn't true; that when Yah said forever he meant, and still means, forever. In a previous chapter, I mentioned this briefly and later in the same chapter referred to prophecy about the coming millennial kingdom where we see people coming to Zion to hear Torah, observing the Sabbath and the feasts, etc. Those ideas take center stage here. Are we to believe that at first Yah said these things were forever, and in the future we know these things will still apply, but for the time being they're suspended? No verses indicate these things will go away for a time but then be re-instituted. Because Yah said they were forever, and because we see them being observed in the past and because prophecy tells us they will be observed in the future, they must still be applicable to us in the present.

How can one insist that the Bible is true if one turns right around and says that it's not true that the feasts are forever, and it's not true that we should remember the Sabbath, and it's not true that Torah is written on our hearts?

What about verses like Amos 3:7:

> *Surely the Lord GOD does nothing Unless He reveals His secret counsel To His servants the prophets.*

If it was Yah's intention to abolish Torah we should either expect to find that eventuality recorded by the prophets or Yah did something without revealing it to them, which would make Amos 3:7 untrue.

How about Deuteronomy 13:1-5:

> *¹ "If a prophet or a dreamer of dreams arises among you and gives you a sign or a wonder, ² and the sign or the wonder comes true, concerning which he spoke to you, saying, 'Let us go after other gods (whom you have not known) and let us serve them,' ³ you shall not listen to the words of that prophet or that dreamer of dreams; for the Lord your God is testing you to find out if you love the Lord your God with all your heart and with all your soul. ⁴ You shall follow the Lord your God and fear Him; and you shall keep His commandments, listen to His voice, serve Him, and cling to Him. ⁵ But that prophet or that dreamer of dreams shall be put to death, because he has counseled rebellion against the Lord your God who brought you from the land of Egypt and redeemed you from the house of slavery, to seduce you from the way in which the Lord your God commanded you to walk. So you shall purge the evil from among you.*

Pay particular attention to the infractions described in verse 5. Yah specifically tells them to kill a prophet who would presume to *"counsel rebellion against the Lord"* and *"seduce you from the way in which the Lord your God commanded you to walk?"* Incidentally, this is a passage that stands as a monumental barrier to presenting the mainstream Christian gospel to our Jewish friends and neighbors. Sadly, I believe the mainstream Christian presentation of the gospel, as it stands today, is also what Paul warned about when he warned of anyone who would *"preach a different Christ than we preached"*.

Allow me to explain. If it's true that Yeshua taught that Torah was abolished and should no longer be followed, He perfectly fits the description of one who *"seduces you from the way in which the Lord your God commanded you to walk"*. Either Yeshua taught no such thing, or Yah ordered His people not to follow Yeshua and to kill Him for what Yah knew He'd come and preach. That makes little, if any, sense. The third option of course is that what Yah advises in this passage is simply not true. That He, for some reason, warned about prophets who would come along and encourage "Torahlessness" even though His plan was to send His son to do exactly that, and His intention was always for people to ignore His words in Deuteronomy 13:5 and follow the one counselling *"rebellion against the Lord"*. I don't believe that's the case.

At a higher level, consider simple statements like Psalm 111:10:

> *"The fear of the Lord is the beginning of wisdom; A good understanding have all those who do His commandments; His praise endures forever."*

Is it no longer true that *"a good understanding have all those who do His commandments"*? Those who preach against Torah seem to think those of us who follow Torah lack understanding. Which is true? Many people quote from Proverbs, which indicates that they believe what they're quoting to still be true. I'm sure many of us have quoted Proverbs 16:18,

> *"Pride goes before destruction, and a haughty spirit before stumbling."*

Perhaps Proverbs 10:16 sounds familiar:

> *"The wages of the righteous is life, but the earnings of the wicked are sin and death."*

It should sound familiar since Paul referred to it in the popular verse, Romans 6:23. Why are these two verses true and applicable today but not the first few verses of Proverbs 3?

> ¹ *My son, do not forget my teaching,*
> *But let your heart keep my commandments;*
> ² *For length of days and years of life*
> *And peace they will add to you.*

When the Bible says Yah changes not (Malachi 3:6), is it true? If it is, why is so much anti-Torah doctrine reliant on the idea that He changed? The same people who tell us the Bible is the true, inerrant word of God sure put a lot of effort into explaining how even though it might have been true once, it isn't anymore. That stinks of the spirit of relativism.

A primary foundation of the concept of truth as the Bible and Yeshua presents it, is that truth is immutable. If it was true yesterday it will be true tomorrow and will still be true millennia from now. In contemporary culture, the idea that truth is relative is increasingly pervasive, but from the perspective of a Biblical world view, truth does not change from place to place or from time to time. Yet that's exactly what we have to believe to accept what mainstream Christianity teaches.

For instance, in Jeremiah 2:20 we read:

> [20] *"For long ago I broke your yoke*
> *And tore off your bonds;*
> *But you said, 'I will not serve!'*
> *For on every high hill*
> *And under every green tree*
> *You have lain down as a harlot.*

If Torah is bondage, then it isn't true that Yah *"long ago broke your yoke and tore off your bonds"* is it? Those who teach against Torah would have us believe that long ago Yah placed them under the bondage of Torah. Which teaching is true? As we've already seen, Torah obedience is related to liberty in Psalm 119:45. Psalm 119:142 says that Torah is truth, which is interesting when one considers Yeshua's words in John 8:31-32:

> [31] *So Jesus was saying to those Jews who had believed Him, "If you continue in My word, then you are truly disciples of Mine;* [32] *and you will know the truth, and the truth will make you free."*

We've also already looked at James 1:25 and 2:12 where James refers to the "Torah of liberty". Is it not compelling that both Old and New Testament passages pair Torah and obedience to it with liberty?

So, what of bondage? There's a passage in the second chapter of 2 Peter that's quite illuminating:

> [19] *While they promise them liberty, they themselves are the servants of corruption: for of whom a man is overcome, of the same is he brought in bondage.* [20] *For if after they have escaped the pollutions of the world through the knowledge of the Lord and Saviour Jesus Christ, they are again entangled therein, and overcome, the latter end is worse with them than the beginning.* [21] *For it had been better for them not to have known the way of righteousness, than, after they have known it, to turn from the holy commandment delivered unto them.* (KJV)

Peter is talking about false prophets and is warning readers that there will be those who come teaching a lifestyle they say leads to liberty when, in fact, it leads to bondage. In verse 21, Peter makes clear these false teachers know the way of righteousness, a direct reference to Torah, but have turned from the holy commandment.

Allow me to paraphrase. Peter is saying there are those who know Torah but have abandoned it and, having abandoned it, they act in the world as false teachers compelling others to abandon *"the way of righteousness"*. They accomplish this by selling people on the idea that Torah is bondage and disobedience is liberty. Peter specifically says this teaching has things backwards, which is absolutely true according to the Scripture references we've looked at, but this is precisely what mainstream Christianity teaches today.

Yeshua was well-known for explaining things through parable and metaphor so, I'll take a page from His playbook to illustrate the relationship between Torah, lawlessness, liberty and bondage. Consider the difference between a prison population and the population at large. What's the primary difference between the two groups that explains where each group is? Is it not true that those in prison, or in bondage, are those who have broken the law? And is it not also true that those who are free are, generally speaking, those who live in obedience to the laws of the land? To take it one step further, how does one who has been bound in prison qualify for parole if not by turning from his lawless ways? In other words, returning to the boundaries of law, one finds freedom! It shouldn't be surprising that the physical world is a reflection of spiritual reality.

To bring this to a more personal level, I don't break the laws that exist at the local, state and federal level. One result of this is that I'm not in jail. I enjoy liberty as a result of my obedience. If I did break the law, I would rightly be placed in prison. In other words, my disobedience would leave me in bondage. Taking this idea one step further, no one accuses me of legalism because I abide by the laws that apply to me, I'm simply being a good citizen of my community. Why is it then, when I strive to follow the instructions that govern Yah's kingdom, and encourage others to do the same, I *am* accused of legalism? That's no more true spiritually than it is physically. Obeying Torah simply makes one a law-abiding citizen of Yah's kingdom. Just as it does in the physical world, this obedience leaves one in a state of liberty rather than bondage. This is exactly as Scripture describes Torah obedience from Genesis to Revelation.

Section IV

Rest, Feasts, and Food

CHAPTER **10**

His Ways His Way

When I started writing this book, my goal was very simple. My intention was to write a few pages to explain to my parents and my grandmother why my wife and I decided to stop celebrating Christmas and Easter. As I reasoned through the explanation in my mind I realized that I had spent years studying, praying, and pouring over Scripture to arrive at the decision to abandon traditions both my wife and I grew up with, and ones we had strong, positive memories of and emotions toward. As a result, it wouldn't suffice to simply say we believe we're instructed against it. I would have to explain why certain verses apply to us even though they appear in the Old Testament, why abrogation, a concept that permeates Islam, doesn't apply to the Bible, and why instructions and promises given to Israel thousands of years ago applied to me, a Christian in the 21st century. To explain all of this, I'd have to take on a lot of the things I was taught, some by my well-meaning, God-fearing parents. The result is the last three sections and all of what you've read thus far has laid the foundation for this section. I've written a lot about what I disagree with, what I believe the chasms are between mainstream Christianity and the Biblical record, and all the things I believe are not true.

I'd like to turn now to what I do believe and how I believe the Bible instructs us to live out our faith. A lot of this will be a history lesson of sorts. For instance, to explain the shift of the primary day of worship from the last day of the week to the first requires an examination of the state of Christianity and the Roman empire in the third and fourth centuries, specifically decrees made by Constantine and various Catholic church councils. Many people don't know there's a stark difference between the Sabbath and Sunday worship, assuming it's all the same thing, there's just disagreement on which day of the week it falls on. The history of such things will go a long way in explaining why I take the position I do on things like the Sabbath, Christmas and Easter, and dietary instructions. So, without further ado, let's begin.

Tradition has it there are 613 laws included as part of Torah. If you look for a simple list of these 613 laws, you'll find a few, the most common being a list recorded in the Mishneh by Rambam but you'll find that quite a few instructions on any given list repeat in a sense. For instance, one states farmers "should not gather gleanings" from a harvest and another says "leave the gleanings for the poor", both derived from Leviticus 19:9. One is to "not harvest an entire field" while another is to "leave the corners of the field unharvested" also both derived from Leviticus 19:9. While I don't mean to offend any of my orthodox readers, all four of these are the same thing at their core. Expressing the same idea four ways does not make four instructions. My point is if you've heard of these 613 laws and you're tempted to think "who could keep up with all that", be comforted by the fact that on the one hand, in my opinion, that's an inflated number, and on the other hand, when it comes down to it, no one has to keep all of the instructions in Torah anyway. This is another misunderstanding of what it means to be Torah obedient. To put it succinctly, we're to obey the instructions that apply to us and only if they can be done the way Yah instructed them to be done.

Let me elaborate. Of all the instructions in Torah, there are definite groupings. Not the artificial man-made categorizations like ceremonial, moral and civil, but groupings according to application. For example, an enormous amount of Leviticus, only applies to Levites in service of the Temple. I am not a Levite engaged in Temple service, so those instructions don't apply to me. They're interesting and they bear in themselves spiritual truths that are important to my understanding of the character of the Father who put them in place but that's it. They aren't things I can obey, so I'm not obligated to. Similarly, as we've seen, there are instructions for farmers to not harvest to the edges of their fields. This was a social welfare mechanism that we see illustrated in the story of Ruth. Because Boaz operated a farm, this particular Torah instruction applied to him and he obeyed. I am not a farmer so that's not an instruction I can follow even if I wanted to. Sadly, I can't use this as an excuse to not mow the whole yard. It's worth noting that in Boaz's case, as promised, his obedience led to blessing; the blessing of a wonderful relationship with Ruth and a family, in fact, a family that eventually produced King David and further down the line, Yeshua himself.

Similarly, there are instructions that only apply to men, instructions that only apply to women, and a LOT of instructions for priests and judges. While one aspect of obedience is that we're only responsible for those instructions that apply to us, the other aspect is how we obey the instructions that do apply to us. Scripture is absolutely clear that we're not supposed to sort of follow Torah, by which I mean we're not supposed to force certain things by doing them our own way. The sacrificial system is a good example. We know that sacrifices will resume when the Temple is restored and Yeshua's reign on Earth begins so why don't we do it now? Simply put, there is no Temple and Torah is very clear about to whom we're to bring sacrifices, by whom they are to be prepared, and where they are to be offered. None of these mechanisms are in place so we can't obey. Another example is stoning or, more generally, capital punishment. People seem to have this idea that there were stonings all the time in ancient Israelite culture or that stoning was a kind of lynch mob justice and neither of these ideas are true. There are specific instructions regarding how a capital case was to be heard, the number and veracity of witnesses required, and the burden of proof necessary to pass a capital sentence. It was not, as some would have you believe, as simple as whipping a mob into a frenzy and killing someone. That's what happened to Stephen and that example of stoning was distinctly in opposition to Torah instruction.

Aside from the incident with Stephen, this false "mob justice" idea was illustrated twice in the life of Yeshua, once in an encounter He had with an adulterous woman caught in the act of infidelity as recorded in John 8:1-11 and the other in His own trial proceedings. Let's look at the former example first:

> *¹ But Jesus went to the Mount of Olives. ² Early in the morning He came again into the temple, and all the people were coming to Him; and He sat down and began to teach them. ³ The scribes and the Pharisees brought a woman caught in adultery, and having set her in the center of the court, ⁴ they said to Him, "Teacher, this woman has been caught in adultery, in the very act. ⁵ Now in the Law Moses commanded us to stone such women; what then do You say?" ⁶ They were saying this, testing Him, so that they might have grounds for accusing Him. But Jesus stooped down and with His finger wrote on the ground. ⁷ But when they persisted in asking Him, He straightened up, and said to them, "He who is without sin among you, let him be the first to throw a stone at her." ⁸ Again He stooped down and wrote on the ground. ⁹ When they heard it, they began to go out one by one, beginning with the older ones, and He was left alone, and the woman, where she was, in the center of the court. ¹⁰ Straightening up, Jesus said to her, "Woman, where are they? Did no one condemn you?" ¹¹ She said, "No one, Lord." And Jesus said, "I do not condemn you, either. Go. From now on sin no more."*

There are a lot of problems with this encounter. For example, if they caught the woman in the act, shouldn't there be a man brought forth under the same charge of adultery? Leaving this aside, we know there's a trap here because we're told as much in verse 6. So why didn't Yeshua just allow the stoning of this clearly guilty woman? After all, isn't Torah unambiguous in declaring adultery punishable by stoning? And weren't there an adequate number of witnesses to satisfy Torah's requirement? Not exactly.

It's true that, according to Torah, adultery is punishable by stoning, but there are steps that are required to be taken and a process that must be followed. For instance, charges need to be brought in the form of two or more witnesses whose testimony agrees. Once charges are established the lower court should hear the case, according to the Talmud between the morning sacrifice and noon, and if the person is found guilty, the case must be heard by the high court between noon and evening. None of these criteria were met in this case so had Yeshua allowed or condoned the stoning of the woman, He would be doing so in violation of Torah; exactly what the Pharisees were trying to trap Him into doing.

During this encounter, in verse 6, it's said that Yeshua wrote something in the dust on the ground. There's a lot of conjecture about what He wrote and to be fair, the Bible doesn't say so there's no way for us to know. Some say He wrote the names of the mistresses of the men who were trying to trap Yeshua to point out their own adultery. Some say He was writing their sins. My personal favorite theory is that He was writing out the passages in Leviticus and Deuteronomy that laid out the requirements for passing a death penalty judgement, proving His knowledge of Torah, demonstrating that what they were suggesting was a violation of Torah, and, by extension, exposing His understanding of their attempt to trap Him. The scribes and Pharisees knew what Torah said about such a matter, and Yeshua knew they knew. Remember, after all, how He responded to Satan during His trials in the wilderness. Yeshua responded to each of Satan's three temptations by quoting from Deuteronomy. It seems fitting that here, too, Yeshua would invoke His Father's words. As I said though, there's no way to know for sure.

It would be remiss of me not to at least briefly mention Yeshua's parting words to the woman. After proclaiming her forgiven He says, *"Go and sin no more"*. As I'm fond of repeating, James defined sin as transgression of the Law or, in other words, disobedience to Torah. Yeshua said to the woman, "Go and disobey Torah no more". This is useless advice if Torah was about to be abolished, no? And does this relate to us today. Once we're forgiven, does the advice to *"go and sin no more"* apply to us? Most would agree that yes, once a person has been redeemed by Yeshua, that person should *"sin no more"* without understanding the implications of what sin means. A popular way of describing sin is it's missing the mark. That's very interesting because it begs the question, according to the Bible, what does it mean to hit the mark? The word Torah itself comes from the Hebrew root word "yarah", which means "to point out", as one would point to something with their finger, or "to shoot", which has in mind aiming an arrow at a target. In other words, while sin is missing the mark, Torah points us to the bullseye and provides the mechanism for us to take aim and hit the mark, or standard, that Yah wants for us for our good and His glory.

How is this related to Yeshua's trial? It's essentially the same story. Yeshua was arrested on orders from the Sanhedrin but it wasn't for them to bring charges. While the Sanhedrin was responsible for hearing cases, charges on the testimony of two or more witnesses were supposed to be established first. Instead, they had Him arrested and tried to gather some charges once He was in custody. In Matthew 26 we read the following:

> [59] Now the chief priests and the whole Council kept trying to obtain false testimony against Jesus, so that they might put Him to death. [60] They did not find any, even though many false witnesses came forward. But later on two came forward, [61] and said, "This man stated, 'I am able to destroy the temple of God and to rebuild it in three days.'"

The account would be almost humorous if the end weren't so heinous. All the Sanhedrin needed was for two witnesses to agree on an accusation and while they were able to find many people willing to give false testimony, none of the false testimony agreed! In addition to the fact the Sanhedrin arrested Yeshua without formal charges, and made up charges without valid witnesses, they also conducted the proceeding at night, or more accurately in the early morning hours before dawn. That just wasn't done. These types of hearings were supposed to be held in public in daylight, not in secret under cover of night. Just as with the adulterous woman, the men opposed to Yeshua and His ministry had no problem going outside of Torah to get the result they wanted. They wanted Him dead, and the pesky boundaries of Torah were not going to get in their way. When it comes down to it, if they had truly been Torah observant, Yeshua never would have been so much as arrested.

So, what am I getting at with all of this? Christians are often accused of "picking and choosing" and I think that's mostly a valid accusation as it's the natural result of having made up artificial criteria by which one chooses which instructions to follow and which instructions to ignore. I understand that I'm describing a similar end result; some things we're supposed to observe and some things we aren't, but the difference in how one determines what is and is not to be observed means everything. Mainstream Christianity assumes that all of Torah is irrelevant and adds a small subset back in for a variety of reasons I've already covered. What I'm proposing is that the opposite is true. All of Torah is still relevant but for all of us there is a large set of instructions that don't apply on the grounds that we aren't Levites, priests or judges and there's no Temple, while a smaller set don't apply because of gender or occupation. It's not that I've created arbitrary divisions and ejected some of the categories for Biblically unsupportable reasons, it's that Scripture is consistent throughout that Torah doesn't just describe what things to do (and not do), but to whom each instruction applies and how each instruction is to be followed. If they cannot be done the way Yah has instructed in Torah, we shouldn't try to do them at all.

A great, albeit sad, example of this occurs in the first verses of Leviticus 10. At this point in the Biblical record, Aaron and his sons have just been anointed into the priesthood, a position appointed to them and their descendants. At the end of Leviticus 9 the first sacrifice by this priesthood had just been completed. What you'll notice in the chapters leading up to Leviticus 10 is that Yah commanded something, Moses relayed the instructions, and the people acted, but at the beginning of Leviticus 10 there's this event that breaks the pattern:

> *1 Now Nadab and Abihu, the sons of Aaron, took their respective firepans, and after putting fire in them, placed incense on it and offered strange fire before the Lord, which He had not commanded them. 2 And fire came out from the presence of the Lord and consumed them, and they died before the Lord.*

There are quite a few things going on here but the most relevant to our discussion is that Nadab and Abihu took it upon themselves, in a sense, to perform an act of worship. This is not something Yah instructed them to do. They surely meant well but their actions cost them their lives. In verse one, aside from it being pointed out that Yah never commanded their action, it's further explained that they offered "strange" fire. Some translations render this "profane". Regardless of translation, this was, for lack of a better term, ordinary fire. When Yah does give instruction for how to offer incense in Leviticus 16:12 we find that the fire used in the firepans must be from hot coals from the altar. The altar and the sacrifice had been set apart, in other words, made holy, and this fire, also being holy, was the only acceptable offering to a holy God.

There are a few conclusions we can draw from this narrative. First, it's important to wait on Yah. As humans, we have an awful tendency to take matters into our own hands. In this case it was likely the result of their zeal, which, on its own is a good thing but being zealous in one's faith clearly isn't an excuse to act instead of waiting on the Lord. Had they waited on Him, they would have received the instruction regarding proper incense offerings and would have lived. This leads directly to the second conclusion, which is that burning incense isn't all there is to it. There's a very specific way it's to be done and doing it any other way is unacceptable to Yah. In fact, this event is referred to twice in Numbers, once in Numbers 3:4 and again in 26:61 making it clear that Yah intended for the people to remember the importance of waiting on Yah and doing things He's commanded His way.

In terms of our current topic, this would be one of those commandments that we can't obey. There is no temple and no altar, so there is nowhere for us to get holy fire. Among other things, this story illustrates that it's not as simple as just getting a match and lighting some incense as part of one's worship. We can't do it the way Yah instructed, so we shouldn't do it at all because doing it any other way is profane to Him. This should make my Catholic friends question the use of incense and censers in Catholic services, but that's a debate for another time.

CHAPTER 11

Remembering the Sabbath

Having established the importance of not just doing "Torah things" but doing them the way Yah instructed using accounts from both the New and Old Testament, I'd like to take a more in depth look at Sabbath observance by looking at Yah's instructions concerning the Sabbath. Contrary to what you might think, the "setting apart" of the seventh day of the week occurred long before Torah was written at Sinai, all the way back in the second chapter of Genesis.

> *[1] Thus the heavens and the earth were completed, and all their hosts. [2] By the seventh day God completed His work which He had done, and He rested on the seventh day from all His work which He had done. [3] Then God blessed the seventh day and sanctified it, because in it He rested from all His work which God had created and made.*

This makes the language of the fourth commandment in Exodus 20 very interesting:

> *[8] "Remember the sabbath day, to keep it holy. [9] Six days you shall labor and do all your work, [10] but the seventh day is a sabbath of the Lord your God; in it you shall not do any work, you or your son or your daughter, your male or your female servant or your cattle or your sojourner who stays with you. [11] For in six days the Lord made the heavens and the earth, the sea and all that is in them, and rested on the seventh day; therefore the Lord blessed the sabbath day and made it holy.*

When Yah says to remember the Sabbath day, He of course means for us in future generations to remember it, but He's establishing a reminder to His people that He set the last day of the week apart as holy long ago. This is why we find the reference to creation in verse 11. Yah established the Sabbath on the seventh day of creation, not at Mount Sinai. This begs an obvious question. Since Yah set apart the seventh day of the week, why does the vast majority of Christendom meet for praise and worship on the first day of the week? As with everything I'm writing about, there are several aspects to address. Does it matter what day of the week we rest on? Does it matter what we do on the Sabbath? Was the Sabbath moved, or was something different established, and whichever is the case, under whose authority were such changes made?

The answer to the first two should be obvious having examined the sad fate of Nadab and Abihu. Bluntly stated, yes, it does matter on which day we observe the Sabbath and, yes, it does matter what we do on that day. Doing Torah things in Torah ways is the theme here so let's look at what Yah has said on the matter. First, let's look at Exodus 31:

> *12 The Lord spoke to Moses, saying, 13 "But as for you, speak to the sons of Israel, saying, 'You shall surely observe My sabbaths; for this is a sign between Me and you throughout your generations, that you may know that I am the Lord who sanctifies you. 14 Therefore you are to observe the sabbath, for it is holy to you. Everyone who profanes it shall surely be put to death; for whoever does any work on it, that person shall be cut off from among his people. 15 For six days work may be done, but on the seventh day there is a sabbath of complete rest, holy to the Lord; whoever does any work on the sabbath day shall surely be put to death.16 So the sons of Israel shall observe the sabbath, to celebrate the sabbath throughout their generations as a perpetual covenant.' 17 It is a sign between Me and the sons of Israel forever; for in six days the Lord made heaven and earth, but on the seventh day He ceased from labor, and was refreshed."*

Personally, I think it's significant that these are Yah's final words before handing over the two stone tablets to Moses, but hopefully what jumps out is the specificity of instruction. Yah lays out why they should observe Yah's Sabbaths. It's to be a sign between Yah and His people so they'd know by whom they are sanctified. Yah set apart the seventh day and instructed us to remember it so we'd remember who it is that has set us apart. As we've already discussed, in verse 12, Yah says, *"throughout your generations"*. In verse 16, He calls it a *"perpetual covenant"*. He didn't say until Messiah comes, or until I replace the Sabbath. He said in all generations, perpetually. That seems very clear to me. Yah is also very specific in reiterating that the Sabbath is to be observed on the seventh day. To those who believe it doesn't matter which day we rest, just so long as we set a day aside for rest, He doesn't say six days you shall work and one day you shall rest, as if it's up to us to choose. As He did earlier in Exodus, and even earlier in Genesis, He specifies the seventh day as the Sabbath day.

I'd like to pause for a moment and make an important distinction that will continue to come up in this chapter. I'm not saying it's wrong to praise and worship Yah on Sunday, or any day, or every day, but there is a problem with replacing what Yah has set apart with something different, especially something man-made. It's one thing to say, I observe the Sabbath on Saturday, but I attend church services on Sunday. It's something quite different to replace what Yah has made holy with something else, and that's what most of Western Christianity has done. I have several Torah observant friends who attend Sunday services but also observe the seventh day Sabbath. For them Sunday services don't act as a replacement for Sabbath observance and personally, I don't see anything in the Bible that makes this wrong. It's not Sunday worship services that are the problem (although the root of worshiping on "sun" day is problematic as we'll see), it's the "instead of" or "in the place of" mentality that's the problem.

In light of this "replacement" idea, let's get into our first bit of history and look at whether or not Sunday worship was ever intended as a sort of New Testament Sabbath. The idea some Christians promote is that they do observe the Sabbath, they just do it on Sunday. Most don't really know when Sunday worship started, it's just been done for so long now that it's Christian tradition and no one digs any deeper. Jews go to synagogue on Saturday, Christians go to church on Sunday. Everyone just knows that, but the lesser known reality is, it wasn't always so. For the first 3-400 years following Yeshua's death and resurrection early Christians, whether they were formerly Jew or Gentile (Galatians 3:28, Ephesians 2:14-15), worshipped on Saturday and observed the seventh day Sabbath. So, what happened?

Before we get to the historical record, I'd like to point out that, contrary to all the passages in the Bible that place the Sabbath on the last day of the week, there isn't a single verse or passage that supports a shift of the Sabbath to the first day of the week. In fact, as opposed to the over 70 verifiable Biblical accounts of early followers of Yeshua keeping the Sabbath up to 60 years after his resurrection, there are only 8 references at all to the first day of the week, and none that show anyone observing worship services or keeping a Sabbath on Sunday. We've looked at what the Bible says about the Sabbath so let's look at what it says in those 8 passages about the first day of the week. Out of 8 references to the first day of the week 6 center around the same event, and 4 of them essentially say the same thing. Starting with Matthew:

> Matthew 28:1 - Now after the Sabbath, as it began to dawn toward the first day of the week, Mary Magdalene and the other Mary came to look at the grave.

This passage clearly states that the first day of the week was after the Sabbath, making it clear that there was a distinction between the two, so no change yet. The same account, and reference to the first day of the week, is given in Mark, Luke, and John.

> Luke 23:56 – 24:1 - Then they returned and prepared spices and perfumes. And on the Sabbath they rested according to the commandment. But on the first day of the week, at early dawn, they came to the tomb bringing the spices which they had prepared.

> Mark 16:1-2 - But on the first day of the week, at early dawn, they came to the tomb bringing the spices which they had prepared.

> John 20:1 - Now on the first day of the week Mary Magdalene came early to the tomb, while it was still dark, and saw the stone already taken away from the tomb.

Another reference to the first day of the week appears in Mark where it's made clear that Yeshua had risen early on the first day of the week.

> Mark 16:9-11 - *Now after He had risen early on the first day of the week, He first appeared to Mary Magdalene, from whom He had cast out seven demons.*

It was this same day that Yeshua appeared to the disciples according to John.

> John 20:19 - *So when it was evening on that day, the first day of the week, and when the doors were shut where the disciples were, for fear of the Jews, Jesus came and stood in their midst and said to them, "Peace be with you."*

As a brief side note, I'll point out that many will claim Sunday is observed as a day of worship because Yeshua was raised on the first day of the week; that shifting from the seventh day to the first is a sort of homage to Yeshua's resurrection. I would actually argue the opposite. Because Yeshua had work to do upon His resurrection, it makes a lot of sense that He didn't take His life up again on the Sabbath but continued His work of salvation on the first day of the week; the day after the Sabbath. Even in His death and resurrection, Yeshua was keeping Torah!

The remaining references are as follows:

> Acts 20:7-11 - *On the first day of the week, when we were gathered together to break bread, Paul began talking to them, intending to leave the next day, and he prolonged his message until midnight.*

> 1 Corinthians 16:1-2 - *Now concerning the collection for the saints, as I directed the churches of Galatia, so do you also. On the first day of every week each one of you is to put aside and save, as he may prosper, so that no collections be made when I come.*

In Acts, we see Paul gathering with fellow believers on the first day of the week for a meal and a message, and in Corinthians we see Paul asking fellow believers to put aside money for an offering on the first day of the week.

That's it. Those are all the references there are in the Bible to the first day of the week and the only mention of the Sabbath in any of them are references that make clear that the first day of the week came after the Sabbath day. In my humble opinion, that should be enough to at least cause concern. On the one hand, we have ample scriptural support for the Sabbath being on the last day of the week, including Yah's own words, and plenty of examples of Yeshua, Paul and other believers keeping the Sabbath on the last day of the week, the latter continuing to observe the Sabbath after Yeshua's death and resurrection. On the other hand, we have zero scriptural support for a Sunday Sabbath, nor any reference to any believer observing a Sabbath on any day other than the last day of the week, save for special Sabbath's like Passover, Yom Teruah, etc., nor any support for a change in the day. Regarding the passages in Acts and Corinthians, which are commonly, albeit incorrectly, used as biblical evidence of Sunday worship, the claim in both cases is the same and relies on reading into the text information that isn't there. Of Acts, it's said that because they broke bread and Paul delivered a message, this was clearly a church service. Of Corinthians, it's said that since Paul is taking up a collection, it must be a church service. On the basis of these two assumptions we're expected to believe the Sabbath has been changed. I remain unconvinced.

There are many times I've shared a meal with friends and talked about Christianity and faith, as I'm sure have many of you. Does that mean we've held a church service? Does that qualify as observing a Sabbath? Hopefully we can agree that's a stretch without additional information to support that conclusion. It's even more of a stretch when you consider Acts 2:46,

> "Day by day continuing with one mind in the temple, and breaking bread from house to house, they were taking their meals together with gladness and sincerity of heart".

By the same logic, wouldn't this make every day the Sabbath? Maybe breaking bread and talking about faith does not a Sabbath make. That Paul had dinner and spoke about Yeshua on the first day of the week is, at best, anemic evidence that the Sabbath had been moved, and cannot be considered evidence at all if we take into account all the places in Acts where we see Paul keeping the Sabbath on the last day of the week.

Finally, there exists a misunderstanding of Hebrew time keeping. In Hebrew culture, one day ends and another begins at sundown, not at midnight, as we're accustomed to today. The problematic assumption is, Paul preached all day Sunday until midnight and left Monday morning. The first day of the week, though, started at sundown Saturday. What's actually being described here is a Havdalah observance; a traditional way to end the Sabbath and welcome the new week where candles are lit, and a meal is shared. This was an evening meal at the start of the first day of the week, which, according to our form of timekeeping, is not Sunday but Saturday after sundown. That's a problem because this argument hinges on the idea that Paul gathered with these believers sometime Sunday, spoke until late Sunday night and left Monday morning, when in fact, that would be the second day of the week, not the first. If Paul started speaking in the evening following the Sabbath, that would be, in our way of keeping time, Saturday after sundown. He then spoke until what we would call midnight Saturday and planned to leave during the next daylight period, which would be Sunday morning. This is a great illustration of the problems that arise from reading and interpreting the Bible without understanding the Hebrew culture from which it was born.

When it comes to the passage in Corinthians, yes, Christian's do traditionally take an offering during Sunday services, but can we extrapolate backwards in history and assume that because Paul took a collection on the first day of the week, it was a Sunday worship service? Even if that was a reasonable conclusion, which it isn't, it's still wrong. Paul didn't take up a collection at all. In fact, he advises putting this money aside specifically *"so that no collections be made when I come"*, as going around collecting donations on the Sabbath would be considered work. So, the argument is that Paul's recommendation to the brethren to put some money aside on Sunday is evidence that the Sabbath had been moved? My wife and I put money aside as soon as we get paid because we know that things come up and that money will go somewhere else by the time we intend to make our offering. Does that make pay day the Sabbath? To say that's a stretch would be putting it mildly. Paul is simply giving wise advice. If you want to make an offering, put the money aside early so you'll know it will be there when the time comes to offer it. Nothing about this revokes or changes Yah's definition of, or instruction regarding, the Sabbath.

Is there any other evidence from Scripture we might turn to? There's only one additional passage I've seen used to support the change in Sabbath and, shockingly it's the biggest stretch of them all. The verse is Revelation 1:10:

> I was in the Spirit on the Lord's day, and I heard behind me a loud voice like the sound of a trumpet.

The premise is, in contemporary culture, Sunday is often referred to as "the Lord's day" so this must be talking about Sunday, and you see, John was in the Spirit and isn't that what we do on Sunday? We get in the Spirit? The fact that man-made tradition co-opted the phrase "the Lord's day" and began using it to refer to the first day of the week some 2-300 years after Revelation was written does not make this evidence of the Sabbath being moved to Sunday. History is replete with the meaning of words being commandeered and altered over time. We must be careful to understand what a word or phrase meant when it was written rather than applying a contemporary meaning and then making assumptions from there.

Before I get to a more in-depth discussion of "the Lord's day", what that has come to mean, and what it originally meant in the context John was using it, let's look at an article that speaks in support of this misguided view. The following is from BlueLetterBible.org:

> The passage in Acts has the Christians gathering together on the first day of the week to break bread. The grammar here makes this out to be a regular occurrence. And so, this, if not the day during which the Church was observing the Sabbath, needs to be explained. Also, John, being in the Spirit on the Lord's day demonstrates that the first day of the week bore enough significance to merit such a familiar nomenclature as "the Lord's day" and John speaks of this day as if it were a normal occurance [sic]. These are just some reasons.
>
> Here are a couple more based upon Biblical Theological models for interpretation. The original Sabbath is based in the seven days of the Old Creation: God worked six days and then rested on the LAST day of the week. Whereas the Sabbath falling on the last day of the week was indicative of the Old Creation, the Christian practice of observing the Sabbath on the FIRST day of the week is a congruent with God's New Creation. Christ rose

on the first day of the week and began His Sabbath rest then (cf. Hebrews 4).

Also of interest is the fact that the two versions of the Sabbath are typological of the two covenants that go along with each Creation. With the Old Creation, Adam was given a covenant of works whereby he would work for a time and then receive his heavenly rest. Adam failed in this and God uses the institution of the Sabbath falling on the first day of the week to demonstrate that with His New Creation, man begins in his rest and the good works follow.

These are all fair reasons I think that we, as Christians, celebrate the Sabbath on the Lord's day (i.e., Sunday). (Blue Letter Bible)

If this is what passes for sound theology, I want no part of it. In the second sentence, the writer says: "And so, this, if not the day during which the Church was observing the Sabbath, needs to be explained." Apparently, the writer can't imagine any explanation but a Sunday Sabbath when in fact, the simplest explanation is that it was no more than the Bible says it is: Fellow believers sharing a meal and a word about Yeshua. According to this article, the fact that they ate together regularly can't be anything else except a Sunday Sabbath. As I've pointed out, the explanation is simple: It was a Havdalah observance; a very common and well-known custom among Jews that occurred at the end of every Sabbath.

Of particular note though is the lack of scriptural support for anything the author asserts in the second paragraph. He takes oblique ideas that are true, strings them together as if they go together, which they don't, and then draws conclusions about what it all must mean. That fact is stated outright in the second paragraph's first sentence, where the appeal is not to Scripture but to "Theological Models", which is really a fancy way of saying doctrinal tradition. You'll also notice that in the "typological evidence" sentence the author makes the mistake we discussed at length by asserting that Torah and obedience was an old way of salvation that didn't work. As I've proven, the Bible supports no such conclusion about the purpose or nature of Torah, so the entire typological comparison is based on a faulty understanding of Torah, or worse, total ignorance of what the Bible says about Torah, deferring instead to traditionally held, but biblically unsupportable, ideas. Contrary to the author's final statement, these are not at all "fair reasons" to celebrate the Sabbath on Sunday. These are arguments that man's traditions trump Yah's words. If you'll remember, Yeshua had something to say about that topic in Mark 7:9:

> "He was also saying to them, "You are experts at setting aside the commandment of God in order to keep your tradition.""

Is this not exactly what is being suggested here? That we set aside Yah's actual words and rest our faith on "typological theories" and "theological models"? I think I'll stick with Yah's instructions, thanks.

So, what about this reference to the Lord's day in Revelation? The article presents it as commonly known in John's day that "the Lord's day" referred to the first day of the week (which isn't true) but is that what John is referring to? First, let's enjoy another exercise in letting the Bible define the Bible. There are really two ways one could go in this analysis. The first, and for contextual reasons I believe the one least likely to be correct, might be to ask if the Lord has a day and, if so, what day is that? In Matthew 12 we read this in the eighth verse (also Luke 6:5):

> "For the Son of Man is Lord of the Sabbath."

If Yeshua is the Lord of the Sabbath, doesn't that make the Sabbath "His day"? Maybe that's a bit too much of a stretch. After all, it's only a single verse. Let us also consider Isaiah chapter 58:

> 13 *"If because of the sabbath, you turn your foot*
> *From doing your own pleasure on My holy day,*
> *And call the sabbath a delight, the holy day of the Lord honorable,*
> *And honor it, desisting from your own ways,*
> *From seeking your own pleasure*
> *And speaking your own word,*
> 14 *Then you will take delight in the Lord,*
> *And I will make you ride on the heights of the earth;*
> *And I will feed you with the heritage of Jacob your father,*
> *For the mouth of the Lord has spoken."*

In the second stanza of verse 13, Yah clearly says the Sabbath is "My holy day", and in the third stanza it's called "the holy day of the Lord". The Sabbath is set apart as holy by Yah in Genesis, codified in writing at Mt. Sinai after the Exodus, referred to as His holy day in Isaiah and Yeshua claims to be the Lord of it. This adds up to a compelling case that, according to Scripture, if the Lord has a day, that day is the Sabbath, and the Sabbath is the seventh day of the week.

While all of this is true, I don't think this is what John is referring to in Revelation. The context of Revelation, and this passage in particular, makes clear that *"the Lord's day"* in this case is simply another way of saying *"the day of the Lord"* or, the day when Yeshua returns. Let's look at the wider context of Revelation 1:10:

> *9 I, John, your brother and fellow partaker in the tribulation and kingdom and perseverance which are in Jesus, was on the island called Patmos because of the word of God and the testimony of Jesus. 10 I was in the Spirit on the Lord's day, and I heard behind me a loud voice like the sound of a trumpet, 11 saying, "Write in a book what you see, and send it to the seven churches: to Ephesus and to Smyrna and to Pergamum and to Thyatira and to Sardis and to Philadelphia and to Laodicea."*
>
> *12 Then I turned to see the voice that was speaking with me. And having turned I saw seven golden lampstands; 13 and in the middle of the lampstands I saw one like a son of man, clothed in a robe reaching to the feet, and girded across His chest with a golden sash. 14 His head and His hair were white like white wool, like snow; and His eyes were like a flame of fire. 15 His feet were like burnished bronze, when it has been made to glow in a furnace, and His voice was like the sound of many waters. 16 In His right hand He held seven stars, and out of His mouth came a sharp two-edged sword; and His face was like the sun shining in its strength.*

What I want to point out here is that in verse 12, John is already in the vision, so to speak. In other words, John isn't describing hearing this voice in 9-11, and then he's taken to the kingdom and into the presence of Yeshua from verse 12 forward, it's all a vision starting from the beginning of verse 10. When John says in verse 10, "I was in the Spirit on the Lord's day", he's not saying he was doing something spiritual on the first day of the week and in the course of his "Sunday worship" he had a vision, as some teach. He's saying that he had an experience whereby he was whisked away in spirit to the future and was allowed to see, and instructed to describe, what that "Lord's day" would be like. It's actually quite surprising that anyone would think "the Lord's day" in a first century context would refer to Sunday considering the thousands of years of prophecy that refer to the same event John writes about in Revelation. Consider the following passages:

> *Isaiah 2:12 - For the Lord of hosts will have a day of reckoning against everyone who is proud and lofty and against everyone who is lifted up, that he may be abased.*
>
> *Isaiah 13:6 - Wail, for the day of the Lord is near! It will come as destruction from the Almighty.*
>
> *Isaiah 13:9 - Behold, the day of the LORD is coming, Cruel, with fury and burning anger, to make the land a desolation; And He will exterminate its sinners from it.*
>
> *Ezekiel 13:5 - You have not gone up into the breaches, nor did you build the wall around the house of Israel to stand in the battle on the day of the Lord.*
>
> *Ezekiel 30:3 - For the day is near, even the day of the Lord is near; It will be a day of clouds, a time of doom for the nations.*
>
> *Joel 1:15 - Alas for the day! For the day of the Lord is near, and it will come as destruction from the Almighty.*
>
> *Joel 2:1 - Blow a trumpet in Zion, and sound an alarm on My holy mountain! Let all the inhabitants of the land tremble, for the day of the Lord is coming; surely it is near,*
>
> *Joel 2:11 - The Lord utters His voice before His army; surely His camp is very great, for strong is he who carries out His word. The day of the Lord is indeed great and very awesome, and who can endure it?*
>
> *Joel 2:31 - The sun will be turned into darkness and the moon into blood before the great and awesome day of the Lord comes.*
>
> *Amos 5:18 - Alas, you who are longing for the day of the Lord, for what purpose will the day of the Lord be to you? It will be darkness and not light;*
>
> *Amos 5:20 - Will not the day of the Lord be darkness instead of light, even gloom with no brightness in it?*
>
> *Obadiah 1:15 - For the day of the Lord draws near on all the nations. As you have done, it will be done to you. Your dealings will return on your own head.*

> *Zephaniah 1:7 - Be silent before the Lord God! For the day of the Lord is near, for the Lord has prepared a sacrifice, He has consecrated His guests.*
>
> *Zephaniah 1:14 - Near is the great day of the Lord, near and coming very quickly; listen, the day of the Lord! In it the warrior cries out bitterly.*
>
> *Zechariah 14:1 - Behold, a day is coming for the Lord when the spoil taken from you will be divided among you.*
>
> *Malachi 4:5 - Behold, I am going to send you Elijah the prophet before the coming of the great and terrible day of the Lord.*

I'd like to take a moment to point out the various authors don't always use exactly the same wording. Most of the time this is referred to as the day of the Lord but in Isaiah 2:12 it simply says, *"the Lord of hosts will have a day"* and goes on to describe the same thing that's described in Revelation and the other prophets. Similarly, in Zechariah it says, *"a day is coming for the Lord"* and again goes on to describe the same event or series of events. In fact, the KJV renders both of these passages with the *"day of the Lord"* phrasing. The point is, it's not uncommon, especially when translations are being used, for the wording to be shuffled around a bit but clearly the Lord having a day, "a day for the Lord" and "the day of the Lord" are describing the same event. Furthermore, John calls it *"the day of their wrath"* in Revelation 6:17, and *"the day of God almighty"* in Revelation 16:14. Speaking of the New Testament, Acts 2:20 quotes from Joel but there are a handful of original references:

> *1 Thessalonians 5:2 - For you yourselves know full well that the day of the Lord will come just like a thief in the night.*
>
> *2 Thessalonians 2:1-2 - Now we request you, brethren, with regard to the coming of our Lord Jesus Christ and our gathering together to Him, that you not be quickly shaken from your composure or be disturbed either by a spirit or a message or a letter as if from us, to the effect that the day of the Lord has come.*
>
> *2 Peter 3:10 - But the day of the Lord will come like a thief, in which the heavens will pass away with a roar and the elements will be destroyed with intense heat, and the earth and its works will be burned up.*

My intention with all of these quotes is to demonstrate just how frequently this prophetic event was described and referred to. This was something John would have understood well, so is it more likely that he made it a point to record that it was on a Sunday that he had his vision, or was it simply that when he was caught up in the spirit he knew exactly what he was being shown and described it using familiar language? I see no reason why the day on which John had his vision would be important enough to record, however, specifying that what he wrote referred to the same thing other prophets had foreseen is quite important. For those of you keeping score, that's 16 Old Testament and 6 unique New Testament passages, including 2 in Revelation itself where this language is used to describe the exact same future event, yet somehow, we're supposed to believe that this one verse, using similar wording and written in the context of describing that same event, is referring to Sunday instead? Combine this with the fact that, extra-Biblically, there's no record of Sunday or the first day of the week being referred to as "the Lord's day" until some 2-300 years later. It makes much more sense given the context and, frankly just the plain text of the rest of Revelation, that *"the Lord's day"* in the first chapter is a reference to the return of the Messiah which takes us back to zero references for a "set-apart" first day of the week.

Earlier, I mentioned we'd get into the historical record to explain the shift in the primary day of worship from the last day of the week to the first. We've established there are myriad references to early Christians observing the Sabbath and doing so on the last day of the week as instructed by Yah through Torah. We've also established that there are zero references to anyone in the Bible observing the first day of the week as a holy day. The question we're left with is, if Yah, under His own authority set aside the last day of the week as holy, under whose authority was the last day of the week declared "normal" and the first day of the week set apart as holy instead?

The short answer is, mankind did and, to put it bluntly, that should be the end of this topic. Yah said the last day of the week is holy and a perpetual covenant, a sign between Him and His people, and man came along in the late 300's AD and said, no, no, we'll set aside the first day of the week instead. Matthew 15:9 comes to mind:

In vain do they worship me, teaching as doctrines the commandments of men.

The history of this is very simple and is really a sad illustration of man's fallen state expressing itself through the anti-Semitism of Rome and the early Catholic church. Yeshua's death and resurrection, among other things, tore down the middle wall of partition between Jew and Gentile. It did not take long for man, in his brokenness, to try to put that dividing wall back up leaving early Christians in a precarious position. While Christianity was made illegal and early followers of Yeshua were being persecuted (see Acts 8), Judaism was somewhat tolerated, albeit abusively and oppressively, so long as Jews obeyed Roman laws and paid their taxes. When the Jews rebelled, and the temple was destroyed as a response to that rebellion in 70 A.D., that limited tolerance came to a harsh close. At the time, Rome's predominant religions were forms of sun worship, where rest was taken on "the day of the sun", or Sun-day; the first day of the week. For Jews and first through third century Christians, the practice of observing the Sabbath made one stand out from the cultural crowd, and clearly identified a person as either Jew or Christian and, to the Roman Empire, either was an acceptable target. Essentially being a Sabbath keeper put one's life at risk, so in the early centuries, many Christian's stopped observing the Sabbath and began keeping Sun-day "holy" because it was safer to blend in. Remember what Yeshua had to say about those who would seek to save their lives in this way (Matthew 16:25, Mark 8:35, Luke 9:24).

Finally, as the legend goes, Constantine became a Christian and made Christianity the official religion of the Roman Empire after having a vision. Sadly, all that narrative seems to be is a legend. The historical facts indicate that Constantine was just as pagan throughout his life, until his death, as he was prior to his so-called conversion. The reality is, Constantine hated Jews and the Jewish sect that came to be called Christianity. In his anti-Semitism he sought to condemn any who would associate themselves with Hebrew people or practices. Doing "Jewish" things or observing "Jewish" customs came to be known as Judaizing, and in Constantine's Rome, that type of behavior would not be tolerated. What Constantine was doing was creating a new state religion, which he called Christianity, but which bore very little resemblance to the Torah observant life of the Jewish carpenter from Nazareth or the Torah observant lifestyle of this Jewish Messiah's followers.

One might say Constantine started the very first ecumenical movement with the intention of pulling the various religions across the empire into a single universal faith. The Christianity that Constantine created would, in time, come to include a sort of Roman Jesus that was only superficially similar to Yeshua. This new religion mixed Jewish wisdom, Gospel truth, and Roman paganism to create something that was distinctly different than the faith of Paul, Peter, Stephen, et al. To this end, one of the first things he did to establish this religion was to codify its own day of rest distinct from what he saw as the "Jews day of rest". Thus, on March 7 of the year 321, borrowing from familiar Sun worship traditions, Sunday was made the official day of worship for Roman Christianity with the following declaration:

> "On the venerable Day of the Sun let the magistrates and people residing in cities rest, and let all workshops be closed."

A few decades later, in 364, the Catholic Church officially adopted Sunday, co-opting the term "the Lord's day" to describe the new "Christian" day of rest emphasizing that to observe the Sabbath was to "Judaize"; a derogatory term for daring to believe and follow Yah's Biblical instruction rather than accede to the Catholic church's authority. At the Council of Laodicea, Canon 29 was ratified which read:

> "Christians must not judaize by resting on the Sabbath, but must work on that day, rather honouring the Lord's Day; and, if they can, resting then as Christians. But if any shall be found to be judaizers, let them be anathema from Christ."

And with that, Sunday became official from both a state and a religious perspective as a holy day. Just to be clear, this is not some sort of hidden history that only those on the fringes would believe nor a conspiracy theory with no basis. Quite the contrary. These are facts of which the Catholic Church is quite proud. Consider the words of archbishop James Gibbons from his book, "The Faith of our Fathers":

> "You may read the Bible from Genesis to Revelation, and you will not find a single line authorizing the sanctification of Sunday. The Scriptures enforce

the religious observance of Saturday, a day which we [the Catholic Church] never sanctify." (Gibbons, p. 89)

When questioned about this statement, H.F. Thomas, Gibbons' Chancellor, responded saying:

"Of course the Catholic Church claims that the change [Saturday Sabbath to Sunday] was her act... And the act is a mark of her ecclesiastical authority in religious things"

Now, almost 1700 years later, it is such an old tradition that no one questions it. But it should absolutely be questioned and then immediately abandoned. First and foremost, under what authority did the Catholic Church overrule Yah in not only establishing a new holy day but in condemning the day Yah made holy? Their answer is fascinating:

"Question: How prove you that the Church hath power to command feasts and holydays?

Answer: By the very act of changing the Sabbath into Sunday, which Protestants allow of; and therefore they fondly contradict themselves, by keeping Sunday strictly, and breaking most other feasts commanded by the same Church." (Tuberville, p.58)

Did you catch the logic there? The claim of authority to change Yah's holy days is proven by the fact that they changed Yah's holy days! What? That's like me stealing your car and then saying my proof of ownership of the car is the fact that I took it. Here it is again:

"Q. Have you any other way of proving that the Church has power to institute festivals of precept?
A. Had she not such power, she could not have done that in which all modern religionists agree with her; —she could not have substituted the observance of Sunday the first day of the week, for the observance of Saturday the seventh day, a change for which there is no Scriptural authority. (Keenan, p. 174)

And again:

"Question: Why do we observe Sunday instead of Saturday?
Answer: We observe Sunday instead of Saturday because the Catholic Church transferred the solemnity from Saturday to Sunday." (Geiermann, p. 50)

And one more:

> "Sunday is our mark of authority... the church is above the Bible, and this transference of Sabbath observance is proof of that fact" (Catholic Record of London, Ontario Sept 1, 1923).

Sure. The Catholic Church's ability to transfer the Sabbath had nothing to do with a Roman power structure behind the church that would hunt you down and either crucify you or throw you in the Colosseum if you were a Christian caught resting on the Biblical Sabbath because you were "Judaizing". This is one of the many places where the Protestant reformation didn't go far enough in separating itself from Catholicism. Just note the choice of words that begin that statement (and end H.F. Thomas' statement). "Sunday is our mark of authority". As we've seen, the Bible says the Sabbath was established as Yah's mark of authority which places these Catholic assertions at the very center of a spirit of rebellion against Him.

I'm surprised by how many Protestants aren't familiar with where Sunday worship came from. Considering the sola scriptura (Scripture alone) concept of the five solas of the Protestant reformation, one would think that the lack of Biblical support for such a shift would have immediately put the fourth commandment back on the table and Protestants would have returned to observing the last day of the week as holy. For some reason, that hasn't happened. This fact has not gone unnoticed by the Catholic Church. Here are a few quotes that should give my Protestant friends serious pause (emphasis mine):

> "The [Roman Catholic] Church changed the observance of the Sabbath to Sunday by right of the divine, infallible authority given to her by her founder, Jesus Christ. **The Protestant claiming the Bible to be the only guide of faith, has no warrant for observing Sunday.** In this matter the Seventh-day Adventist is the only consistent Protestant." The Catholic Universe Bulletin, August 14, 1942, p. 4.

> "But since Saturday, not Sunday, is specified in the Bible, isn't it curious that non-Catholics who profess to take their religion directly from the Bible and not the Church, observe Sunday instead of Saturday? Yes, of course, it is inconsistent; but this change was made about fifteen centuries before Protestantism was born, and by that time the custom was universally observed. **They have continued the custom, even though it rests upon the authority of the Catholic Church and not upon an explicit text in the Bi-**

ble. That observance remains as a reminder of the Mother Church from which the non-Catholic sects broke away - like a boy running away from home but still carrying in his pocket a picture of his mother or a lock of her hair." (O'Brien)

"If Protestants would follow the Bible, they would worship God on the Sabbath Day. **In keeping the Sunday they are following a law of the Catholic Church.**" (Smith, February 10, 1920)

"**The observance of Sunday by the Protestants is homage they pay**, in spite of themselves, **to the authority of the [Catholic] Church.**" (Segur, p. 213)

"The Sabbath was Saturday, not Sunday. The Church altered the observance of the Sabbath to the observance of Sunday. Protestants must be rather puzzled by the keeping of Sunday when God distinctly said, 'Keep holy the Sabbath Day.' The word Sunday does not come anywhere in the Bible, so, **without knowing it they are obeying the authority of the Catholic Church.**" (Spirago, p. 89)

A tract from the Library of Christian Doctrine drives to the heart of the matter rather forcefully, making the same point I'm making here even going so far as acknowledging what I've proven out in the previous section; that there is no portion of Scripture that supports the altering or abandonment of the seventh day Sabbath.

> What Important Question Does the Papacy Ask Protestants?
> Protestants have repeatedly asked the papacy, "How could you dare to change God's law?" But the question posed to Protestants by the Catholic church is even more penetrating.
> Here it is officially: ""You will tell me that Saturday was the Jewish Sabbath, but that the Christian Sabbath has been changed to Sunday. Changed! but by whom? Who has authority to change an express commandment of Almighty God? When God has spoken and said, Thou shalt keep holy the seventh day, who shall dare to say, Nay, thou mayest work and do all manner of worldly business on the seventh day; but thou shalt keep holy the first day in its stead?
> This is a most important question, which I know not how you can answer. You are a Protestant, and you profess to go by the Bible and the Bible only; and yet in so important a matter as the observance of one day in seven as a holy day, you go against the plain letter of the Bible, and put another day in the place of that day which the Bible has commanded.
> The command to keep holy the seventh day is one of the ten commandments; you believe that the other nine are still binding; who gave you authority to tamper with the fourth? If you are consistent with your own

principles, if you really follow the Bible and the Bible only, you ought to be able to produce some portion of the New Testament in which this fourth commandment is expressly altered."" (Library of Christian Doctrine, p. 3, 4)

Finally, it pains me to agree with archbishop Gibbons but he's absolutely right when he asserts the following:

"Reason and sense demand the acceptance of one or the other of these alternatives: either Protestantism and the keeping holy of Saturday, or Catholicity and the keeping holy of Sunday. Compromise is impossible." (Gibbons, The Catholic Mirror, December 23, 1893)

The choice we all have, whether the history of these things has been previously known by us or not, is whether we will bend the knee to Yah and obey His instruction once the truth is revealed to us. Considering how clear the Bible is, on the day of judgement I seriously doubt that "I never knew" or "no one ever told me" will be a valid defense for anyone, let alone anyone with a Bible in his or her own language.

CHAPTER 12

Holidays or Holy Days

Part of the goal of this book is to encourage everyone who reads it take a closer look at what they've been told the Bible says, and dig deeper into it to determine if what they were taught is accurate. Whether you agree with me or not, we all need to understand how our practices came to be, studying the Word to see if our traditions fit with the truth of Scripture. Anything that doesn't has to go. Which leads us to quite possibly the most inflammatory subject I'll bring up: Christmas and Easter.

If you recall, at the beginning of the chapter we looked at the story of Aaron's sons, Nadab and Abihu, who were consumed by holy fire for presuming to worship in a way they weren't instructed. To summarize my position regarding contemporary Torah observance I would simply characterize it as, "doing Bible things in Bible ways" to explain why certain things, like the Sabbath, are observed by those who believe as I do, but we don't follow all of Torah, for instance we can't observe Temple rites because there's no Temple. Since we can't do those things the way Torah instructs us to, we wait until Yeshua's return to do them as the prophets tell us we will. Among other things, we learn from Nadab and Abihu's example that it's better to wait on Yah than it is to try and strike out on our own and do Bible things our own way.

A slightly different but conceptually similar problem is in attempting to adapt and apply what we learn from the culture in which we live to our worship. It's another example of doing Bible things our own way but instead of coming up with something new, as did Nadab and Abihu, we borrow from the world around us. Torah warns us against this in Deuteronomy 12:

> [29] "When the Lord your God cuts off before you the nations which you are going in to dispossess, and you dispossess them and dwell in their land, [30] beware that you are not ensnared to follow them, after they are destroyed before you, and that you do not inquire after their gods, saying, 'How do these nations serve their gods, that I also may do likewise?' [31] You shall not behave thus toward the Lord your God, for every abominable act which the Lord hates they have done for their gods; for they even burn their sons and daughters in the fire to their gods.

Notice here that the intention behind verse 30 could be explained away as good, just as Nadab and Abihu's zeal could be considered a positive thing had it not led to their deaths. Yah recognizes that His people will want to offer Him praise and worship and, in their zeal, may look to the practices and customs of the people in the land Yah is giving them so He warns them to stick to His instructions and not incorporate other forms of worship or pagan practices into their veneration of Him. Perhaps the reason Yah issued this warning is because this problem had already come up.

Back in Exodus, while Moses is up on the mountain with Yah, the mixed multitude ran into an interesting problem that caused a great deal of strife. They thought Moses had died and became concerned about who would mediate between them and Yah in Moses' place. It's likely a familiar story to many of you, however, if you're like me, some truths about the story have been left out of your Christian education. The story is that of the golden calf relayed in Exodus 32:

> [1] Now when the people saw that Moses delayed to come down from the mountain, the people assembled about Aaron and said to him, "Come, make us a god who will go before us; as for this Moses, the man who brought us up from the land of Egypt, we do not know what has become of him." [2] Aaron said to them, "Tear off the gold rings which are in the ears of your wives, your sons, and your daughters, and bring them to me." [3] Then all the people tore off the gold rings which were in their ears and brought them to Aaron. [4] He took this from their hand, and fashioned it with a graving tool and made it into a molten calf; and they said, "This is your god, O Israel, who brought you up from the land of Egypt." [5] Now when Aaron saw this, he built an altar before it; and Aaron made a proclamation and said, "Tomorrow shall be a feast to the Lord." [6] So the next

> day they rose early and offered burnt offerings, and brought peace offerings; and the people sat down to eat and to drink, and rose up to play.
>
> [7] Then the Lord spoke to Moses, "Go down at once, for your people, whom you brought up from the land of Egypt, have corrupted themselves. [8] They have quickly turned aside from the way which I commanded them. They have made for themselves a molten calf, and have worshiped it and have sacrificed to it and said, 'This is your god, O Israel, who brought you up from the land of Egypt!'" [9] The Lord said to Moses, "I have seen this people, and behold, they are an obstinate people. [10] Now then let Me alone, that My anger may burn against them and that I may destroy them; and I will make of you a great nation."

Throughout my Protestant upbringing I was taught that this was a story warning of the dangers of idolatry. That somehow the Israelites had forgotten the miracles that had just happened and by whom they were performed and endeavored to make themselves a new god distinct from Yah. Is that true? Not quite, but the mistake is understandable in a sense because of the translation in play and centuries of misguided teaching. In verse 1 we find the people asking Aaron to *"make us a god who will go before us"* and in verse 4, of the golden calf Aaron says, *"This is your god…"*. So why isn't this a simple case of idolatry? Well the key that there's something else happening is verse 5 when Aaron proclaims, *"Tomorrow shall be a feast to the Lord"*. This indicates that whatever they're doing, they aren't doing it to worship and make offerings to a false god, or idol, their intention is to honor Yah. The problem is with the common but mistaken understanding of the word translated "god" in the previously referenced verses. To clarify this, let's look back at what Yah said to Moses at the burning bush in Exodus 4:

> [14] Then the anger of the Lord burned against Moses, and He said, "Is there not your brother Aaron the Levite? I know that he speaks fluently. And moreover, behold, he is coming out to meet you; when he sees you, he will be glad in his heart. [15] You are to speak to him and put the words in his mouth; and I, even I, will be with your mouth and his mouth, and I will teach you what you are to do. [16] Moreover, he shall speak for you to the people; and he will be as a mouth for you **and you will be as God to him**. [17] You shall take in your hand this staff, with which you shall perform the signs."

If you recall from the discussion of the word "elohim" in the first chapter of this book, the word means "strong leader" and while it often refers to THE strong leader, Yah, it is used in other ways as we see here. Additionally, remember that the word "as" is not present in the original Hebrew text. It should read "and you will be elohim to him". There's just no need to add a word here, as the translators have done, unless you've replaced the word instead of translating it. Remember the word "God/god" has been used in place of the word "elohim" rather than simply translating elohim as strong leader.

This idea is repeated in Exodus 7:1:

> Then the Lord said to Moses, "See, **I make you as God to Pharaoh**, and your brother Aaron shall be your prophet.

Again, if we leave the word "elohim" untranslated it would read, "I make you elohim to Pharoah" or, if we translate it properly, "I make you a strong leader to Pharoah". Clearly Yah has not made Moses God in the sense that we normally think of the word "God". Also, I don't believe it should be capitalized in English translations. What's actually being described is something more like an intermediary; Yah's representative.

Another aspect to understand about Yah is the Hebrew character that represents Yah in the Hebrew alphabet. Originally, Hebrew was a pictographic language and the symbol, if you will, for elohim was the head of an ox or bull. It represented the idea of the strong leader and ties in with the yoke metaphors used in Scripture (Matthew 11:29-30).

With these two concepts about the word "elohim" in mind, let's take a closer look at what's happening in the story of the golden calf. In the first verse of Exodus 32, we're informed of the problem:

> Now when the people saw that Moses delayed to come down from the mountain, the people assembled about Aaron and said to him, "Come, make us a god who will go before us; as for this Moses, the man who brought us up from the land of Egypt, we do not know what has become of him."

The people had obviously been witness to the plagues of Egypt and the parting of the Red Sea but they've been somewhat insulated from direct contact with Yah because Moses had acted as an intermediary. Just as Yah said, Moses had become elohim to them – a strong leader that represented them before Yah. With Moses gone, presumed dead, they're pretty nervous. They did not, as many teach, ask Aaron to make them a false god. They actually said, "Come, make us a strong leader who will go before us". This is why, in the span of two verses Aaron can say "this is your elohim, O Israel" and "Tomorrow shall be a feast to YHVH".

> *⁴ He took this from their hand, and fashioned it with a graving tool and made it into a molten calf; and they said, "This is your god, O Israel, who brought you up from the land of Egypt." ⁵ Now when Aaron saw this, he built an altar before it; and Aaron made a proclamation and said, "Tomorrow shall be a feast to the Lord."*

What Aaron made was not a new god, nor was it an idol of a false god. It was an intermediary to stand in place of Moses. A strong leader replacement, as it were. In the four hundred years the descendants of Jacob had spent in Egypt they learned how the Egyptians worshipped their gods which included fashioning an intermediary that was in some way a representation of the deity. They would then pray to, worship and make offerings to the intermediary because they feared direct contact with the god itself. It shouldn't be surprising that when the 3 million plus people became concerned that Moses might be dead, they fell back on what had become familiar to them in Egypt, which was to simply make an intermediary, and of course, a representation of a strong leader, or elohim, would have to be an ox or bull. In this case, a golden calf.

All of this explanation is intended to point out that this event was not simple idol worship. The infraction was that they tried to worship Yah in the way that pagan nations worship their gods. They hadn't magically forgotten everything they had just witnessed, nor were they under the impression that the golden calf was Yah. They had an honest desire to continue in their communion with Yah but didn't know how to do that without Moses, so they made a Moses the only way they knew how; the Egyptian way.

What does all of this have to do with Christmas and Easter? We've already looked at how Constantine and the early church declared a shift in the primary day of worship from the Sabbath to the first day of the week and the history of Christmas and Easter follows a similar pattern. There were so many pagan religions that were foundationally sun worship cults that it made pragmatic sense to co-opt the already established day of worship and simply say, "last Sunday we worshipped all these sun gods, this Sunday we'll worship Jesus". And just like that, a pagan practice was "Christianized", as if one can take something Yah has not made holy and declare it holy on man's authority alone. This fact is stated plainly in Job 14:4:

> "Who can make the clean out of the unclean?
> No one!

I'll leave it for my readers to research the details of Christmas and Easter on their own simply because the pagan origins of Christmas and Easter are universally recognized and nearly undisputed. The only debate is whether those origins pose a problem or not. Modern Christianity says those origins do not pose a problem for a variety of reasons. From here forward I'll pick on Christmas but the same objections I'll raise apply equally to Easter. Consider an article about Christmas from "Christianity Today":

> Q: A friend says her church doesn't celebrate Christmas because it began as a pagan holiday. Why then do most churches celebrate Christmas? — Brian Smith, via the Internet.
>
> A: Was the event we now call Christmas originally a "pagan holiday"? In some ways. Does that mean the church should discard it, along with its lights, tinsel, and increasing commercialism? Only if we are prepared to abandon many other holidays and common Christian practices that the early church co-opted for its own purpose of glorifying Christ
>
> Christmas has its origins in the fourth century. December 25, which Christians now herald as Jesus' birthday, was actually the date on which the Romans celebrated the birth of the sun god. (Christianity Today)

From the start, you should notice a big problem. The author acknowledges that Christmas was based on pagan observances and asks if that means the church should discard it. The author's conclusion is no, on the grounds that so many other pagan things would have to be ejected as well. What? So, we shouldn't get rid of pagan things in our worship of a holy God because there are so many pagan things to get rid of? That is fascinating reasoning. Back to the question though, should the church discard a practice because it was originally pagan? According to Yah's actual words, yes, we should discard it along with everything else that has been co-opted from pagan practices.

In addition to the concepts of not worshipping any way we please and not worshipping Yah the way pagans worship their gods, there are three other relevant concepts here. One is the idea of leavening, another is the relationship between light and darkness and the last is worshipping in truth. In Galatians 5 we find the following passage:

> [2] Behold I, Paul, say to you that if you receive circumcision, Christ will be of no benefit to you. [3] And I testify again to every man who receives circumcision, that he is under obligation to keep the whole Law. [4] You have been severed from Christ, you who are seeking to be justified by law; you have fallen from grace. [5] For we through the Spirit, by faith, are waiting for the hope of righteousness. [6] For in Christ Jesus neither circumcision nor uncircumcision means anything, but faith working through love.
>
> [7] You were running well; who hindered you from obeying the truth? [8] This persuasion did not come from Him who calls you. [9] A little leaven leavens the whole lump of dough. [10] I have confidence in you in the Lord that you will adopt no other view; but the one who is disturbing you will bear his judgment, whoever he is. [11] But I, brethren, if I still preach circumcision, why am I still persecuted? Then the stumbling block of the cross has been abolished. [12] I wish that those who are troubling you would even mutilate themselves.

I've included the entire passage so as not to be accused of leaving out important truths, and some may look at verses 2-6 and suggest they refute everything I've written. As I explained in a previous chapter, Paul is not preaching against circumcision here, he's addressing the same concept that he addressed in Romans where some were insisting that circumcision was a pre-requisite to salvation through Yeshua. Paul is being very clear here in saying that if you are trying to gain salvation by your obedience, Christ is of no benefit to you. He's not suggesting that no one should get circumcised as an obedient response to salvation. To verify this, simply jump ahead to verse 11. If he's teaching against circumcision why would he say, *"why am I persecuted even though I still preach circumcision"*? The distinction he's making is between obedience as a result of salvation and obedience as a means to secure salvation. He's not saying obedience (in this case in matters of circumcision) is no longer necessary, nor is he saying those who attempt to obey Torah have made Christ meaningless. He also says, *"you who are seeking to be justified by law; you have fallen from grace"* but people like me, for instance, are not seeking to be justified by the Law. I endeavor to obey the Law because I have already been justified by grace and as such I'm free of the yoke of sin that once ruled my life and drove me to disobedience. That doesn't mean I have no yoke, it means I share the yoke of Yeshua, the strong leader who teaches me how to walk by the way He walks – according to Torah.

With that made clearer, let's look closely at verses 7-9. Paul is saying (if Paul were a Southerner), "y'all were doing pretty good, who filled your head with these false ideas that are causing you to stumble". To illustrate this, Paul uses the metaphor of leaven. Just as leaven when added to a batch of dough will spread to the whole lump, so too will false ideas about Yah spread and contaminate the life of a believer. The mixing of ideas is clearly in view here. In the context of Christmas, Easter, and, for that matter, the abandoning of the Sabbath in favor of Sunday worship, there has clearly been a mixing of the pagan with the holy. Not only is there no biblical basis for embracing such a mixing, the Bible specifically instructs against it. There's a similar concept enshrined in the Levitical instruction against mixing cotton and linen. Practically speaking the two threads shrink at different rates so if you have clothing that's a mixture, it will wear out more quickly because the fabric that shrinks more quickly will pull at and tear apart the other. Beyond the practical wisdom of this lies the spiritual truth that if one tries to mix wickedness with righteousness, the wickedness will pull at and tear apart one's life. Again, the principal is clear. What Yah has set apart as holy is not to be mixed with that which is contrary to Him and that includes pagan practices and the ways non-believers worship their gods.

The other way the Bible expresses this concept is the contrast between light and darkness. Perhaps the most well-known is 2 Corinthians 6:14:

> Do not be bound together with unbelievers; for what partnership have righteousness and lawlessness, or what fellowship has light with darkness?

In other translations, verse 14 begins, *"Do not be yoked with unbelievers"*, which gives us a better sense of what this passage is talking about and what it means in the last half of the verse when it asks, *"what fellowship has light with darkness?"* It's talking about the same idea of walking together or learning the way that Yeshua talked about when He offered us rest if we would but *"take His yoke upon us and learn from Him"*. Whereas Yeshua was inviting us to learn His ways, Paul is warning us not to walk the way unbelievers do and proceeds to point out a list of things that simply don't mix starting with light and darkness. The contrast is well established in the Old Testament, for instance Proverbs 4:18-19 says:

> [18] But the path of the righteous is like the light of dawn,
> That shines brighter and brighter until the full day.
> [19] The way of the wicked is like darkness;
> They do not know over what they stumble.

Or, compare Isaiah 2:3,5:

> [3] And many peoples will come and say,
> "Come, let us go up to the mountain of the Lord,
> To the house of the God of Jacob;
> That He may teach us concerning His ways
> And that we may walk in His paths."
> For the law will go forth from Zion
> And the word of the Lord from Jerusalem.
> ...
> [5] Come, house of Jacob, and let us walk in the light of the Lord.

with Isaiah 8:20:

> [20] To the law and to the testimony: if they speak not according to this word, it is because there is no light in them. (KJV)

Between the two, we see the contrast between light and darkness where, in Isaiah 2:5 the invitation to come learn and walk according to Torah is summarized in the phrase, *"Come, let us walk in the light"*, while in Isaiah 8:20, those who don't walk according to Yah's instructions are related to darkness.

As an aside, both of these verses are talking about a time during Yeshua's reign on earth after His second coming, indicating that in the future, whether a person walks in the light or in darkness is measured by Torah obedience. As I've said before, if walking as Yeshua walked, according to Yah's instructions, was the measure of light and darkness before Yeshua's death and resurrection, and will be the measure upon His return, it's reasonable to believe it's the measure today.

Returning to the point, the contrast between light and darkness is continued in the New Testament. For instance, John 8:12 says:

> [12] *Then spake Jesus again unto them, saying, I am the light of the world: he that followeth me shall not walk in darkness, but shall have the light of life.*

And in 1 Peter 2 we find the following:

> [9] *But you are a chosen race, a royal priesthood, a holy nation, a people for God's own possession, so that you may proclaim the excellencies of Him who has called you out of darkness into His marvelous light;*

What's important to notice about these references is, it's one or the other. There's no half way. There's no mixing light and darkness and while Paul does a succinct job of describing that in the first verse we looked at, 2 Corinthians 6:14, Isaiah 5:20 leaves no uncertainty:

> *Woe to those who call evil good, and good evil;*
> *Who substitute darkness for light and light for darkness;*
> *Who substitute bitter for sweet and sweet for bitter!*

As it relates to Christmas and Easter, no matter how much they've been polished up with a Christian veneer, the traditions and practices Christian's engage in on these days are firmly rooted in the darkness of ancient paganism. Is that not calling evil, good? And from what we've learned about the goodness of Torah, is abandoning Yah's set apart times on the grounds that

Torah is bondage not calling good, evil? Bluntly put, in replacing His holy days with man's holidays have we not tried to substitute light with darkness?

Finally, what of worshipping in truth? Yeshua said the following in the fourth chapter of John:

> [23] But an hour is coming, and now is, when the true worshipers will worship the Father in spirit and truth; for such people, the Father seeks to be His worshipers. [24] God is spirit, and those who worship Him must worship in spirit and truth."

Yeshua was not born on December 25th so is worshipping him for his birthday on a day he wasn't born worshipping in truth? Is it a problem that, as the ChristianityToday article referenced previously acknowledges, "December 25, which Christians now herald as Jesus' birthday, was actually the date on which the Romans celebrated the birth of the sun god."? Isn't that calling darkness, light? The truth is nearly ALL of the trappings of Christmas are grounded in falsehoods. Gift giving, stockings, Santa Claus, Christmas trees, gingerbread men, December 25th, all of it comes from a variety of pagan celebrations, and none of it has anything to do with the objective truth of Yah. For those who have ever lamented that we should "put Christ back in Christmas", I would suggest that He never should have been put there to begin with. Sadly, like so many things, it happened so long ago that the majority of Christians don't question it. But clearly it should be questioned.

Let's do a little thought experiment to remove the time factor from these traditions. At issue here is the idea of taking a holiday celebrated by a non-Biblical religion, putting a Christian spin on it and calling it a "holy day". The largest religion in the world next to Christianity (Catholic and Protestant combined) is Islam. In Islam, the month of Ramadan is observed as a month of fasting to commemorate the revelation of the Quran to Mohammed. What if I were to tell you that this year, I'll be observing Ramadan, but I'm not Muslim, I'm simply going to fast in commemoration of the revelation of the New Testament. In essence, I'm going to Christianize Ramadan and then celebrate it in the name of Yeshua. That would be crazy, right? There's no biblical basis for it, my Muslim friends would probably be offended, and my

Christian and Jewish friends would be, at best, very confused. But, let's say it catches on for some reason and 1,000 years from now Christians the world over celebrate Ramadan. Would that be a problem? Be careful with your answer because if you don't think it's appropriate to observe Ramadan in the name of Yeshua, it's not appropriate to observe Christmas or Easter in His name either. The temporal separation we have from the original Christianizing of pagan practices is no excuse for our continuing to apply pagan forms of worship to our worship of Yah.

There is another problem with these so-called holidays. As we've seen, it's good to observe that which Yah has instructed but not so good if we try to modify or add to it. It's worse to ignore that which Yah has instructed and observe man made celebrations instead. Just as Sunday worship didn't just change the primary day of worship but essentially ended and replaced Sabbath observance for Christians, so too have Christmas and Easter not just added to Yah's 7 holy days, but they've effectively replaced them and ended their observance among believers. Sadly, much has been lost as a result, most importantly as it affects our relationship with, and understanding of, Yeshua.

The Hebrew word for Yah's holy days is moadim, which means "appointed times" and in Exodus seven appointed times are outlined: Passover, The Feast of Unleavened Bread, Firstfruits, the Feast of Weeks (Shavuot/Pentecost), The Day of Trumpets (Yom Teruah), the Day of Atonement (Yom Kippur), and The Feast of Tabernacles (Sukkot). The first 4 are known as the spring feasts while the latter 3 are known as the fall feasts. Interestingly, Yeshua illustrated and fulfilled the true meaning of the spring feasts in His first coming. That pattern combined with prophecy about His second coming makes it quite reasonable to believe that He will fulfill the true meaning of the fall feasts when He returns. When I say true meaning, what I mean is each of the moadim was established to commemorate an event or teach an important truth when they were established but each one also foreshadows future events in the life of the Messiah. Let's look more closely at each one.

I already covered many of the similarities between Passover and Yeshua's death and resurrection previously, but to summarize, Passover was to act as a commemoration of the Exodus but it also foreshadowed the Messiah coming as a spotless lamb whose blood would cover us and protect us from Yah's wrath, just as the blood of the lamb over the doorposts of one's home protected Yah's people from the tenth plague. Consider Exodus 12:5 and 1 Peter 1:18-19:

> Exodus 12:5 - Your lamb shall be an unblemished male a year old; you may take it from the sheep or from the goats.
>
> 1 Peter 1:18-19 - knowing that you were not redeemed with perishable things like silver or gold from your futile way of life inherited from your forefathers, but with precious blood, as of a lamb unblemished and spotless, the blood of Christ.

Add to that Exodus 12:46 and John 19:33-36

> Exodus 12:46 - It is to be eaten in a single house; you are not to bring forth any of the flesh outside of the house, nor are you to break any bone of it.
>
> John 19:33-36 - but coming to Jesus, when they saw that He was already dead, they did not break His legs. But one of the soldiers pierced His side with a spear, and immediately blood and water came out. And he who has seen has testified, and his testimony is true; and he knows that he is telling the truth, so that you also may believe. For these things came to pass to fulfill the Scripture, "Not a bone of Him shall be broken."

In addition, the lamb was to be brought into the home on the 10th day of the first month, the very day that Yeshua rode into Jerusalem on a donkey. Finally, the lamb was to be inspected and only sacrificed if found spotless. This directly mirrors the trials of Yeshua, where His life was inspected and time and time again He was found perfectly innocent; spotless. In Matthew 26 we find the results of Yeshua's inspection by the very same priests that were examining lambs for the coming Passover sacrifices.

> [59] Now the chief priests and the whole Council kept trying to obtain false testimony against Jesus, so that they might put Him to death. [60] They did not find any, even though many false witnesses came forward.

And, of course, we find Pilate's conclusion, and by proxy, Herod's, in Luke 23:13-15 (also see John 19:4):

> [13] Pilate summoned the chief priests and the rulers and the people, [14] and said to them, "You brought this man to me as one who incites the people to rebellion, and behold, having examined Him before you, I have found no guilt in this man regarding the charges which you make against Him. [15] No, nor has Herod, for he sent Him back to us; and behold, nothing deserving death has been done by Him.

Beyond these details, the core of Passover is our deliverance from bondage. In the Exodus, it marked freedom from slavery to Egypt while Yeshua's death freed us from the bondage of slavery to sin.

Next comes the Feast of Unleavened Bread, which is a week-long observance where all the leaven is to be removed from one's house, leaven being a symbol of sin or, more particularly, thoughts, concepts, and behaviors that have crept into our lives but have no place in our lives as followers of Yeshua. This feast serves as a demonstration of ridding one's life of those things that are contrary to our holy calling and pointed forward to the time when the Messiah would sweep our records clean of the leaven of our disobedience.

The third spring feast is a harvest celebration where we take the first fruits or the first and best of our bounty and offer it to Yah. This points to Yeshua being the first to be resurrected from the dead, the first and best of a coming harvest. While the original instruction used the physical harvest as a teaching tool, the intent was to point forward to the spiritual harvest Yeshua referred to in Matthew 9:

> [36] Seeing the people, He felt compassion for them, because they were distressed and dispirited like sheep without a shepherd. [37] Then He said to His disciples, "The harvest is plentiful, but the workers are few. [38] Therefore beseech the Lord of the harvest to send out workers into His harvest."

In this spiritual harvest, someone had to be raised first, and of course that someone was Yeshua, as Paul pointed out in 1 Corinthians 15:20:

> But now Christ has been raised from the dead, the first fruits of those who are asleep.

Finally, we have Shavuot, or the Feast of Weeks, more commonly known in the Christian world as Pentecost. As originally ordained, Shavuot acted as a commemoration of Yah giving instruction to His people in the form of Torah fifty days after Passover. In the life of Yeshua, this foreshadowed the pouring out of the Holy Spirit fifty days after Yeshua's death, which happened on Passover, and marked Yah's writing His Torah on our hearts.

As remarkable as these correlations between the spring feasts and important events in the life of Yeshua are, what's even more remarkable is the timeline that these events followed. The Spring feasts essentially acted as a roadmap to when and why Yeshua's death, burial and resurrection, as well as the pouring out of the Spirit, would happen. What Yah had done in instructing His people to observe the spring feasts was give them an annual demonstration of what was to come. By the time Yeshua was born into this world, the Israelites had been rehearsing the events of His life for thousands of years and many of them still missed it although it's worth noting that many did not and became followers of Yeshua. Is it possible that because Christians have abandoned Yah's feasts in lieu of Christmas and Easter we will miss important details of His return? If those who had rehearsed these moadim for so long missed their true meaning as it unfolded in front of them, what chance is there for those who know nothing about them?

The first of the fall feasts, the Feast of Trumpets (or Yom Teruah in Hebrew) is a rather interesting example as Yah really doesn't say much about what's to be done. Leviticus 23:23-25 describes Yom Teruah simply as a day of rest, *"a reminder by blowing of trumpets"*. It was likely a reminder of Yah's presence at Mt. Sinai which was accompanied by a great and increasing trumpet blast (Exodus 19:16). As we should expect based on the pattern of the spring feasts, it foreshadows an event in Yeshua's life. It points to the announcing of the return of Yeshua which will likewise be marked by the blowing of trumpets as Yeshua described in Matthew 24:

> [30] And then the sign of the Son of Man will appear in the sky, and then all the tribes of the earth will mourn, and they will see the Son of Man coming on the clouds of the sky with power and great glory. [31] And He will send forth His angels with a great trumpet and they will gather together His elect from the four winds, from one end of the sky to the other.

The most astonishing aspect of Yom Teruah is the timing of it. All the other feasts are very precise and calculable. Passover, Unleavened Bread and Firstfruits all start on a specific day in the Hebrew month of Nisan. Several others are what I'll call calculated dates. Shavuot, for instance, is always exactly 50 days after the second day of Passover. Yom Kippur is observed 10 days after Yom Teruah. Sukkot is observed five days after Yom Kippur. They all have very precise and predictable timings. So, what's so unique about Yom Teruah as it relates to the blowing of trumpets preceding Messiah's return? It's to be observed on the first day of the month of Tishri, and the first day of a month cannot be known with precision. To mark out months, the Israelites used a lunar calendar which means a new month starts with the new moon. Obviously, they didn't have the technology we have today so the question becomes, how does one mark the emergence of a new moon and thus mark the first day of a month? Tradition holds that the moment two Israelites see the first sliver of a new moon, that moment starts the month. In other words, no one knows the day or the hour! That should sound very familiar and couples this appointed day even more tightly with Yeshua's return. Speaking on the topic, Yeshua himself said in Matthew 24:36,

> "But of that day and hour no one knows, not even the angels of heaven, nor the Son, but the Father alone."

Based on the fact that the dates I've outlined in Yeshua's life perfectly matched the dates of the spring feasts, I don't think it's a stretch to predict that He'll return on the first day of the Hebrew month of Tishri of some indeterminate future year, but from year to year, no one can say exactly what day or hour that will be.

Following the Day of Trumpets, the next fall holy day, the Day of Atonement (or Yom Kippur), was the only day when the High Priest would enter the holy of holies to offer atonement for the sins of the people. It was a day of judgement and so it will be when Yeshua returns. While some may be under the mistaken impression that believers will face no judgement, Scripture says differently. For instance, in Romans 14:10-12, Paul is speaking to believers when he says:

> [10] But you, why do you judge your brother? Or you again, why do you regard your brother with contempt? For we will all stand before the judgment seat of God.[11] For it is written, "As I live, says the Lord, every knee shall bow to Me, And every tongue shall give praise to God." [12] So then each one of us will give an account of himself to God.

And in 2 Corinthians 5:10, Paul says:

> For we must all appear before the judgment seat of Christ, so that each one may be recompensed for his deeds in the body, according to what he has done, whether good or bad.

While we will face the judgement seat of Christ, for those who follow Yeshua, Yom Kippur is an opportunity for us not only to take stock and repent of those areas in our lives where we need to turn to Him and away from our sins, but also to celebrate the atoning sacrifice of Yeshua on our behalf.

Finally, we come to the Feast of Tabernacles, sometimes called the Feast of Booths, or in Hebrew, Sukkot. The Hebrew word sukkah, the plural of which is sukkot, refers to a temporary dwelling and, in terms of commemoration, acts as a reminder of the temporary dwellings the Israelites lived in following the Exodus. In terms of what it foreshadows, there are actually two important truths regarding the life of Yeshua. The first is that Scripture points to Sukkot as the actual time Yeshua was born, not December 25th. Isn't it fascinating that, when Yeshua came as a human and "tabernacled" among us, it just so happened that there was no room for Mary and Joseph at the inn, forcing them to stay in a temporary dwelling – a sukkah! As it relates to Yeshua's return, this coincides with the marriage supper of the lamb marking the beginning of the millennial kingdom. Again, it's a time when Yah will tabernacle with us as was prophesied by Ezekiel in Ezekiel 37:

> [26] I will make a covenant of peace with them; it will be an everlasting covenant with them. And I will place them and multiply them, and will set My sanctuary in their midst forever. [27] My dwelling place also will be with them; and I will be their God, and they will be My people. [28] And the nations will know that I am the Lord who sanctifies Israel, when My sanctuary is in their midst forever."'"

Understanding what the Feast of Tabernacles points to in Yeshua's life, we can better understand why Yeshua said what he did in John 7:2-8:

> [2] Now the feast of the Jews, the Feast of Booths, was near. [3] Therefore His brothers said to Him, "Leave here and go into Judea, so that Your disciples also may see Your works which You are doing. [4] For no one does anything in secret when he himself seeks to be known publicly. If You do these things, show Yourself to the world." [5] For not even His brothers were believing in Him. [6] So Jesus said to them, "My time is not yet here, but your time is always opportune. [7] The world cannot hate you, but it hates Me because I testify of it, that its deeds are evil. [8] Go up to the feast yourselves; I do not go up to this feast because My time has not yet fully come." [9] Having said these things to them, He stayed in Galilee.

His time had not come, because it will be on His return that He will fulfill the true purpose of Sukkot. It was not time for that during His first coming so He stayed in Galilee while His disciples went to Judea. Finally, let's not forget that Sukkot will be celebrated by all nations when Yeshua reigns in His kingdom on Earth (Zechariah 14:16-17).

I'd like to take brief moment to explain a small nuance as it relates to the previous point. At this point in history Israelites would take a pilgrimage to the Temple for Sukkot, Passover and Shavuot, to comply with Torah instruction. So, when Yeshua stayed in Galilee was He breaking Torah? It's important to note that the instructions in Torah don't say to go to Jerusalem or to the Temple, but to go into Yah's presence. At the time, Yah's presence was external and dwelt in the Temple. Because Yeshua was always in Yah's presence it was entirely legitimate for Him to stay in Galilee without breaking Torah. This also helps to explain why I, and others like me, don't go to Jerusalem today. In those days, Yah's presence was external so one had to go to where He was, but today, for those of us who are saved, Yah's presence is internal through the indwelling Spirit. I've said before that we shouldn't attempt Torah instruction our own way, so it's important to understand that not taking a pilgrimage during Sukkot as was necessary in Yeshua's day, doesn't in any way break Torah's guidelines on observing Sukkot (or Passover and Shavuot) today.

In contrast to what I've described about Yah's holy days, what do Christmas and Easter teach us about Yeshua? I understand that many take the opportunity to read the story of Yeshua's birth during Christmas or perhaps study Scriptures regarding Yeshua's death and resurrection during Easter but what do the days or traditions themselves teach us? In a word, nothing. They are empty save for what any individual chooses to fill them with but have no intrinsic value. The events of Yeshua's first coming perfectly mirrored the dates, timeline, and purpose of the spring feasts. By contrast, nothing in Yeshua's life had anything to do with the winter solstice, December 25th or any of the traditions that are part of Christmas, nor do the date and traditions of Easter have anything to do with His death and resurrection. We're left, then, with an important question. If so much of Yeshua's first coming and return is wrapped up in Yah's appointed times, does it sound wise to have abandoned them in favor of holidays invented by ancient Rome that relate far more to their pagan origins then they do to Yeshua, His life, or His purpose? Simply put, from a spiritual perspective, Christmas and Easter are left void next to the days and times Yah appointed as holy and established as sign posts for us.

CHAPTER 13

There's No Such Thing as Junk Food

The final topic that deserves close scrutiny has to do with Yah's instructions regarding what is and isn't food. As the story goes, since Torah has been abolished, we can eat whatever we'd like regardless of Yah's advice. As you'll see, support for this idea is more of the same: misunderstandings, half-truths, and verses taken out of context. These instructions are given in Leviticus 11 with some additional details and clarifications provided in Deuteronomy 14 and are collectively known as "kashrut", from the Hebrew root word "kasher", which means "fit". In other words, they describe the distinction between those things that are fit to eat and those things that aren't. There's a common misunderstanding that the distinction is between clean foods and unclean foods but that's not correct. There are clean animals and unclean animals, and while the former are to be considered food, the latter are not. It's a subtle distinction but a vitally important one, as we'll see.

Before I get into the practical reasons for Yah's distinction, I'll start by addressing the common objections to these dietary instructions. One of the primary passages used to support the abolishing of Yah's food laws concerns a vision Peter had in Acts 10:

> [9] On the next day, as they were on their way and approaching the city, Peter went up on the housetop about the sixth hour to pray. [10] But he became hungry and was desiring to eat; but while they were making preparations, he fell into a trance; [11] and he saw the sky opened up, and an object like a great sheet coming down, lowered by four corners to the ground, [12] and there were in it all kinds of four-footed animals and crawling creatures of the earth and birds of the air. [13] A voice came to him, "Get up, Peter, kill and eat!" [14] But Peter said, "By no means, Lord, for I have never eaten anything unholy and unclean." [15] Again a voice came to him a second time, "What God has cleansed, no longer consider unholy." [16] This happened three times, and immediately the object was taken up into the sky.

Most people, including pastors and teachers, stop there and say, "see, there's clean and unclean animals and Yah said to eat any of them". It seems compelling. Unless you keep reading. In verse 17-20, we find the following:

> [17] Now while Peter was greatly perplexed in mind as to what the vision which he had seen might be, behold, the men who had been sent by Cornelius, having asked directions for Simon's house, appeared at the gate; [18] and calling out, they were asking whether Simon, who was also called Peter, was staying there. [19] While Peter was reflecting on the vision, the Spirit said to him, "Behold, three men are looking for you. [20] But get up, go downstairs and accompany them without misgivings, for I have sent them Myself."

I'll pause here to point a few things out. First, isn't it interesting that back in verse 14 Peter protests, saying he'd never eaten anything unclean. This was at least 10 years after Yeshua's death and Peter obviously had no notion that the event had somehow cancelled Yah's instructions regarding what is and isn't food. He was still eating kosher.

Additionally, far from concluding that Yah had declared all foods clean through his vision, Peter remained *"greatly perplexed"* about the meaning. It didn't seem possible to him that Yah would contradict His own previous instructions as we're taught today, so what could it possibly mean? The other thing to take note of is the Spirit saying, *"accompany them without misgivings"*. Why would Peter have misgivings? Is it simply because these were strangers to him? Not quite. At this point in history, Jewish tradition held that Gentiles were unclean. We've already seen an illustration of this during Paul's legal troubles in Acts when his accusers charged him with defiling the temple by bringing Gentiles into it (though it's worth pointing out that this too was a false accusation as Acts 21:29 says, *"they assumed that Paul had brought [Trophimus] into the temple"*). Understandably, this was causing some division among the followers of Yeshua. There's even a record of Paul admonishing Peter for refraining from eating with Gentiles when Jews were around (Galatians 2:11-21). Knowing that Peter was prone to think of Gentiles as unclean, Yah knew Peter would have misgivings about associating with the Gentiles Yah was sending.

Getting back to the vision, if we continue to Acts 10:28-29 we find Peter's interpretation:

> [28] And he said to them, "You yourselves know how unlawful it is for a man who is a Jew to associate with a foreigner or to visit him; and yet God has shown me that I should not call any man unholy or unclean. [29] That is why I came without even raising any objection when I was sent for. So, I ask for what reason you have sent for me."

So, there it is. The vision Peter had was not about animals or food at all, but about man, specifically Gentiles. Torah includes no instructions distinguishing between clean and unclean people. Those ideas were added by Rabbinic teaching and the vision Peter was given was Yah's way of telling Peter that He had not declared any man unclean, so Peter had no right to treat anyone as if they were. Yah was preparing Peter's heart for the Gentiles that would come to him. As a result, in the rest of Acts 10 we're given the account of the first Gentiles to be baptized.

This leaves us in an awkward position as it relates to this passage. We can believe what theologians say is the interpretation, or we can believe Peter's interpretation. As usual, I'll stick with the Biblical record and believe Peter interpreted his own vision correctly, and it had nothing to do with food. If there's evidence that the food laws have been abolished, it's not to be found here, so let's move on.

Another primary passage used to support the idea that the food laws are no longer to be obeyed is Romans 14, specifically verse 14:

> I know and am convinced in the Lord Jesus that nothing is unclean in itself; but to him who thinks anything to be unclean, to him it is unclean.

Again, seems pretty cut and dry, but as I continue to point out, it's not a good idea to hang a doctrine on a single verse, so let's look at the context a bit more closely. We looked at part of this passage in chapter 9, and if you'll recall, this section is talking about certain optional fast days:

> [5] One person regards one day above another, another regards every day alike. Each person must be fully convinced in his own mind. [6] He who observes the day, observes it for the Lord, and he who eats, does so for the Lord, for he gives thanks to God; and he who eats not, for the Lord he does not eat, and gives thanks to God.

Paul is pointing out that these fast days are important to some and not to others, but their observance is not required according to Torah so those who observe the day by not eating shouldn't judge those who don't. Let's look at the rest of the verses surrounding verse 14:

> [13] Therefore let us not judge one another anymore, but rather determine this— not to put an obstacle or a stumbling block in a brother's way. [14] I know and am convinced in the Lord Jesus that nothing is unclean in itself; but to him who thinks anything to be unclean, to him it is unclean. [15] For if because of food your brother is hurt, you are no longer walking according to love. Do not destroy with your food him for whom Christ died. [16] Therefore do not let what is for you a good thing be spoken of as evil; [17] for the kingdom of God is not eating and drinking, but righteousness and peace and joy in the Holy Spirit. [18] For he who in this way serves Christ is acceptable to God and approved by men. [19] So then we pursue the things which make for peace and the building up of one another. [20] Do not tear down the work of God for the sake of food. All things indeed are clean, but they are evil for the man who eats and gives offense. [21] It is good not to eat meat or to drink wine, or to do anything by which your brother stumbles. [22] The faith which you have, have as your own conviction before God. Happy is he who does not condemn himself in what he approves. [23] But he who doubts is condemned if he eats, because his eating is not from faith; and whatever is not from faith is sin.

This is a large passage and there is a lot to cover but the summary is, there are some aspects of what Paul is saying that have simply been lost in translation. First let's take a look at two Greek words: "Koinos" and "akathartos". "Akathartos" is the Greek word used in the New Testament to describe unclean animals, while "koinos" is used to refer to things that are, for a variety of reasons, for lack of a better term, contaminated. When we looked at Peter's vision, both words are used in Acts 10:4 when Peter says, *"I've never eaten anything common or unclean" (KJV)*. In the original Greek that would be, *"I've never eaten anything {koinos} or {akathartos}"*. The point is, "koinos" isn't referring to things that were declared unclean by Yah and thus weren't to be considered food, it refers to things that are suspect in their purity but that aren't unfit as food according to Yah's definition. Think of ground beef that's been left out a bit too long. Cattle is a clean – aka edible – animal so the beef is not "akathartos", but it may be "koinos" and for that reason it may be wise to avoid eating it. In verse 14 when Paul says, *"I know and am convinced in the Lord Jesus that nothing is unclean in itself"*, guess what the Greek word is? You got it. "Koinos", not "akathartos", and in this, Paul is absolutely correct; nothing Yah has declared fit as food is suspect in and of itself.

If Paul isn't talking about eating animals Yah told us weren't to be considered food, what is he talking about? To better understand this passage, we have to jump over to 1 Corinthians 8:

> *⁴ Therefore concerning the eating of things sacrificed to idols, we know that there is no such thing as an idol in the world, and that there is no God but one. ⁵ For even if there are so-called gods whether in heaven or on earth, as indeed there are many gods and many lords, ⁶ yet for us there is but one God, the Father, from whom are all things and we exist for Him; and one Lord, Jesus Christ, by whom are all things, and we exist through Him.*
>
> *⁷ However not all men have this knowledge; but some, being accustomed to the idol until now, eat food as if it were sacrificed to an idol; and their conscience being weak is defiled. ⁸ But food will not commend us to God; we are neither the worse if we do not eat, nor the better if we do eat. ⁹ But take care that this liberty of yours does not somehow become a stumbling block to the weak. ¹⁰ For if someone sees you, who have knowledge, dining in an idol's temple, will not his conscience, if he is weak, be strengthened to eat things sacrificed to idols? ¹¹ For through your knowledge he who is weak is ruined, the brother for whose sake Christ died. ¹² And so, by sinning against the brethren and wounding their conscience when it is weak, you sin against Christ. ¹³ Therefore, if food causes my brother to stumble, I will never eat meat again, so that I will not cause my brother to stumble.*

We see here a lot of the same language Paul uses in Romans 14, which shouldn't be surprising considering Paul wrote the two letters very close to one another and actually wrote the letter to the Romans from Corinth where this issue first came up. For instance, compare Romans 14:15 and 1 Corinthians 8:9 and 13:

> *Romans 14:15 - For if because of food your brother is hurt, you are no longer walking according to love. Do not destroy with your food him for whom Christ died.*
>
> *1 Corinthians 8:9 and 13 - But take care that this liberty of yours does not somehow become a stumbling block to the weak...Therefore, if food causes my brother to stumble, I will never eat meat again, so that I will not cause my brother to stumble.*

If you compare the two passages in their entirety, you'll see the same subject is being discussed in both. What's in view is not the eating of clean and unclean animals, but the eating of otherwise clean animals that have been sacrificed to idols. To be more specific, these are animals that were declared fit as food by Torah. The meat in question was not "akathartos" (unfit as food) but there was some question about whether or not it was "koinos" (impure), as a result of having been sacrificed to an idol. Paul is making the point in both letters that idols aren't real, so sacrificing an otherwise clean animal to something that's not real doesn't affect it being fit as food. But, if you're around those who believe those idols are real, it's best not to set what could be perceived as a bad example.

As you'll recall, I pointed out an important distinction between clean and unclean animals and clean and unclean foods. The truth is, there's no such thing as unclean food because the animals that were unclean were not meant to be food. So, in Romans 14:20 when Paul says not to tear down the work of God for the sake of food, he wouldn't be talking about unclean animals because Paul wouldn't have considered them food. This is further supported in the next verse where Paul says it's good not to eat meat or drink wine if it causes a brother to stumble. There was no prohibition against wine in Torah so by context it's safe to assume that Torah cleanness or uncleanness isn't the issue. All that's being addressed are those things that *are* fit for consumption according to Torah. Once again, we have a passage that has nothing to do with whether or not what Yah has declared unfit to eat suddenly became acceptable as food after Yeshua's death and resurrection.

Another often-cited passage used to support the idea of food laws being abolished is in the seventh chapter of Mark where we see Yeshua correcting the Pharisees. In verse 18-19 we find this:

> [18] And He said to them, "Are you so lacking in understanding also? Do you not understand that whatever goes into the man from outside cannot defile him, [19] because it does not go into his heart, but into his stomach, and is eliminated?" (Thus He declared all foods clean.)

Look at that parenthetical statement! On top of Yeshua's words, that seals the deal, right? It couldn't be more plainly stated. Except that the parenthetical statement doesn't appear in the original Greek text, which is why you don't find it in the King James version. The KJV came before translators started adding the statement and when they do they put it in parentheses because it's a bit questionable. In other words, this isn't Mark clarifying what Yeshua was saying, it was added by translators who endeavored to explain what they thought Mark was saying Yeshua was saying. Unfortunately Mark wasn't saying what translators thought he was. For Comparison, here's what the King James says:

> [18] And he saith unto them, Are ye so without understanding also? Do ye not perceive, that whatsoever thing from without entereth into the man, it cannot defile him; [19] Because it entereth not into his heart, but into the belly, and goeth out into the draught, purging all meats? (KJV)

To understand what's actually being discussed, let's look at the wider context by going back to the beginning of Mark 7 where this exchange between Yeshua and the Pharisees began.

> [1] The Pharisees and some of the scribes gathered around Him when they had come from Jerusalem, [2] and had seen that some of His disciples were eating their bread with impure hands, that is, unwashed. [3] (For the Pharisees and all the Jews do not eat unless they carefully wash their hands, thus observing the traditions of the elders; [4] and when they come from the market place, they

> do not eat unless they cleanse themselves; and there are many other things which they have received in order to observe, such as the washing of cups and pitchers and copper pots.) *5 The Pharisees and the scribes asked Him, "Why do Your disciples not walk according to the tradition of the elders, but eat their bread with impure hands?"*

Verse 2 describes what they were eating. Bread. There was obviously no Torah instruction describing bread as unclean. Additionally, verse 3 describes the cultural context so it's clear that what the Pharisees object to is not the disciples eating unclean animals (which they weren't eating anyway), but the disciples eating without first ceremonially washing their hands. This ceremonial hand washing was a tradition that the Pharisees had added. It is not part of Torah. Also, like the previous passages we looked at in Romans and 1 Corinthians, the word used in the Greek for "unclean" in this section of Mark is "koinos" not "akathartos". When Yeshua says, *"whatever goes into the man from outside cannot defile him, because it does not go into his heart, but into his stomach, and is eliminated"*, He's not saying you can eat unclean animals and you'll be fine. He's saying that if you eat without washing your hands, you'll be ok because the body's digestive system will eliminate any contaminants that may be consumed as a result.

Humorously enough, since the Pharisees, Yeshua, and all the Jews who witnessed the encounter would not have considered unclean animals food, the parenthetical statement of Mark 7:19 is true in a sense. All food is clean because if it's unclean it's not considered food. It's a bit like the contemporary idea that there's no such thing as junk food. It's either junk or it's food. What we have here is a third passage used to support the idea that we can eat unclean animals when the passage has nothing to do with unclean animals. All of the support for abolishing food laws relies on misinterpretations and misunderstandings about the difference between unclean animals and culinary impurities, misconceptions about what the Hebrew mind would have considered food and would not have considered food, and individual verses ripped from the context of the passage in which they appear. If that's the best evidence there is, I'd say the "we can eat anything we want" crowd has no case. At least, none that stands on the solid foundation of Scripture.

CHOKING GOATS • 219

There's one more passage that's worth addressing in this discussion and it's Colossian's 2:16-17:

> [16] Therefore no one is to act as your judge in regard to food or drink or in respect to a festival or a new moon or a Sabbath day— [17] things which are a mere shadow of what is to come; but the substance belongs to Christ.

I was taught, as I suspect many of you were, that this is Paul saying, "hey, do what you like and don't let anyone judge you for it". The word translated food here though is "brosis", which refers not to food but to the act of eating, so a better rendering might be, *"no one is to act as your judge in regard to {eating} and {drinking}"*. If we expand our investigation to include more of Colossians 2, we see that what Paul is addressing was the problem of asceticism. Briefly, asceticism was the idea that only the spiritual things of the world had any goodness to them and everything physical was corrupted, so ascetics would do all they could to avoid physical interaction with the world, including refraining from eating and drinking so far as that was possible. This is illustrated in Colossians 2:20-23:

> [20] If you have died with Christ to the elementary principles of the world, why, as if you were living in the world, do you submit yourself to decrees, such as, [21] "Do not handle, do not taste, do not touch!" [22] (which all refer to things destined to perish with use)—in accordance with the commandments and teachings of men? [23] These are matters which have, to be sure, the appearance of wisdom in self-made religion and self-abasement and severe treatment of the body, but are of no value against fleshly indulgence.

What was going on in Colossae at the time was ascetics trying to convince believers that if they were truly spiritually evolved they wouldn't interact so much with physical things, including things Yah had no problem with, like eating clean animals. The last half of verse 21 makes clear that Paul is not talking about Torah instruction, since he specifically states these *"do not taste, do not touch"* ideas were *"the commandments and teachings of men"*. While most people are taught that verses 18-19 are targeting those who encourage Torah observance and saying don't let anyone convince you that you still have to do these things, the reality is, Paul is saying you go ahead and eat Kosher, observe the Sabbaths, and keep Yah's feast days, and don't let the ascetics judge you based on their man-made sense of holiness. How wonderful that it applies to us today in the same way.

Paul hammers this home at the end of verse 23 when he says that the ascetic ideas *"are of no value against fleshly indulgence"* the implication being that obedience to Torah IS of value against fleshly indulgence, which, as we've seen, is a view fully supported by everything the Bible says about Torah and everything Yeshua taught us about following His commandments. Most Christians teach or have been taught that Paul is saying don't let anyone judge you for disobeying Torah when he's saying precisely the opposite! He's saying don't be discouraged by those who would judge you because you follow Torah.

That's zero for four regarding Scripture in support of the abolition of food laws. Now let's look at a verse that supports the idea that Yah's food laws still apply; a verse that's difficult to explain away, Isaiah 66:16-17:

> *16 For the Lord will execute judgment by fire*
> *And by His sword on all flesh,*
> *And those slain by the Lord will be many.*
> *17 "Those who sanctify and purify themselves to go to the gardens,*
> *Following one in the center,*
> **Who eat swine's flesh, detestable things and mice,**
> *Will come to an end altogether," declares the Lord.*

First, let me say that I don't think people who eat pork are going to hell. Salvation and damnation are solely determined by one's relationship with Yeshua, or lack thereof. There are none of us who follow Torah perfectly, and in the areas we don't know about or don't understand fully, thank the Father there is grace to cover our mistakes as part of our relationship with Yeshua. That said, we have to deal with this passage because it speaks of a time during the second coming, where clearly eating unclean things is still on the list of disobedient activities.

For the non-believer, it's one more disobedient act on a long list with no redeemer to stand for them, but for the believer who isn't heeding the dietary instructions of Torah it leaves one in the awkward and spiritually untenable position of knowing for a fact that upon Yeshua's return, disobeying Yah's instructions regarding food will be considered sin, but persisting in that sin anyway. In an earlier chapter I used the analogy of car theft to illustrate the idea that, being pardoned for grand theft auto doesn't abolish the law against stealing cars, but having been shown mercy and knowing how close the thief came to facing justice, doesn't it make sense for the thief to stop breaking the law? And is it not so with us? Having had the debt for our disobedience paid by Yeshua, and having Torah written on our hearts, shall we not cease in our disobedience? However you answer those questions, here's another passage that shows Yah's instructions being relevant in the future, and we know they were relevant in the past. It takes more faith than I have to think that they'd be rendered irrelevant in the relatively short span of time between Yeshua's first and second coming.

The idea is also reiterated by none other than Paul in 2 Corinthians 6:

> [14] *Do not be bound together with unbelievers; for what partnership have righteousness and lawlessness, or what fellowship has light with darkness?* [15] *Or what harmony has Christ with Belial, or what has a believer in common with an unbeliever?* [16] *Or what agreement has the temple of God with idols? For we are the temple of the living God; just as God said,*
>
> *"I will dwell in them and walk among them;*
> *And I will be their God, and they shall be My people.*
> [17] *"Therefore, come out from their midst and be separate," says the Lord.*
> *"And* **do not touch what is unclean**;
> *And I will welcome you.*
> [18] *"And I will be a father to you,*
> *And you shall be sons and daughters to Me,"*
> *Says the Lord Almighty.*

We looked at the first verse of this passage earlier in our discussion of light and darkness. Verse 14 starts with a "yoke" analogy to explain that we shouldn't live the way unbelievers do and goes on to draw several contrasts to illustrate that one cannot mix holiness and worldliness. Paul goes on to quote from several parts of the Old Testament to describe some of the attributes of those who *"are the temple of the living God"*. Among these, Paul includes the instruction not to touch what is unclean in verse 17. This indicates that Paul believes that part of *"coming out of their midst and being separate"*, includes following Yah's instructions regarding that which is clean and unclean.

Having addressed the objections to Yah's food laws and established that they will still be criteria by which one will be judged disobedient in the future, let's look at some practical realities about the animals Yah has declared unclean; animals that are not intended for food. The first thing that jumps out is how many of the animals that are unclean are basically nature's garbage disposals. Shellfish like crab and lobster as well as some fish like catfish live at the bottom of their habitats and consume all the sick, dead and decaying effluvia that floats down there. They play an important role in their ecosystems as trash collectors, but they just don't generally eat healthy live prey. The same is true of hogs. They'll eat anything, and they serve an important function in nature disposing of rotten and decaying things. Ditto birds of prey like vultures. The other thing they tend to have in common is high toxicity loads. One of the primary ways that mammals rid themselves of toxins is through perspiration but some unclean animals like pigs and camels have no sweat glands. As a result, they tend to be highly prone to bacterial infection including bacteria that can survive the high temperatures of cooking. Ask a nutritionist about the nutritional value and toxin load of pork compared to other animals like deer, cattle, or chicken and you'll find it's simply inferior as a food source.

Consider, also, things like mice, rats, and bats that tend to be carriers of disease, and the fact that such a high percentage of humans have shellfish allergies. The more you look into the animals, birds, reptiles and insects that Yah has declared unfit as food, the more it will make sense to you. They're just not good things to be eating if one wants to maximize one's probability of remaining healthy. This brings us back to a topic we've talked about before; the term "law" as it's used when referring to food laws. Instruction is always a better understanding of Torah and in this sense, Yah has given us sound instruction in telling us to stay away from eating these things. He designed them to fulfill a vital and specific role in nature, but the nature of that role makes them poor choices for human consumption.

Before I bring this chapter to a close, I will leave you with one final thought. The very first instruction Yah gave man was a food restriction. I'm speaking, of course, of the fruit of the tree of knowledge of good and evil. In a sense, the first "verse" of Torah relayed to mankind was instruction regarding something that was edible but was not to be eaten. Some might be thinking, surely Yah has more important things to worry about than what I eat, or how big a deal is it, really, to eat that which Yah has instructed us not to. The very first act of man's disobedience, the source of the original sin that plagues us all, and the reason we are in need of salvation is because the first man and woman ignored Yah's instruction against eating something that looked like food but was not intended for consumption. Yah knew that upon eating of the fruit of that tree they would die in spirit and warned them of the terrible consequences. They failed to heed that loving guidance, and in eating that which they were told was not fit for consumption, broke themselves and all of creation with them.

Section V

Conclusion

Having covered so much of the value of Yah's instructions, I feel quite comfortable saying that all of the Scripture I've covered falls under the category of good and edifying including the entirety of Yah's instructions we know as Torah. Contrary to what some would have you believe these are not burdensome boundaries of oppression, but are wonderful, freeing and beneficial things to do and observe. Given the loving nature of the Father who gave us these instructions it should come as no surprise that they quickly become a source of joy, comfort, and education that draw us ever nearer to our Creator.

At the beginning of this book, I invoked the imagery of the Ents from The Lord of the Rings to illustrate the importance of being firmly rooted in our faith. I then asked a series of questions and, in many ways, everything since then has been my conclusion. Early in the history of Christianity a schism formed that deliberately severed the root of our faith from its Hebrew origins. Over the hundreds of years since, so much has been built on that unstable foundation that no one remembers the doctrines that did emerge, emerged based on faulty premises like man's authority to declare things holy or clean, supplant Yah's feasts, and declare an end to Yah's instructions, all in opposition to Scripture. A Rabbi named Mordechai Kraft once illustrated the difficulty of majority opinion saying if you see two roads, and 1,000 people are traveling one road, but only five are traveling the other, it's wise to go with the 1,000. But, he said, what if, on closer examination, one finds that 999 people are blind and only the one person in front knows where they're going whereas the five all know and understand where they're headed. Does that not change the majority equation? Suddenly it's not 1000 to 5 it's 5 to 1.

It's an interesting thought experiment and while Rabbi Kraft, being an orthodox Jew, certainly didn't intend to apply the concept to Christianity, it fits remarkably well. What we're left with today is an enormous body of mainstream Christian believers who are either following those who came before without realizing that those who came before were blind or, without realizing that the things that came before, came about under papal authority, not by the authority of Scripture. This shouldn't be surprising. After all, is it not true that Noah was right and the rest of the world wrong? What was the difference in that case? Noah, having found favor in the eyes of Yah (Genesis 6:8), had eyes to see while the rest of the world, in their disobedience, was blind. In fact, what was the summary charge leveled against the people of Noah's day? We find the answer in Genesis 6:12:

> God looked on the earth, and behold, it was corrupt; for all flesh had corrupted their way upon the earth.

The entire reason for the destruction of the flood was all flesh having corrupted their way. In other words, everyone departed from Yah's instructions and went their own way, save for Noah.

Add to this Yeshua's words in Matthew 7:13-14:

> [13] "Enter through the narrow gate; for the gate is wide and the way is broad that leads to destruction, and there are many who enter through it. [14] For the gate is small and the way is narrow that leads to life, and there are few who find it.

According to Pew Research (pewresearch.org), Christianity is the world's largest religion with a little over 31.5 percent of the world's religious population identifying as Christian. While I realize there are monumental differences between Catholicism and Protestantism, on the topic of Torah's abolishment the two faiths are in lock step. How can this number be so high when Yeshua said that there are few who find the narrow way? Either mainstream Christianity as we know it today is NOT the narrow way that Yeshua is describing or He's a liar. I suppose the other option is that He was surprised to learn that, actually, most people find the narrow way and the small gate, but this seems unlikely. Perhaps that's because "the way" Yeshua was talking about, is the same way Isaiah was talking about when he wrote in Jeremiah 6:16:

> "This is what the LORD says: "Stand at the crossroads and look; ask for the ancient paths, ask where the good way is, and walk in it....""

This is speaking of Torah obedience. Considering that there are so few Christians who follow Torah and so few Jews who believe Yeshua was the

Messiah, this idea would certainly fit with Yeshua's description as *"the way few find"*. I assert that the narrow path is simply the one that doesn't go to the left into legalism, as Jews have done, nor to the right into license, as Christians have done, instead walking the fine line in the middle as a law-abiding citizen of the kingdom where Yeshua sits on the throne.

As I've said before, much of this is the result of mankind trying to rebuild the wall between Jew and Gentile and, sadly, quite successfully. In my opinion, there are two pages in almost every Bible that do not belong in any Bible. The one before Genesis that says Old Testament and the one between Malachi and Matthew that says New Testament. These two pages, and the division they create in the minds of readers have done an enormous amount of damage to our understanding of the story of Yah's relationship to, and activity in, this world. Let us not forget, this is one book that tells one story of one God from beginning to end. There is not a Jewish book and a Christian book. There is not a time where there was a just God followed by a time where there was a merciful God nor was there an angry God followed by a benevolent God. There was not a time where salvation was achieved through obedience followed by a time where salvation was given through grace. Most importantly for the purposes of my thesis, there was not a time where the human heart needed to be changed followed by a time when the Law was changed instead. Torah was the standard of righteousness from the beginning, continued to be the standard throughout human history including the present, and will be the standard until the end and the Bible quite clearly articulates this. Will we embrace the Spirit that allows and encourages us to obey out of love for He who saved us, or will we resist and continue in the disobedience that left us so broken in the first place?

The sad reality is, whether knowingly or unknowingly, for more than 1800 years, instead of nourishing sheep with the sound doctrine of Scripture, mainstream Christian leaders have been choking goats on the garbage of this world and it's time we all take a more serious look at what we're consuming and whom we're following lest we remain spiritual infants in an age that desperately demands holy maturity.

Bibliography

n.a. Catholic Record of London. Ontario, 1 Sep. 1923.

n.a. The Catholic Universe Bulletin, 14 Aug. 1942.

n.a. Library of Christian Doctrine: Why Don't You Keep Holy the Sabbath-Day? Burns and Oates, Ltd, n.d.

n.a. "The Sabbath and the Lord's Day - Study Resources." Blue Letter Bible, n.d. www.blueletterbible.org/faq/sabbath.cfm.

n.a. Synod of Laodicea (4th Century)

n.a. Thayers Greek Lexicon. Hendrickson Publishers, 1995.

Geiermann, Peter. The Convert's Catechism of Catholic Doctrine. B. Herder Book Co., 1946.

Gibbons, John C. The Catholic Mirror, 23 Dec. 1893.

Gibbons, James. The Faith of Our Fathers, 92nd Ed. John Murphy Company Publishers, 1917.

Hackett, Conrad and McClendon, David. "Christians Remain world's largest religious group but they are declining in Europe." Pew Research, 5 Apr. 2017. www.pewresearch.org/fact-tank/2017/04/05/christians-remain-worlds-largest-religious-group-but-they-are-declining-in-europe/

Keenan, Stephen. A Doctrinal Catechism. P. J. Kenedy, 1899.

O'Brien, John A. Faith of Millions: The Credentials of the Catholic Religion. Our Sunday Visitor, Inc, 1955.

Schaff, Philip. History of the Christian Church Volume 3. Edinburgh, 1884.

Segur, Louis. Plain Talk about the Protestantism of Today. Patrick Donahoe, 1868.

Shelley, Bruce L. Directions: Is Christmas Pagan? Christianity Today, 6 Dec. 1999, www.christianitytoday.com/ct/1999/december6/9te085.html

Smith, Albert. Feb 10. 1920. Letter.

Spirago, Francis. The Catechism Explained. Benziger Brothers, 1899.

Thomas, C.F. 28 Oct. 1895. Letter.

Turberville, Henry. An Abridgment of the Christian Doctrine. John Doyle, 1833.

Willard, Dallas. The Problem With Vampire Christianity. ChurchLeaders.com, 2 Jun. 2013. www.churchleaders.com/pastors/pastor-how-to/149646-the-problem-with-vampire-christianity.html

Young, Brad H. Meet the Rabbis: Rabbinic Thought and the Teachings of Jesus. Baker Academic, 2010.

www.ingramcontent.com/pod-product-compliance
Lightning Source LLC
LaVergne TN
LVHW041540070426
835507LV00011B/852